TRIATHLONTRAINING
IN 4 HOURS A WEEK

FROM BEGINNER TO FINISH LINE
IN JUST 6 WEEKS

ERIC HARR

© 2003, 2015 by Eric Harr

Photographs © 2003, 2015 by Mitch Mandel/Rodale Images

Illustrations © 2003 by Phil Guzy

Rodale books may be purchased for business or promotional use or for special sales. For information, please write to: Special Markets Department, Rodale, Inc., 733 Third Avenue, New York, NY 10017

Printed in the United States of America

Rodale Inc. makes every effort to use acid-free ♾, recycled paper ♻.

Book design by Joanna Williams

Library of Congress Cataloging-in-Publication Data number: 2003003927.

ISBN 978-1-62336-559-2 hardcover

Distributed to the trade by Macmillan

2 4 6 8 10 9 7 5 3 1 hardcover

We inspire and enable people to improve their lives and the world around them.
rodalebooks.com

"A happy family is but an earlier heaven."
—George Bernard Shaw

Truer words were never spoken. I dedicate this
to my breathtaking, loving, supportive, fun, beautiful family:
Alexandra, Vivienne and Turner.

You are "but an earlier heaven."

CONTENTS

Introduction: The Hero inside You ... vii

1 20 GREAT REASONS TO DO A TRIATHLON ... 1
2 PUT YOUR EXCUSES TO REST ... 15
3 GEAR UP WITHOUT BLOWING YOUR BUDGET ... 35
4 YOUR TRAINING PROGRAM: AN OVERVIEW ... 49
5 SWIM EASIER ... 67
6 CYCLE STRONGER ... 83
7 RUN FASTER ... 99
8 STRETCH AND STRENGTHEN YOUR BODY ... 113
9 PUT IT ALL TOGETHER ... 161
10 FUEL YOUR ACTIVE BODY ... 189
11 STAY INJURY FREE ... 211
12 PUT YOUR MIND TO IT ... 231
13 SEIZE THE RACE DAY ... 237
14 NOW WHAT? THE MORNING AFTER AND THE REST OF YOUR LIFE ... 251

Triathlon Talk: An Enlightening and Entertaining Glossary of Terms ... 255
Acknowledgments ... 261
Index ... 263
About the Author ... 273

INTRODUCTION

THE HERO INSIDE YOU

"Far better it is to dare mighty things, to win glorious triumphs, even checkered by failure, than to take rank with those poor spirits who neither enjoy much nor suffer much, because they live in the gray twilight that knows not victory nor defeat."

—THEODORE ROOSEVELT

We all look to our heroes for inspiration. My hero has always been my mother. She was a triathlete long before I even knew what that meant.

Each one of us has the potential to be a hero to somebody—and feeling heroic, or "important," is something we all yearn to experience. But unless we happen upon a burning building or someone drowning in icy waters, we rarely, if ever, dig deep inside ourselves and reveal that hero within.

This is where the triathlon comes in.

While it may seem a weak comparison to real-life displays of bravery, training for a triathlon makes you feel heroic on so many levels. For proof, watch any triathlon anywhere in the world and observe the expressions of the racers—mothers, doctors, and account executives of every shape, size, and age—as they cross the finish line. You can use the same words to describe them all: electrified, thrilled, vibrant, and yes, heroic. It is why you will see those same people just minutes after they finish the race—some rushing, some wobbling—making their way to the registration tent to sign up for next year's event.

While there is little doubt that training for and completing a triathlon make you feel heroic in a world that rarely gives us opportunities to feel that way, for many the triathlon appears to be too daunting a task. The moment people consider doing a triathlon, a litany of fears and excuses rises up to extinguish their sense of adventure: "I'm too overweight—I could never do that!" "Are you joking? I don't have the time." "No way. Look at this painful carbuncle on my foot!"

I'm a little hazy on what a carbuncle is, but I am very clear on the power a triathlon has to change your life. It forces you to move beyond excuses and overcome your fears and weaknesses so you can live life to the fullest. It also ignites your inner fire—the hero hidden deep inside you—and inspires you to keep striving for a better life and a better world.

You've got that fire in you. You may not realize it or may have forgotten it, but it's there. It burns within each one of us. And it's not far from your reach. This book can help you ignite and sustain that fire. For life. And the best part is that you won't have to turn your life upside down to do it. The program in this book, which will set all of these things into action, requires just four hours a week for the next six weeks.

WHY A TRIATHLON?

It is widely regarded as one of the world's most physically demanding sports, the Mount Everest of athletic endeavors. Until recently, the triathlon was perceived as an esoteric endeavor braved only by the fitness elite—an image perpetuated by the media's coverage of the infamous Hawaii Ironman torture-fest.

You're likely thinking, "Why do I need to do a full-fledged triathlon to achieve my goals?" You don't. You can undertake an ordinary fitness program, be moderately motivated, and achieve ordinary results. Or you can choose to be extraordinary.

Admittedly, this is no ordinary undertaking—and Chapter 2 provides a "let's be real for a moment" break—but keep in mind that these are not ordinary times, and if you picked up this book, you likely are not an ordinary individual.

This extraordinary quest will not take over your life. I'm asking for 24 hours, just four hours a week for the next six weeks of your life. That's not a lot when you consider the 20 long-lasting payoffs I discuss in Chapter 1. That represents a very high return on your investment.

THE MAKINGS OF A GREAT EVENT

The triathlon is a swim, bike, and run event, in that order. It emerged in the late 1970s and has since lured millions from around the world. The sport is wildly popular in Europe, Australia, and Asia, where the triathlon is tantamount to religion and professionals are revered like NBA players are here. The first known triathlons were organized by members of the San Diego Track Club, intended as little more than playful summer evening pauses from the normal grind of run-only training. Several years later, a few emboldened athletes took this "cross-training" phenomenon across the Pacific where, apparently in a mai tai–induced stupor, they fused three of Oahu's endurance events—the Waikiki Rough Water Swim, the Around-Oahu Bike Ride, and the Honolulu Marathon—into one event: the Ironman. This is the triathlon you've likely watched on television, perhaps shaking your head in disbelief. In 1982, the dramatic footage of Julie Moss crawling to the finish line on her hands and knees triggered an explosion of interest in the sport—and also stigmatized the sport for decades. While the gripping images of Moss and the negative-body-fat-percentage über-people running five-minute miles make for provocative television entertainment, they have very little to do with the collective soul of the sport.

Over the past five years, the triathlon has attracted thousands of new participants of every age, background, size, and shape—people just like you. Maybe you cycle, run, or swim for recreation and have always thought of trying a triathlon but never knew how—or you were too put off by the extreme nature of the sport. Perhaps you're an accomplished single-sporter, such as a runner or cyclist, who wants to move to the "next level" and elevate your performance. Maybe you're a busy executive or parent who wants to get the most possible benefit from your limited exercise time. Or perhaps you just want to lead a healthier, better life and take on a challenge that will excite and inspire you.

Indeed, the triathlon is for each one of us.

Today there are thousands of triathlons held annually in more than 30 countries around the world. One of the most popular iterations is known as the sprint distance, which in most cases is roughly a 400-meter swim, a 12-mile bike ride, and a 3-mile run. This takes the majority of people about 90 minutes to complete.

You bet those numbers are realistic for some of you. And others of you can do more.

THE PROMISE

No matter who you are, if you follow the simple program in this book, there is little doubt that your life will change in a number of positive ways. The total body-mind approach of this triathlon training program will leave you looking and feeling better than you ever have in your life—all within six weeks. It will help you shed more weight than you would from any diet, pill, or exercise gadget. If you suffer from existing pain or injury, cross-training will help reduce or even eliminate your pain and prevent future injury by building a stronger, more flexible, and balanced body.

This program will show you how to stretch your body and your mind to give you a physical and mental edge in everything you do. It will show you how to stay motivated to exercise more. It will teach you everything you need to know about optimum nutrition. The training principles in this book will relax your mind and fortify your spirit. They will build your self-confidence and free you from any limits you may have set for yourself.

This program will help you fit into, and look better in, new clothes. And of course, it will show you how to train for and complete a triathlon. But most of all, it will add fun and focus to your exercise plan and passion and conviction to your life.

How do I know these things? I've met thousands of ordinary people in more than 20 countries who have braved the challenge, and the vast majority have experienced one, or all, of these benefits. Now, how do I *really* know? I *am* one of those people.

MY FIRST TRIATHLON

I discovered the sport of triathlon quite serendipitously in 1994 while working as an overweight legal clerk in the U.S. Virgin Islands. What "law" was I doing there, you ask? Hey, it was the Virgin Islands. I was just out of college.

Since the island I lived on is only 28 miles long, I decided that buying a car would be an act of unqualified laziness, so I rode my mountain bike everywhere: to the grocery store, on dates, to work—often through torrential Caribbean downpours that provided me with daily adventures and the locals with regular comic relief. Picture a plump, lawyerly fellow waddling on his bike to work through driving rainstorms. I'd laugh, too.

An annual event on the island, the St. Croix International Triathlon, lured top athletes from around the world. While I was an accomplished swimmer in college, I had no real background in cycling or running, but I knew that my familiarity with swimming could serve as a foundation upon which to learn the other two sports. The bottom line was that the notion seemed compelling.

I decided to train for the event for no other reason than that I was a fast-fattening guy unwittingly dooming myself to a desk-bound existence. I couldn't imagine a better way to look and feel better in a shorter period of time than by doing a triathlon. I had just shy of six weeks to prepare for the event.

As I trained—and slimmed down—the locals' laughter turned to applause when I sailed by on my bike every morning. Each day I gained more momentum and lost a little more weight. Little did I know that the simple decision to enter that one event would completely redirect the course of my life.

That first triathlon stands out as one of the most enlightening days of my life. After six weeks of training, I found myself toeing the starting line with people a lot leaner, a lot meaner . . . and a lot more prepared than I! I thought to myself: "Whoa, Eric, this time you're in way, way over your head."

When the starting gun went off, I hurled my body into the Caribbean Sea and flailed myself salmonlike toward the brightest object in the water, the first buoy. Out of the swim, I felt great—a little woozy, but great. Onto the bike, I miraculously found myself in ninth place, wedged in between three testy Germans who were screaming at me—presumably because I was breaking up their triumvirate. I held my position through the bike.

Then came the run. For me, it was completely uncharted territory. I think I had done a mere eight or nine actual run workouts before this event. As I rode my bike into the transition area, I spotted my father, who had been working himself into a frenzy during my ride. That frenzy had reached crescendo level by the time I reached him. Add to that his utter disbelief at seeing his boy in ninth; he could barely contain himself.

As I dismounted my bike and donned my running gear, I could hear Dad roughly one foot away behind the barricades screaming at me, "Son, what do you need? Sonwhatdoyouneed? *So-o-o-on, whaddo-o-yo-o-u-n-e-e-ed?*"

I was too focused on the task to answer him. As I left the transition area, there was Dad, running alongside me (he was 260 pounds at the time). This scene was entertaining for other participants and spectators alike. Here was this giant man trying to hand off a glass gallon jug of apple juice and a Heath candy bar to his son during a triathlon. It was so consummately my dad—he was always there to support his boy. Excitable at times, but always there.

At that moment, I reflected on what was happening and realized how impractical either of those food items is in a triathlon. I stopped running . . . and began laughing hysterically. Dad looked down at his apple juice and candy bar—which was fully melted from the Caribbean heat—and he began laughing, too. There we laughed, in the middle of my event, with the Germans running by me. That laughter relaxed me so much that, despite my inadequate run training, I went on to finish a respectable 18th out of a field of over 400.

Of the more than 75 triathlons in 25 countries I've completed, that moment with my father stands as the most memorable and precious of all my experiences. I had never felt a wash of more positive emotions than I did at the finish line. In my postrace stupor, I called my mom and proclaimed, much to her chagrin, that I was going to trade a career in international law for a shot at being a professional triathlete. Six months after that phone call, I was ranked number six on the Triathlon Pro Tour—and Mom & Dad, Inc., was my biggest sponsor. God love them.

The point of this story is that triathlons invariably give rise to memorable stories, perhaps because there are so many variables colliding out there at once. These are precisely the kinds of memories you should expect to come away with from your triathlon day, and they will reward you, and those cheering you on, for the rest of your life.

YOU CAN DO IT, TOO!

Since my first event, I've traveled to more than 25 countries to train with and compete against some of the finest athletes. I've worked alongside respected coaches, sports psychologists, and nutritionists who have helped me hone my craft and reach my potential. Along the way, I gleaned some powerful insights about health, fitness, performance, and living more fully. I learned how to exercise smarter from the Finnish athletes. The Kenyans taught me how to run. The French showed me how to ride. The Italians shared with me their eating secrets. And from the Aussies, I learned to loosen up, have a few beers, and make workouts more fun.

One universal lesson I learned is that top athletes are not a species distinct from you. They are ordinary people simply called to extraordinary circumstances, regular people who have ignited, and sustained, a driving passion for what they do. This is how they achieve such mind-boggling physical feats. You have the same fire inside of you. Regardless of your fitness level, background, or beliefs, *you* can go the distance in a triathlon.

This book will show you how.

In these pages, I turn much of the wisdom I've learned from my personal experience, top athletes, real-life case studies, hundreds of first-time triathletes, and leading experts around the world into simple, practical tips you can understand and use right away in your quest to train for and complete a triathlon.

Over the past 10 years, I've presented the same time-tested principles you will find in this book to tens of thousands of people, from couch potatoes to serious fitness enthusiasts, to help them achieve extraordinary results. I have zero doubt this program will help you, too.

This book is designed for the beginner as well as the serious fitness enthusiast and single-sport athlete looking to take it up a notch and complete a triathlon to the best of their ability. It is not a technical manual for the seasoned triathlete. You will not hear me talk about max V02 or gear inches, and I will not ask you to run a "pyramid set of descending cruise intervals."

What you can expect is this: You will perform better than you ever imagined you could. You will cross that finish line with a profound sense of empowerment, confidence, and achievement. And you will reap all the rewards that come from getting there.

Finally, as you undertake this journey, keep this important tenet in mind: The triathlon, or any organized athletic event for that matter, is a merely a symbol. It is a clear path to self-actualization; to courageously taking on a challenge; to building a stronger, more energetic, more beautiful body; to taking control over your own life; to inspiring those around you by leading through example; and to feeling more heroic more often.

These are universal desires that resonate in the hearts of us all, regardless of age, culture, or gender. They are the core concepts in this book. And if you follow the advice in these pages, you stand to realize them all.

Read on and become somebody's hero.

1
20 GREAT REASONS TO DO A TRIATHLON

"Go confidently in the direction of your dreams. Live the life you
have imagined."

—HENRY DAVID THOREAU

People are motivated to "take the plunge" and do a triathlon for reasons that are as varied as those setting out on this mission. Some are obvious: "to lose weight fast!" Others are personal: "to boost my self-confidence and feel good about myself." Others are spiritual: "to find more meaning in my exercise" or "to live more fully." A few are social: "to brag to everyone in the office that I did a triathlon." And some are inspirational: "to serve as a model for others and show what is truly possible in life."

Although the reasons people do a triathlon differ, the benefits are universal. That's what this chapter is about—it outlines the 20 benefits you can reap from training for and completing a triathlon. The bottom line is that this process is one of the most rewarding things you will ever do in your life, not just physically but also mentally, spiritually, and socially. Ask anyone who has done a triathlon and they will tell you the same thing.

But for all its power to *change* your life, training for a triathlon isn't going to *consume* your life. The training program set forth in this book is designed to blend seamlessly into your busy schedule and requires four hours a week for six weeks—a total of just 24 hours. The payoffs, however, are timeless: You will lose loads of weight, feel better than ever, and gain self-confidence that will last a lifetime.

Lofty promises, indeed. Can doing a triathlon really deliver? Follow the advice in this book and, yes, without a doubt it can. It has for hundreds of thousands of other triathletes, and it will for you, too.

PHYSICAL BENEFIT

For you to consider training for and completing a triathlon, there have to be some serious, long-lasting benefits, right? Well, here they are—20 of them. Let's start with the most observable payoffs: what will happen to your body.

YOU WILL LOSE WEIGHT

The first thing you'll probably notice as a Triathlete-in-Training is that your clothes will become too big. That's because training for a three-sport event will make you as fit and healthy as you have ever been in your life. When you engage in a well-balanced program of swimming, cycling, and running—known as cross-training—you will burn an enormous amount of fat from every area of your body. Better yet, the weight will come off as a natural consequence of your passion-driven quest to complete a

FEEL GOOD AT ANY WEIGHT

Losing weight is a goal coveted by many, and you certainly stand to shed the pounds on this program. But it's also important to accept and enjoy how you look here and now—and every step of the way.

Over the past few decades, the American media has perpetuated an almost hysterical level of irrational obsessive-compulsion with looking thin. That has wreaked havoc on our sense of perspective and our self-esteem, making it virtually impossible for us to enjoy how we look.

The problem is that when you fail to appreciate your body, in this moment, you postpone life enjoyment. It's saying: "I will appreciate my body when . . ." Unfortunately, "when" rarely arrives. But a Triathlete-in-Training is different: Although you're always striving for a better quality of life, and perhaps a better body, you're genuinely satisfied with, and grateful for, the here and now. That way, you can celebrate the destination of a fitter you while having enjoyed your triathlon journey along the way.

triathlon, rather than from a guilt-induced diet, a boring exercise plan, or a bizarre fitness implement.

The principles and strategies in this book are built on passion, not deprivation. As you progress on this program, you will gain momentum: You'll lose a couple of pounds in the first week and you'll begin to feel stronger, which means you can do a little more and lose a little more weight. The workouts will get easier, so you'll be able to go even farther and lose more weight. Before you know it, you'll be sailing!

Keep this in mind: The program in this book isn't based on some untested herbal weight-loss product. The principles at work are basic scientific ones that your body cannot disobey. Like the apple that must fall from the tree, your body must lose weight if you're consistently burning more calories than you're consuming. And *nothing* burns more calories than training for a triathlon.

Plus, you'll likely find that when you're training for such an athletic event, you'll want to eat a healthy, well-balanced diet that supports your training. Overeating or indulging in lots of less-than-nutritious foods will leave you feeling dull and tired during your workouts, so you'll quickly learn to eat what's good for you—and that will accelerate your weight loss even more. (For more on nutrition, see Chapter 10.)

ACTION ITEM: *Ditch the scale and the madness attached to it. Muscle weighs more than fat, so if the numbers on the scale aren't budging, they aren't telling you the right story. Just look in the mirror and decide for yourself if you are making progress. Judge your fitness not by some arbitrary number but by how energetic and positive you feel and how your clothes fit!*

YOU WILL LOOK AND FEEL YEARS YOUNGER

When we neglect our bodies, imperceptibly over time we gradually accept lower standards of fitness, of health, and, therefore, of living. Worse, we don't even realize how bad we feel until we wake up and get fit again.

Training for a triathlon will reconnect you with your body and make you feel like you haven't felt in years: young, energetic, and powerful. You will not only *feel* years younger but also look better than ever. Triathletes are legendary for having some of the best physiques in the fitness world. That is because cross-training shapes the body in complementary ways: Running develops long, lean muscles; cycling builds strength and tones your lower body; and swimming increases your flexibility and sculpts your upper body. Take a look at any triathlete over age 55 and you'll see what I mean. These people have the look—and swagger—of 20- and 30-somethings.

YOU WILL HAVE MORE ENERGY

Energy forms the basis of our existence, yet it seems that we all have less and less of it as our schedules have grown increasingly hectic. Unfortunately for some people, exercise can exacerbate this problem by draining their energy rather than replenishing it. In an effort to get results or lose weight fast, they may wind up overtraining and exhausting themselves.

Not so on this program.

The strategies in this book will show you how to exercise so that each workout refreshes your body and clears your mind, giving you more energy over time so that you can perform better at work and at play. That, I guarantee.

You're likely wondering, "How can training for something as rigorous as a triathlon actually *give* me energy?" This program is for real people, not elite athletes. By following the principles in this book and exercising at the right pace for your fitness level, you'll get fit without fatigue.

When I took a year off my triathlon training program (to write this book!), my energy plummeted. I couldn't believe it. It was as if someone had pulled the plug on my life force. When I returned to consistent training, I felt fully alive again. You will, too.

YOU WILL GET MORE OUT OF YOUR WORKOUTS

In this book, I show you how to exercise more efficiently by using a few simple strategies, such as monitoring your heart rate and breathing properly. Follow these and other techniques set forth in the training program, and you'll get fast results from your workouts without expending a huge amount of effort. It's all about training smart, not hard.

YOU WILL INJURY-PROOF YOUR BODY

When you stick with one sport like running, for example, you continually stress the same parts of your body. That can result in overuse injuries such as shin splints, stress fractures, knee problems, and tendinitis.

Training for a triathlon, however, incorporates three very different sports. This cross-training, as it is called, isn't as hard on the body, because it distributes the stress more evenly to your bones and muscles and develops more balanced fitness. That means less pain, fewer injuries, and a stronger body. Or as Donna Carlysle, a mother of three from Pittsburgh, Pennsylvania, put it: "I like training for the triathlon because of the variety. It strengthens every muscle in my body, and it keeps me fresher as opposed to getting all the aches when I'm just running or biking or lifting weights all the time." (For more on preventing injury, see Chapter 11.)

YOU WILL IMPROVE YOUR HEALTH

According to the American College of Sports Medicine, regular exercise can lower your blood pressure; prevent diabetes, heart disease, and certain cancers; and reduce your risk of osteoporosis and depression—just to name a few. Follow the training program in this book, and you'll spend less time at doctors' offices and more time enjoying your life!

YOU WILL LIVE LONGER

Regular exercise helps you prevent disease and fortifies your body. Training for something as complete as a triathlon lays a foundation of fitness that will ensure your later years are more pain free and fun filled. So you'll not only add years to your life but also add life to your years.

MENTAL BENEFITS

Although the physical payoffs of doing a triathlon are thrilling, the mental rewards you stand to reap are even greater, because they are truly *timeless*. The mental edge you'll develop by becoming a triathlete will never fade.

YOU WILL BE MORE PRODUCTIVE

Training for a triathlon will clear your mind and sharpen your focus. My most lucid and creative thoughts invariably arise during bike rides, after swims, or while running with my dog, Owen, around the lakes of Mount Tamalpais in Northern California first thing in the morning.

You will not only have these "lightbulb" moments *during* exercise but also return to your day feeling refreshed and ready to tackle the tasks that lie ahead of you. Essentially, as your body becomes stronger, your mind will follow.

YOU WILL LEARN TO HANDLE STRESS MORE EFFECTIVELY

In Chapter 12, you will learn the profound skill of developing grace under pressure—that is, increasing your composure as the pressure around you heightens—as well as how to apply that skill to any stressful situation. If you can learn to "relax into" more intense physical efforts during a 45-minute run, for example, you will be more able to maintain mental equanimity during your morning commute. One of the most rewarding outcomes of my triathlon career is that few things in my daily life unsettle me. I am now more mentally resilient. You will be, too.

YOU WILL BUILD ROCK-SOLID SELF-CONFIDENCE

To develop a strong, "in-your-bones" confidence, I believe you must achieve something that deeply challenges you. Training for and finishing a triathlon is certainly a remarkable achievement and a powerful way to build self-confidence that will last a lifetime.

YOUR MOOD WILL IMPROVE

Research shows that exercise improves your mood and lifts your spirits. And no wonder! When you put your body in motion, you can't help but feel alive and invigorated. They don't call it "runner's high" for nothing. Plus, training for a triathlon gets you outdoors, and spending time in the beauty of nature is bound to boost your mood!

YOUR MOTIVATION TO EXERCISE WILL SOAR

Studies on exercise adherence show that many people quit their exercise routines because they become bored or burned out. This can happen when you do the same

Mark Allen, widely considered the greatest triathlete of all time, once summed up why he loved the sport of triathlon and why he was willing to sacrifice so much to pursue triathlon professionally for 15 years: "I love triathlon because it's *real*. It's just you and you out there. It's a raw reality. It's like no other experience in life, and I treasure that."

Our daily lives are often dictated by external forces—bosses, co-workers, friends. In a triathlon, you are in total control of your destiny. You have complete autonomy, which is hard to come by these days.

The process of training for and finishing a triathlon can give you insight into who you really are and what you're really made of, free from the limits imposed on you by others. In this regard, it might be seen as a vision quest—with aid stations!

---

thing day in and day out. Incorporating three different sports into your weekly exercise plan helps you to avoid burnout. When you grow tired of swimming along that godforsaken black line in your local pool, you can go for a run, a hike, or a bike ride around town or through the countryside. After all, each of these activities directly contributes to your triathlon success.

If the variety of training for a triathlon isn't enough to keep you motivated, don't worry. In Chapter 2, I give you several other strategies for keeping your enthusiasm high throughout your training.

Not only that. The training program in this book will help you redefine how you see and do exercise so that you can alter your long-term view of physical fitness. You will begin to see each triathlon training session for what it can be: a unique opportunity for personal growth, a celebration of life, and a relaxing pause in your otherwise hectic and stressful life. You'll learn to make exercise about letting go, stepping out into the world, getting sunshine on your face, and having fun.

YOU WILL LEARN TO STRENGTHEN YOUR WEAKNESSES

As we age, we begin erecting physical and psychological walls, brick by brick, made of our fears, doubts, and excuses. And we do it without realizing it. This wall begins to widen the distance between ourselves and our human potential. Before we know it, we're nowhere close to the person we once were or to the person we wanted to become. That can be a very scary realization later in life.

Training for and finishing a triathlon forces you to smash through that wall and deal with your weaknesses (for example, chronic knee pain, poor self-image, fear of failure). When you strengthen your weaknesses, you become more capable of setting aside your fears and doubts to achieve other extraordinary things in your life.

SOCIAL BENEFITS

Whether you train for your triathlon alone or with others, you're sure to meet fellow triathletes along the way. You'll find that the camaraderie within the triathlon world is unmatched in any other sport. In addition to making new fitness friends, you stand to reap other social rewards as well.

YOU GET TO RUB SHOULDERS WITH THE BEST ATHLETES IN THE WORLD

In a triathlon, everyone completes the same course: mother of three, 56-year-old age-group competitor, world-champion professional. That's one of the truly unique things about this sport. Can you imagine golfing alongside Tiger Woods? No way. But you can compete in the same triathlon as Ironman world champion Tim DeBoom. You may not be immediately impressed with that, but when a pro like Tim DeBoom gives you a thumbs-up or a pat on the back as he goes by, you'll get chills.

YOU WILL JOIN THE FITNESS ELITE

If you complete just one triathlon, you will become one of the fitness elite no matter what your finishing time. You will have accomplished something that only 1 percent of the population even dare try. That puts you in more of an elite class than a Hollywood star. Now that's sure to impress your friends and co-workers, not to mention anyone you're meeting for the first time.

INSPIRATIONAL BENEFITS

Perhaps the most profound benefits of all to training for a triathlon are those you least expect. Setting out on this mission will not only shrink your waistline and give you more confidence but also transform your life in ways you never imagined.

YOU WILL HAVE AN INCREASED SENSE OF PURPOSE IN YOUR LIFE

There are times in our lives when we find ourselves unfulfilled on deep, intangible levels, and we cannot explain why. We may have everything we want: a fulfilling career, a wonderful family, a strong network of loving friends. We just can't put our finger on our underlying restlessness.

Focusing your attention on an exciting, positive, and challenging goal such as a triathlon can breathe renewed purpose into your life and channel away some of that restlessness. The triathlon is a noble pursuit and an outside-the-box undertaking, and because of that people tend to wake up each morning feeling that they are on a mission.

YOU WILL BECOME THE BEST YOU THAT YOU CAN BE

Are you tired of others telling you (or implying) that you shouldn't, you can't, or you won't? Daily life rarely, if ever, provides us with the opportunity to be truly courageous, to show the world what we're really made of, and to be recognized for our own greatness. Completing a triathlon will provide you, and those around you, with physical proof that you are capable of more than anyone realizes.

In this quest, pushing past what you thought was possible might be your barometer of success. For others, it might be setting a personal record. Regardless of your goals, you will glimpse your true potential by completing a triathlon.

Steve Prefontaine, one of the best competitors of all time, saw a race not so much as a competition against other people but as a test to see how far the human heart can go.

That is what participating in a triathlon is all about.

TRIATHLON TALE:
TRAINING FOR A TRIATHLON CHANGED HER LIFE

Maureen was a 44-year-old university professor and mother of two. But her career success had come at a price: her body. She didn't recognize, and certainly didn't appreciate, the "strange, amorphous shell" hiding her real figure. She used to run consistently and had always been in decent shape. She never dreamed she could fall out of shape so quickly. Yet it was happening. And fast.

Maureen knew that consistent exercise was the answer to her fitness predicament, but like the rest of us, she faced three almost insurmountable obstacles: Her busy work schedule left her with little time or energy to exercise; when she did manage to exercise, she didn't know how to get the most benefit from her workouts; and, perhaps the toughest challenge of all, she could not stay motivated to exercise consistently. Every year she would begin a new exercise program like gangbusters in January only to lose steam by mid- to late January.

As Maureen's weight climbed, her self-esteem plummeted. She wanted nothing more than to change the way she looked and felt and to fit into her clothes again. She wanted to feel younger and to have more energy to do the things she loved.

She searched for reliable answers. On TV she was bombarded with questionable weight-loss products, exercise gadgets, and fitness "experts" who seemed more focused on selling than helping. In bookstores, she was overwhelmed by the sea of health and fitness publications, none of which seemed to provide her with long-term motivation or lasting results. She tried the fad diets. She felt lost, and with each fitness failure her self-confidence took increasingly devastating blows.

Like the rest of us, Maureen needed a totally different approach—one that was fresh, inspiring, simple, and applicable, not just to the fitness elite or the complete couch potato but to real people like her. It needed to give her fast results and keep her motivated over the long term.

Maureen never dreamed she should, or could, do a triathlon. But her best friend had completed one the past summer and it changed more than her waistline—it changed her life. It also sparked in Maureen an irrepressible "what if?" Now she was holding this book in her hands, which made the prospect a clear possibility.

"I used to run in high school, and I completed a couple 5-Ks years ago. But I had fallen so far out of shape, I didn't know how to get back to it, how to start," she says. "I had watched a couple multisport events, and each time I was struck by the diversity of people participating. Moreover, I was moved by the expressions of joy on their faces. I was someone who could barely motivate myself to run once a week. What had these people discovered that I had not?"

The reports of skyrocketing obesity in the country—and the fact that she couldn't keep up with her kids—troubled Maureen and forced her to think about dealing with her body. Then came 9-11.

"September 11 was a spark for me, that get-up-and-take-action event. I realized that life is so unpredictable. One must live right now. I also felt like I needed to 'strengthen' or 'fortify' my body, mind, and spirit against an increasingly stressful and violent world. That is why I decided to pursue a total-body venture, the triathlon."

Like most people, Maureen had four serious doubts: "I don't have the time, training for a triathlon will be too painful, I'm too old, and I'm too overweight!"

Fortunately, each one of her "obstacles" could be easily surmounted. As for the lack of time, a simple investment of four hours per week for six weeks was realistic to Maureen. She freed up that extra time by making two simple streamlining moves. First, she cut one day of television viewing a week. Then she quit her gym and started conducting workouts straight from her front door.

Next, Maureen learned that by exercising smart, not hard, she could get more results from her workouts with less pain and fatigue. (She loved that!)

Maureen was pleased to discover that her triathlon event would only last an hour—she could do that—and that more than half the people who finished triathlons were, in fact, just like her.

She realized that building toward a tangible race day would keep her excited, motivated, and focused on her goal. It would also provide her with a host of benefits in addition to losing weight and toning up.

Maureen built a strong support network of exercise buddies, all roughly her age, who kept her going on her journey.

During the training process, Maureen got back in touch with her body as exercise became an enriching part of her life rather than another task on her already brimming to-do list. "I began to understand why it was so important to move my body. Training became less about 'exercise' and more about giving myself the pause each day to quiet my mind. During that time, I was liberated from the doubts and fears and worries that always seemed to plague me. I didn't have a boss telling me what to do. There were no 'office politics' to deal with."

The result? Maureen exercised four to five hours per week every week for those first six weeks, and she enjoyed every minute. She finished her first triathlon, an event that changed her life in ways she hadn't expected.

"For those six weeks of training, I was so swept up in the excitement of exercising again that I didn't notice the weight coming off. Twenty-two pounds. I never focused on calories, though. I just focused on enjoying the workouts. When my race day arrived, I was electrified. I hadn't felt that alive in years. The race was tough, but spectators, volunteers, and other participants supported me every step of the way. That was incredible," she says.

"Crossing the finish line with my arms in the air and my husband and children watching sent chills down my spine and tears down my face. I didn't finish anywhere close to the leaders, but that didn't matter. I had finished what was, to me, a superhuman endeavor. And it was one of the most gratifying moments of my life.

"I walked away from that experience with more self-confidence. I felt 15 years younger. I looked great. I could fit into new clothing. I even started turning heads again! Call me crazy, but that felt fantastic. Most of all, I had a newfound desire to live life with more gusto. That is what my triathlon was all about. Living with gusto. Now I tell all my friends to do a triathlon. I say to them, 'No matter what your fitness level or goals, the triathlon will change your life in ways you cannot imagine.'"

YOU WILL BE A HERO TO YOUR KIDS

If your children watch you finish a triathlon, they may never look at you the same way. How do I know? My mom was a triathlete back in the formative years of the sport—the early 1980s. At that time, people knew very little about how to train for the triathlon; trailblazers like my mom were making it up as they went along.

When I watched my mom train and compete, I gazed at her like I did at any celebrity sports figure. I remember thinking, "Honest to God, Fleer should make a 'Judith Harr, Triathlete' card with stats and everything on the back." As I've grown older, my admiration for what my mom did as a triathlete only grows. She's even more heroic to me now.

YOU WILL MOTIVATE AND INSPIRE THOSE AROUND YOU

The courage and determination you show in pursuing a triathlon may inspire those around you to elevate their fitness and their lives. Or at the very least, your quest will spark in others the possibility that they can do more. ("Hey, if this bozo can do it, surely I can!") Bringing people to that realization is a wonderful gift. Knowing that you have set an example for someone to go after their dreams or to make a positive change in their life is a reward that simply cannot be matched.

YOU WILL SET OTHER POSITIVE THINGS IN MOTION— THINGS YOU NEVER IMAGINED

I know from personal experience that training for a triathlon event can totally transform your life. In 1994, when I decided to train for my first triathlon in the U.S. Virgin Islands, the extent of my exercise was walking to the local mango stand for lunch. It took courage to register for the race, but taking that one simple step set dozens of other unforeseen, positive steps into motion. I began eating better, I had more energy, and I grew more sensitized to the joys of everyday life. I was a much more passionate and giving person because I felt so good about myself. That meant I could begin giving to others more. It may sound trite, but I began racing on behalf of animal welfare, something I likely would never have done if I hadn't pursued the triathlon.

The moment you finish a triathlon, you will be astounded at the new realm of possibilities that open up to you. The only obstacles barring your way are your self-imposed excuses, fears, and doubts. Overcoming them, and moving past them to where your real power dwells, is what the next chapter is about.

2
PUT YOUR EXCUSES TO REST

"The prudent see only the difficulties, the bold only the advantages, of a great enterprise; the hero sees both, diminishes the former and makes the latter preponderate, and so conquers."

—JOHANN KASPAR LAVATER, 18TH-CENTURY POET

I am a tireless optimist, but after Chapter 1, I think we need a "let's be real for a moment" pause.

Although the benefits you stand to reap from training for and completing a triathlon are impressive, is this thing really possible? Just think of all the excuses and reasons you've already enumerated as to why you cannot, should not, and will not do a triathlon. I bet you have a million. I sure did when I began.

It's funny, really. That we tend to approach new challenges with more trepidation than optimism is an adult phenomenon. When we were kids, we thought anything was possible. We didn't give much thought to our own limitations. We'd see a tree and climb it (and get stuck in it!). Yet as we grow older and take on more responsibilities, we start believing less is possible. That belief can chip away at our spirit, our sense of adventure, and our ability to have fun and feel youthful.

This is especially true of a triathlon. Think about it: The first time you picked up this book, you were likely intrigued at the prospect, but didn't you also instantly think of reasons not to do it? Try to approach your triathlon more like a child excited to embark on an adventure than an adult who sees obstacles.

This chapter will help you tear down those obstacles that could keep you from training for a triathlon by listing and providing solutions to each one. More broadly, this chapter talks about how and why we limit ourselves and how we can stand up to our self-imposed excuses and fears. It's about wiping away your excuses and putting yourself first—at least for the next six to eight weeks.

NO MORE EXCUSES

Most barriers to success are self-imposed. We tend to make our excuses bigger than they really are, and that prevents us from living fully.

Take out a sheet of paper and write down every reason why you cannot or should not do this triathlon. (Do this for anything in your life, and you'll find that many of

TRIATHLON TALE: HE TACKLED A TRIATHLON

Former NFL lineman and Super Bowl champion Darryl Haley weighed more than 330 pounds. As a pro football player, he was fit in the traditional sense of the word—he could run laps, lift weights, and pulverize stuffed dummies. But Darryl often felt lethargic, sore, and unhealthy. He performed well on the football field, but he didn't like the way his body worked off the field.

In 1997, when Darryl watched the Hawaii Ironman on television, he was struck by how efficiently the competitors moved, regardless of their body shape. He longed for the same freedom of movement.

So Darryl pushed aside all the reasons he couldn't do it and dared to dream. He set out to train for his first triathlon—a sprint-distance event in upstate New York. When Darryl began, he couldn't get across the swimming pool without gasping for air. He couldn't find a bicycle to fit his colossal frame. Running long distances hurt his knees, joints

that had taken too many thrashings from opposing running backs during his football career. But he kept at it.

As the weeks progressed, Darryl began swimming with more graceful fluidity; he found a custom-frame builder to make a bike for him; and he lost nearly 50 pounds, which eased the pressure on his knees. Undeniably, the triathlon was forcing Darryl to strengthen his weaknesses and find solutions to his excuses. That process was, in itself, very rewarding for him.

Ten weeks after he began, on January 14, 1998, Darryl Haley crossed the finish line of his first triathlon hand in hand with someone he didn't know, but with whom he shared a look of sheer, unabashed joy.

"The feeling I had was as exhilarating as when we won the Super Bowl," says Darryl. "In fact, even better. I overcame my personal demons and physical obstacles—on my own—to finish this triathlon. It was all me. And that was incredible."

your excuses for not doing a triathlon match those you use in other areas of your life.) Use the examples provided in this chapter as a guide and add some of your own.

After you've completed your Excuse List, look at each excuse objectively. Acknowledge the part that is true and root out the lie. Then, use the information below to write a rebuttal for each excuse, like this:

Excuse: I can't do a triathlon because I don't have time.

Rebuttal: My time is limited, but I can watch a little less TV each week and streamline my exercise program. I will look and feel better than I ever have in my life.

Finally, record each excuse and rebuttal on a separate three-by-five-inch index card. Refer to these cards as you find yourself giving the same excuses later on. You'll find it much more difficult to procrastinate when your solutions are staring you in the face.

Now, let's take a look at the most common excuses that stop people from tackling the triathlon, along with simple solutions to each.

EXCUSE NUMBER 1:
I DON'T HAVE TIME

Between work, family, and other activities, most of us are considerably time-pressed. But how is it we have no time to exercise, yet we've seen every episode of *The West Wing* since it began? The truth is, we make choices each day that determine our quality of life and our health and fitness. Some of us simply choose not to spend part of our free time exercising. The psychology is simple: When it comes to leisure, we make time for what we enjoy, and we put off—or avoid entirely—what we don't.

SET YOUR PRIORITIES

Because we all have less time these days, it's vital to focus on our most important life priorities, which likely include these four core areas:

1. Career/money/security
2. Family/friends
3. Health
4. Fun/happiness

Look objectively at how you prioritize your time. A week consists of 168 hours. You spend about 50 working and 50 sleeping. What do you do with the other 68? Even if you were to evenly divide the above priority areas into those 68 hours, it would give you 17 each week to devote entirely to your health. This triathlon training program takes only four!

> **ACTION ITEM:** *Figure out where your time goes each day by creating a Time Journal. Over a 24-hour period write down every activity you do—including eating, watching TV, talking on the phone, driving, bathing, and so on. Once people see their day plotted out on paper, they're often surprised by how much time they waste each day and how little they devote to their priorities. Does your daily to-do list correspond with your life priorities? Figure out what doesn't and move it to the bottom of your list. Your priorities should rise to the top.*

Although many people consistently rate health as one of their three highest life priorities, their daily schedules typically do not reflect that. Sadly, as we've put off regular exercise, we've accepted a lower standard of health over time. Though you may not immediately feel the effects of relegating exercise to the end of your to-do list, your body is keeping track. And one day, it'll demand payment—with interest.

Committing to "get back in shape" is not enough. To regain permanent control of your body and your health, you must block out periods of time for physical fitness each week.

> **ACTION ITEM:** *Write your scheduled workouts into your daily planner and assign them high priority. Be vigilant and selfish in protecting this exercise time, because the demands of daily life will threaten to take it from you. Treat these commitments to yourself like any important business appointment that you wouldn't consider missing.*

FREE UP SOME TIME

As you begin to schedule your workouts, ask yourself this: To what extent is your busy schedule the result of simply filling your days with more to-do items? Can your life be simplified? Few, if any, daily schedules are so demanding that there isn't room for four hours a week.

Here are several things you can do to free up time over the next six weeks.

TURN OFF THE TV. Of all the time- and energy-saving strategies I know, I believe this one has the most potential to instantly liberate your time and improve your mental well-being and quality of life. The average American watches 27 hours of television each week. This says nothing of the cost in mental currency: The relentless barrage of negative TV images can exhaust you.

The first TV-free week will bring on withdrawal-like symptoms, and you may wander the house wondering what to do with your newly liberated time. After a couple of weeks, however, you'll begin to enjoy the quiet and the quality time with your family, yourself, and your training.

ACTION ITEM: Call your cable company and request that they suspend your service for six weeks. You can even request an automatic resumption after that time so that you can relax, knowing it will return. If you need to stay abreast of the news, do it online or via newspapers.

PUT EXERCISE FIRST. Get up an hour earlier and exercise first thing in the morning. Studies have shown that people are four times more likely to exercise in the morning than in the evening. This is probably because putting off a workout until later in the day makes it too easy to skip in favor of accomplishing other things. As a bonus, the solitude and peace of a morning exercise session nourishes your soul, making you more productive all day.

SIMPLIFY YOUR WORKOUT. Streamline your fitness approach by reducing the "friction" in your training program. If you drive 30 minutes to the gym, change clothes, wait for machines, lift weights, chitchat with complete strangers, shower, get dressed, and drive home, you're only spending a fraction of your time actually working out.

ACTION ITEM: Examine your exercise habits and eliminate time-wasters. For example, work out at home instead of at a gym. Run or bike earlier in the morning or after the evening rush hour when fewer people are on the road. Store all of your gear in one place—like a closet or trunk—so you can find everything you need and be out the door in 10 minutes. Keep your cycling gear in good working order so you aren't wasting time on your rides making repairs.

DO MORE RUNNING. Of the three triathlon sports, running requires the least amount of preparation. Just strap on your shoes and head out the front door. At work, use your lunch break to fit in a nice, steady 30- to 45-minute run. Do this once or twice a week and you'll go a long way toward fitting in all of your training workouts. Take your running shoes and heart rate monitor with you on business trips, and you'll have the world's most efficient "portable gym."

Running is also one of the most effective sports for building aerobic fitness. So if you need to substitute runs for bike rides or swims, that's fine. Just be sure to maintain your feel for the other sports by doing them at least once each week.

DOUBLE UP. You can double your fitness benefits by doing workouts that give you both strength and aerobic benefits concurrently. For example, run in the hills, cycle with extra weight on your bike, or swim with paddles.

GET FIT WITH YOUR FAMILY. One of the more daunting challenges triathletes face is fitting training around family responsibilities. When you find yourself skipping exercise because of family obligations, it may be time to integrate your children and partner into your exercise life.

TRIATHLON TALE: ▰ ▰ ▰ ▰ ▰ ▰ ▰ ▰ ▰ ▰ ▰ ▰ ▰ ▰ ▰
SHE MADE IT A FAMILY AFFAIR

Sharon Egan, 43, is a single mother of two beautiful daughters: Tara, 13, and Makayla, 11. Sharon is vice president of communications at Trinity Springs in Paradise, Idaho, the world's leading marketer of geothermal water. She invests a lot of hours in her job, which has exacted its toll on her health and fitness—and on her spirit.

Sharon used to be an avid cyclist and basketball player, but on a recent run, she had to stop after just five and a half minutes. She hadn't realized how far her fitness had slipped.

In addition, as her children grow more independent, Sharon, like most good parents, has begun to grow anxious over the loss of their family time together. She also finds herself worried about the negative social influences on her kids, such as drugs and alcohol, violence and promiscuity in the media, and "contagious" depression stemming from spiritual disconnectedness.

I offered to train Sharon for a triathlon on one condition: that she train with her daughters. This would address three important issues facing the family. First, it would help Sharon get into the best shape of her life. Second, it would provide her, Makayla, and Tara with a common goal, bonding them more deeply. Third, and perhaps most important, the process of training for a triathlon would keep the kids focused on a positive, healthy endeavor—and make their confidence and self-esteem soar.

Sharon snapped up the offer. I helped her design a simple, streamlined triathlon program that integrated her daughters into almost every workout. For example, the younger Makayla rode her bike as Sharon and Tara ran.

Six weeks after we first talked, Sharon finished her triathlon with Makayla and Tara in tow. All three beamed with pride and excitement as they crossed the finish line together, holding hands. It was an achievement they will remember fondly for the rest of their lives.

Sharon says of the endeavor, "Tara, Makayla, and I experienced what the triathlon is all about: commitment, self-esteem, empowerment, joy, and health!"

Record-low levels of physical activity have led to record-high rates of child obesity. This threatens the long-term health of our nation: Today's overweight children are likely to become tomorrow's obese adults, placing them at risk for various health problems, including high blood pressure, heart attack, and diabetes. Meanwhile, parents are busier than ever and have less time for exercise.

That's the bad news. Here's the good. These two serious and pervasive problems can be improved concurrently with one simple move: Do your triathlon training with your children.

"Integrating family and fitness is probably the single most effective way to boost your children's health and liberate more exercise time for you," says Steve Bennett, co-author of *365 TV-Free Activities You Can Do with Your Child*.

One reason children may avoid exercise is that it's often not as much fun as it should be. School coaches, overzealous parents, and a culture that places a premium on winning engender performance anxieties in our children. We all want our children to grow into healthy adults. For that to happen, they must develop positive associations with physical activity early on. Experts say that telling kids to "go exercise" isn't as effective as saying "Let's go play." So redefine your perception of exercise. Any running, cycling, or swimming you do will lead you to your triathlon goal, whether you are jogging on a treadmill at the gym or running through a park with your child in a high-energy game of hide-and-seek. Think—and play—like a kid again.

Another great strategy is to ride tandem with your children. Adams Trail-a-Bike is a great product that turns your bicycle into a child-friendly tandem (a bicycle built for two). This unique attachment allows you to safely share the excitement of cycling with children ages 2 to 12. If your kids are younger, use a bike trailer or a baby jogger to train with them in tow.

Getting your partner involved as well is another great way to combine training with family. Even if your partner isn't a triathlete, the two of you can still go for a hike, run, or bike ride together. Working out with a friend or loved one will provide some rewarding moments. Of the more than 10,000 workouts I've done, the most fulfilling ones have been the easy runs alongside my wife on her mountain bike across the trails of Mount Tamalpais. We enjoy taking in the breathtaking scenery together, and we both get a great workout.

EXCUSE NUMBER 2:
THE TRIATHLON IS A LONG, GRUELING EVENT THAT TAKES HOURS TO COMPLETE

After "lack of time," this is probably the most common excuse for not doing a triathlon. That's because most people don't realize that triathlons come in all distances—and some take only 90 minutes or less to complete.

Granted, the Ironman distance (a 2.4-mile swim, 112-mile bike, and 26.2-mile run) can take up to 17 hours to finish. But one of the most popular triathlons is the sprint distance: a 400- to 600-meter swim, a 10- to 15-mile bike ride, and a 2- to 4-mile run. This book will help you finish a sprint-distance triathlon—and even a more taxing Olympic-distance or half-Ironman, if you so desire.

> *ACTION ITEM: Once you choose an activity to do together, schedule time to do it on a regular basis— no excuses. Make this an ironclad commitment. With today's hectic lifestyle, people often advocate "quality over quantity" in relationships. That's a cop-out. You must have lots of quantity to deepen the quality of your relationship. And your triathlon training sessions provide the ideal time for that.*

EXCUSE NUMBER 3:
I CAN'T STAY MOTIVATED

Lagging exercise motivation is a common problem that all of us—even champion athletes—face at times. Sometimes, no matter how dedicated you are, you have to sell yourself on working out.

PUT TOGETHER A GREAT BENEFITS PACKAGE. Research has shown that people are more likely to commit their time and energy to an activity when they can identify its benefits in advance. So the key to maintaining a long-term exercise program is identifying the benefits of working out. They can be physical ("This run will burn a half-pound of pure body fat" or "I'm going to take 20 seconds off my mile time"), emotional ("This swim will release all of my stress from work"), or social ("I get to catch up with Jenn and John on our bike ride today!"). Focusing on such results provides intrinsic motivation. This is what motivates world-class athletes to train seven hours a day for years on end. When you learn to tap your intrinsic motivations, you will rarely lack the will to work out.

I witnessed true intrinsic motivation when I ran alongside a few of the Marathon Monks of Japan's sacred Mount Hiei. For a period of 100 days, these "running Buddhas" cover 52.4 miles daily. That's twice the length of an Olympic marathon—each day. The prize they seek isn't a slimmer waistline or a few fleeting moments of glory. It is to capture the greatest thing they feel a human being can achieve: enlightenment. That's light-years away from how most of us view exercise, but it's a prime example of intrinsic motivation.

External motivation can also be a powerful thing. This can take the form of rewards you give yourself after particularly successful workouts. For example, to motivate herself to run every day for two weeks, my wife promised herself a new item of clothing at the end of that time period. (Of course, implicit in this plan was that I would pay for the clothes.) She was on a mission: I watched her storm out the door every day—and if I got in her way, she'd hurl her diminutive frame, linebackerlike, right at me. For those two weeks, the prospect of wearing a new dress motivated my wife.

The point is that to achieve lasting fitness success, you must use all the tools at your disposal, leveraging both your intrinsic and external motivations. Don't plan a mere "one-hour run." Instead, schedule a "one-hour stress reduction activity" or "one-hour speed development activity." Incorporate external rewards into your program as well: Set a goal to run a mile in under six minutes, and promise that when you achieve that goal, your reward will be a weekend getaway with your friends or a loved one. You'll be more motivated to break that six-minute barrier—and you'll have supporters cheering for you the entire way.

APPROACH EACH WORKOUT AS IF IT WERE YOUR LAST. If the events of September 11, 2001, taught us anything, it's that life can take an unimaginable turn in seconds. Now more people are "living for today" than ever before. They are turning to the things that matter most: love, family, health, quality of life.

If someone told you that beginning tomorrow morning you were going to be paralyzed from the waist down, how would you spend the remainder of today? You'd likely appreciate every single movement you can make, touching your legs and being infinitely grateful for them.

Almost every time I begin an exercise session, I picture myself not being able to move a single, solitary muscle in my body. I try to imagine what that must feel like. Then and only then do I start running. My perspective completely shifts to deep appreciation and gratitude. I become aware of each part of my body, and I feel so deeply thankful for it. At that point, exercise becomes less of a requirement and more of a privilege.

Exercise provides us with a tangible time each day to pause, to take stock of our lives, to appreciate life, and to nurture our minds, bodies, and souls. Approaching each workout with the attitude that it could be your last is one of the most immediate and enduring ways to redefine your relationship with physical fitness.

EXCUSE NUMBER 4:
EXERCISE IS BORING

I believe this is one of the main reasons why America is the most obese nation in the world. We simply don't enjoy exercise. Here in America, exercise has become less about being the best you can be and more about counting the calories you burn. This type of exercise disconnects our body, mind, and spirit and makes physical fitness just another task to cross off our daily to-do list.

DO IT FOR THE RIGHT REASONS. Take an honest look at what you dislike about exercising. Often, negative feelings stem from the notion that you must live up to somebody else's standards. Exercise to please yourself, focus on your health instead of your weight, and quit counting the calories you burn. Redefine your relationship with exercise. It must be passion driven rather than guilt induced.

MAKE IT FUN. When we were children, physical activity was all about play. Kickball, tag, Boogieboarding—we spent hours, without thought, playing our favorite sports. I used to Boogieboard at Stinson Beach well beyond the point of my lips turning blue. I had no idea that in those two hours of kicking wildly in the ocean, I burned 1,200 calories. The calories burned were a natural consequence of having fun, not the focus of the activity.

That passion for sport is one reason why children are so energetic all the time, why they sleep so soundly, and why they are always so full of excitement.

So when did we stop playing and start "working out"? I suspect it happened sometime in our late teens to early twenties. Exercise became another form of work. That's too bad, because physical activity isn't meant to be work. You work enough! It's time to get out there and play again.

You'll notice that when you play your favorite sport, time fades away, just as when you were a kid. You become fully immersed in the activity, and as a result, you lose your self-consciousness. That's how you want to feel during workouts.

ACTION ITEM: Do you remember how you felt when you were 10 years old? During your next workout, try to capture that feeling, if only for fleeting moments. Be passionate! The only rule is that you have to let go of all rules and expectations. This technique of "play" takes practice, but it's very well worth it. For those of you serious about performance, it will help you reach your potential by opening up your body and mind and relaxing your approach.

GIVE YOURSELF A CHANGE OF SCENERY. In exercise, as in real estate, the key is location, location, location. It's a big, exciting world out there, yet many of us confine our workouts to limited venues. We do the same old walk every day. Our bike rides follow the same route over the same roads. We crowd into gyms and wait for overbooked stairclimbers when there's a perfectly good hiking trail just 10 minutes away.

Working out in the same place over and over can eventually lead to exercise ennui—and boredom is the death knell of a fitness program. Physical activity should be fun and adventurous; it should provide you with emotional and spiritual payoffs as well as physical ones. "The environment in which we exercise determines, in large part, our enjoyment for that activity and how well we perform," says Kelly Brownell, PhD, Duke University dean and former Yale University psychology professor. "Our moods are often shaped by where we are. The feeling you get at the beach is very different from how you feel in an office building."

ACTION ITEM: At least twice a month make an effort to exercise somewhere new. The change of scenery will keep you enthused about your exercise program and prevent boredom from setting in.

EXCUSE NUMBER 5:
I DON'T HAVE THE ENERGY

Many of us are so busy that, at the end of a long day, we'd rather sink into the couch than run up a mountain. The notion of completing a triathlon can seem downright impossible.

The low-energy, minimal-exercise routine is a vicious cycle. It works like this: The less energy you have, the less you want to exercise. The less you exercise, the less energy you have. Follow the training program in this book and you'll not only break this vicious cycle but also set a new one in motion. Study after study shows that engaging in physical activity actually makes you feel *more* energized, decreases stress and tension, and promotes better sleep.

That's right. Training for a triathlon can actually give you more energy, in essence "adding" time to your day. Follow this book's program and you'll have at least 10 percent more stamina, resiliency, and energy. Imagine how much more you'll be able to do each day with that extra vigor. You'll be able to train for the triathlon *and* find time to watch the latest episode of your favorite show.

EXCUSE NUMBER 6:
I WILL EMBARRASS MYSELF

In the sport of triathlon, more value is placed on finishing than on performing. That's why when you watch a triathlon, you'll witness something distinctive in the sports world: The roar of the crowd grows louder as the event goes on. I don't know of any other sport in which the last finishers get more cheers than the first.

As a professional, I always marvel at the people who finish near the back of the pack—and most pros feel this way. Full-time triathletes get to nap and train all day. That's not all

TRIATHLON TALE: ▰ ▰ ▰ ▰ ▰ ▰ ▰ ▰ ▰ ▰ ▰ ▰
HIS ENERGY SKYROCKETED

Forty-something Martin Keller is a father of three and a successful attorney at a major law firm. He's a high-powered man who had been suffering from a low-powered energy supply.

"As I grew older, I found that I was much less energetic," he says. "I could get through a workday just fine, but when I was finished, I had little or no energy for what matters most—my family. "When I began training for a triathlon using Eric Harr's principles, my energy levels skyrocketed. I could not believe it. I felt 15 years younger. And now, honest to God, my kids have to try to keep up with me!"

that impressive. The part-time triathletes—the moms, the accountants, the construction workers, the people with full-time jobs—are the real heroes of the sport. They manage to train for a triathlon despite their busy lives and are highly revered at triathlon events.

Most people who do triathlons are first-, second-, or third-timers, just like you. So there's no need to worry about embarrassing yourself. Even if you finish dead last, you'll be a hero to those watching.

EXCUSE NUMBER 7:
I HAVE AN INJURY/PAIN/ILLNESS

Pain and injury present seemingly insurmountable obstacles to better fitness and quality of life. When you're sick or injured, you may *want* to exercise and you may *try* to exercise, but the injury or pain stops you in your tracks. You don't need me to tell you how this destroys motivation.

There are two ways to approach preexisting pain or injury as it relates to your triathlon. You can either let it stop you completely or let it motivate you. You can say, for example:

1. "My knees hurt when I run, therefore I cannot train for this event."
2. "I've been living with this knee pain for years, and I'm going to do this triathlon. I will find the best doctors and be relentless in eliminating the pain once and for all, so I can enjoy my life."

Which do you think I'm going to suggest? Number two, of course. In the words of author Robert Louis Stevenson: "You cannot run away from a weakness; you must sometimes fight it out or perish; and if that be so, why not now and where you stand?" A big part of training for a triathlon is strengthening your weaknesses.

Granted, none of us likes to face our weaknesses, let alone work on them. But ignoring them can reduce your ability to reach higher levels of health, performance, and quality of life. If you have bad knees and commit to finishing a triathlon, you'll become determined to fix your knees. Otherwise you may never be compelled to address that pain and you may go through life needlessly suffering from it.

In trying to overcome your pain or injury, you may need to look for less traditional ways to train for and complete the triathlon. Did you know that water running is a

TRIATHLON BY THE NUMBERS

Triathlons—long considered the domain of the super-fit elite—have been soaring in popularity. Before you think the sport is beyond your reach, check out these numbers.

- USA Triathlon, the governing body of the sport, estimates that more than 200,000 people ages 6 to 84 completed their first triathlon in 2001. Of those, 98 percent had nine-to-five jobs.
- At age 81, Lew Hollander finished the 2011 Hawaii Ironman (a 2.4-mile swim, 112-mile bike, and 26.2-mile run) in 16 hours, 46 minutes, becoming the oldest athlete ever to finish the Ironman World Championship race.
- Former NFL lineman Darryl Haley weighed nearly 300 pounds when he finished his first triathlon. Since then, he's finished more than 14, including four Ironman events.
- John MacLean, paralyzed from the waist down, has completed more than 50 triathlon events powered by just his two arms.
- Paralympic athlete Rudy Garcia-Tolson had his legs amputated at age 5, finished 21 triathlons by the age of 14, and at age 26 is the first double amputee to complete a full Ironman triathlon.

great way to train for your event or that most pros walk at some point during the triathlon? You can even walk the entire run portion of your event if you want to. Remember, triathlons attract people of all shapes and sizes, including those who have sustained serious injuries and those who use a wheelchair. (For more information on overcoming pain or injury, see Chapter 11.)

EXCUSE NUMBER 8:
I'M TOO FAT/THIN/TALL/SHORT/OLD/YOUNG

Let me remind you of the prerequisites for becoming a triathlete.

1. An ability to set aside your self-imposed limits and allow yourself to dream—for just six weeks
2. A willingness to follow the program in this book

That's it. Notice there are no requirements related to size, age, background, ability, gender, or fitness level in those prerequisites. There simply is no perfect triathlon body type. True, the top professionals are lean, but they all have very different bodies. Some are short and sturdy, others tall and lanky. Watch the "middle of the packers" and you'll notice a rich tapestry of body builds. I guarantee that you'll see at least one person just like you: same weight, same build, same age. If that person can do it, so can you.

Speaking of age, did you know that some of the best marathon runners in the world are in their mid- to late thirties and early forties? Train your body properly and you can perform well into your forties, fifties, and sixties. You're older than that? Hundreds of people over age 70 actually *race* Ironman-distance triathlons. It isn't about age; it's about attitude. Shift yours.

> "Look at me. I'm the 'anti-triathlete.' These people are iron men and women; I'm an aluminum man. But that's what's so cool about this sport—it doesn't matter who you are or how you're built. Just that you're there. So get out there and give one a try."
>
> —ROBIN WILLIAMS

EXCUSE NUMBER 9:
MY SPOUSE/FAMILY/FRIENDS WON'T SUPPORT ME

Break this excuse down. It essentially means that the people who love and care about you won't support an endeavor that will make you a healthier, fitter, more confident and happier human being. That seems very strange.

If the people in your life won't support this admirable and incredibly positive quest, you have three choices: (1) Ignore them, (2) get them involved, or (3) seek the company of people who *will* support you. Throughout this book, I note the benefits of training with others. Find fitness enthusiasts who share your passion for exercise. They will instantly become your support system.

EXCUSE NUMBER 10:
THE WHOLE THING JUST COSTS TOO MUCH

A triathlon is made up of three sports, so it requires more equipment than other sports. But what if I told you that gearing up for a triathlon can cost you less than buying a single exercise machine—and provide you with better results and greater enjoyment?

As you'll learn in Chapter 3, you need only 14 items to train for and complete a triathlon, and much of this gear can be borrowed from friends and family or bought used. For information on how to get discounts on everything from gear to the race entry fee, turn to page 259.

EXCUSE NUMBER 11:
I LIVE IN A CLIMATE THAT MAKES TRAINING DIFFICULT

Did you know that three of the best Ironman triathletes in the world live in inhospitable climates, yet they manage to train more than 25 hours a week? Peter Reid lives in Vancouver, British Columbia. Tim DeBoom lives in the Rocky Mountains. Luc Van Lierde lives in Belgium. All are Ironman World Champions. Do you think these guys make excuses?

Putting this excuse to rest is a simple exercise in overcoming adversity and making the best of your situation. It just takes a little creativity and determination. Realistically, you may have to do a lot of your workouts indoors, but there are ways to make those workouts more enjoyable. For example, ride your bike on an indoor trainer while watching your favorite TV show or listening to a new CD. Join a Spinning class to work on cycling technique. During particularly cold or wet stretches, focus on building aerobic fitness by swimming in an indoor pool.

And as you'll learn in Chapter 9, training too much or too strenuously during the cold winter months may be counterproductive anyway. Reserve most of your focused exercise for spring and summer, when Mother Nature will facilitate your success, not thwart it.

EXCUSE NUMBER 12:
I'M OUT OF SHAPE, AND I HAVE NO BACKGROUND IN THESE SPORTS

This is your opportunity to achieve the best physical shape of your life and master three exciting sports. If you have no background in swimming, cycling, or running, now is your chance to learn. It's easy to give in to pessimism and do nothing. Or you

ENJOY THE JOURNEY

When you let go of focusing on a performance or a destination and instead do your best and appreciate every moment, very special things happen to you.

In 1999, I had high hopes of finishing on the podium (the top three) at the Ironman Canada Triathlon. I trained maniacally toward that goal for 40 hours a week for six months. By the time I toed the start line on the cool waters of Okanagan Lake, in Penticton, British Columbia, I was so nervous that my entire body trembled and I grew dizzy. I was completely blind to the beauty of the race site, the positive collective energy of the other racers, and the fact that I was about to embark on one of the great challenges of my life. I should have been excited, but I was too busy focusing on the finish line.

The race progressed well for me initially. After the 112-mile bike portion of the event, I was in fourth place and running strong. Then, at the precise moment that winning became possible, things quickly disintegrated. My body began slowing down gradually and inexorably to a walk. I slid from fourth to eighth to tenth overall. It was embarrassing.

I was so set on a top three finish that when it became clear it wouldn't happen, I lost my heart—and my body followed. I refused to acknowledge the amazing people cheering for me and the pats on the back from other participants. Instead I thought, "How can you be supporting me? I'm *walking*!"

All of that changed at mile 18 of the run, when I caught up with the early leader, Tony O'Hagan from New Zealand, who was also walking and in bad shape. I put my arm around him and said, "Tony, it isn't about winning anymore, it's about finishing." He barely had the energy to nod in acknowledgment, but he did—and my wife, following me on her mountain bike, began crying uncontrollably.

That's when my entire perspective shifted. It was as if a haze had been cleared from my field of vision. I began to glimpse the power of the triathlon, what every triathlete told me was so special about the sport. I looked around and thought, "This is really unbelievable—all of these people from around the world coming together to brave this monumental challenge. I am going to enjoy every remaining moment of the day."

The racers at the back of the pack who were just heading out on the run, in the opposite direction from Tony and me, cheered for us despite their fatigue and pain and the long road ahead. I began to see the soul, the indomitable spirit of these people. They were ordinary people doing an extraordinary thing. That made me very emotional. I was swept up in the humanity of the triathlon—and for the first time in my career, six years after my first triathlon event, I finally understood what the whole thing meant: The triathlon is about real people, in the midst of their own authentic experiences, courageously working through their doubts, fears, and excuses to give, and to be, their best.

Ironically, at the moment I turned my attention to the present, I began performing better. My body became loose, my spirit felt free, and I began running—all the way to the finish.

Whatever your goals, the primary objective of your training should be to experience the joy of the process. Go at it this way and you cannot fail.

can say, "Damn right I'm out of shape and I don't know how to do these sports—all the more reason to do a triathlon!"

EXCUSE NUMBER 13:
I JUST CAN'T TAKE THAT FIRST STEP

My coach ingrained in me a powerful phrase that I repeat to myself whenever I lose the confidence to keep going: "Motivation follows action." In other words, the best way to overcome your fear of taking that first step is to take that first step. That may sound like oversimplification, but it's right on the money. If you embark tomorrow on the program in Chapter 9 and establish a little momentum, you'll be surprised at how your motivation will grow.

As with any difficult or long endeavor, shift your focus to the process rather than the destination. After all, the destination of a triathlon is a very small part of your total journey. As you progress, take it one small step at a time. If you haven't exercised for a long time, your first step is to refamiliarize yourself with physical movement. Dust off your bike and warm up to it again, like an old friend. In the first few weeks, you may move two steps forward and then one back, but by approaching the process in this manner, you're never too far from your next step—which is the only one you need to take.

You can decide right this very moment to step out your front door and start training. Even if it's just a walk around the block, that courageous, all-important first step will set a series of other steps into motion.

EXCUSE NUMBER 14:
I HAVE NO GUIDANCE

You hold in your hands all the information you need to finish—or reach your potential in—a triathlon. In the pages that follow, I walk you through each week of training, help you prepare for your triathlon, and even take you through your race day minute by minute. No coach could be more accessible!

GET BACK INTO THE FITNESS SWING

Little will deflate your exercise motivation more than staring at a pair of running shoes you haven't laced up in months. Those shoes can conjure up a litany of doubts, fears, and excuses. And you may even succumb to them with a comforting pint of ice cream and a cozy visit to the couch, extending both the cycle of inactivity and the circumference of your waistline.

Here's how to get back into the fitness swing after a long layoff.

TOSS THE ALL-OR-NOTHING APPROACH. Exercising too much too soon could lead to pain, injury, and, worst of all, burnout that puts you right back on the couch with ice cream in hand.

Instead, increase your exercise volume slowly, 5 to 15 percent a week. For example, if you run 2 hours during your first week back and that feels good, increase that amount to 2 hours and 15 minutes the next week, then assess how you handled the increase. This may seem like slow progress, but gradually increasing your exercise—and taking days off when you need them—is essential to creating a fitness program you can stick with.

SHIFT YOUR FOCUS. From now on, view your body as a work of art and think of your training as an artist's tool. In other words, any work you do on your body will improve its beauty. Every workout is positive, no matter how short

DON'T BEAT YOURSELF UP. Let go of any layoff-related guilt, which can derail you from your fitness program. Guilt is a disempowering emotion that has no place in your life. Say you decide to skip a workout. Yes, you miss out on fitness benefits, but guilt only compounds that and can jeopardize your entire program. After you miss a few workouts, you lose steam and give up on your fitness program entirely.

People often say to me, "Eric, I began a great new exercise plan and stuck to it for three weeks. Then I quit. I failed." My response is, "Are you crazy? Three weeks of training is fantastic. You just improved your life by 21 days!"

Look, you are in complete control of your decisions. Either go for your scheduled run—right now—or sit your butt down, watch television, and enjoy it. If you decide to skip your workout, skip it with passion and feel confident about it. Enjoy the fact that you are playing hooky. Make the most of that downtime, and then commit to getting back to business and giving a little more effort in your next workout.

Of course, if you wish, you also can team up with other first-time triathletes and train with them under the watchful eye of an experienced coach. To locate a group near you, log on to triathlon.competitor.com.

So there you have it. No more excuses.

Now you can move on to the next step. Turn the page and I'll show you how to gear up for a triathlon without tearing through your life's savings.

3
GEAR UP WITHOUT BLOWING YOUR BUDGET

"Distrust any enterprise that requires new clothes."

—HENRY DAVID THOREAU

Triathletes are famous for their propensity to use the latest, greatest, highest-technology gear—and for the spending that goes with it. But most of us don't have a large stash of money to fork over for slickly produced athletic clothes and gadgetry. So you'll be glad to know that I kept Thoreau's words in mind when I wrote this chapter.

Granted, the three-sport triathlon requires more gear than a simple bike race. But the truth is, gearing up for a triathlon does not require tons of technology or new clothing. In fact, you only need about 14 items, plus a few other optional accessories. And there are ways to get this gear without spending a fortune.

The smartest and most economical way to pull together the gear you need is to borrow it from friends or family. This accomplishes two important things: (1) You get the gear you need at no cost to you, and (2) you build a support network by getting your friends and family involved in your training.

If you discover you truly love the sport after your triathlon (and you likely will), then go ahead and invest in your own gear—but choose slightly used items over those that are brand new.

"Most competitive triathletes are obsessed with having the latest, coolest gear. You can benefit from this," says Tim DeBoom, Ironman world champion. "To make room for the newest stuff, many triathletes will sell last year's gear, in perfectly good shape

PERSONAL TRAINING

Like a hot new piece of gear, personal trainers have become status symbols in this country. But do they really help us achieve long-term fitness results?

Granted, social facilitation—the notion of being accountable to someone else—is a powerful motivator. If you respond best to having a coach or personal trainer guide you, by all means pursue it.

But you know your body better than anyone else does, and you can become your own trainer. If you're reading this book, you're already doing just that. Of course, if you have a medical question, consult the real expert: your doctor. And if all you need is a little company when you work out, enlist a friend or family member.

---

at affordable prices. Some pros will even sell off their sponsored gear when they sign new sponsors for the following season."

You'll find such gear offered for sale in triathlon magazines or on such Web sites as Craigslist and eBay. These sites now have strong consumer-protection policies in place to safeguard your purchases, so there's no need to worry about shady dealings. Despite conventional wisdom, avoid secondhand athletic gear stores; they often inflate their prices.

Now that you have strategies for keeping your spending in check, you're likely wondering which gear is worth the dough you're willing to spend. As a professional triathlete with 20 years of competing under my bike tires, I've tried and tested hundreds, if not thousands, of products. My livelihood has relied on my ability to separate fact from fiction and to find what works best—in the real world, not just in focus groups. I've noted below the products I've found to be among the best performing, most reliable, and highest quality products. But that's all they are: my picks. I cannot choose the best products for you. That is your job. But it's my belief that you can't go wrong with the brands I suggest.

WARMUP SUIT

WHAT TO LOOK FOR: A light sweat suit or warmup suit to wear before and after workouts and on race day before the race begins. You may want to wear tight-fitting stretch pants, which warm your muscles without adding bulk to your legs—you can even wear them when warming up on your bike. To save money, wear your warmup suit after the race as well, instead of buying a separate postrace outfit for that purpose.

WHAT IT COSTS: Don't spend more than $100 for both top and bottoms.

WHAT I RECOMMEND: First, you want to be comfortable. So start there. Fashion comes next. You want to look good and feel good. You cannot go wrong with these three brands: Garneau, Craft, or Pearl Izumi.

SWIMSUIT

WHAT TO LOOK FOR: A sleek suit in which you feel comfortable. For women, a one-piecer works great for training sessions and for the duration of the event. For men, if you want to "go old school," then by all means rock the Speedo-type brief. You can also choose what's known as a drag suit (baggy trunks that provide resistance) for a better training effect.

WHAT IT COSTS: Women, $40; men, $20.

WHAT I RECOMMEND: For training, you can't go wrong with TYR, Speedo, or Zoot.

RACING SUIT

WHAT TO LOOK FOR: There are one-piece tri suits that are suitable (pun intended) for racing and offer reduced friction in the water. You can also ride and run in them on race day to save time. If you're more comfortable in a two-piece racing outfit, those are available as well.

WHAT IT COSTS: Women, $100 to 150; men, $100 to 150.

WHAT I RECOMMEND: For you competitive men out there, the one-piece Garneau and 2XU are excellent for races.

SWIM CAP (OPTIONAL)

WHAT TO LOOK FOR: Wearing a swim cap can make you sleeker in the water, not to mention that it protects your hair from chlorine damage. If you choose to wear a swim cap when you train, stick with one that's made with silicone or Lycra. Those won't break down from the chlorine like a latex cap. (You will be required to wear a swim cap for the event, and one will be provided for you.)

WHAT IT COSTS: Silicone, $5 to $10; Lycra, $8 to $10. Go to www.swimoutlet.com for an assortment of colors and styles.

GOGGLES

WHAT TO LOOK FOR: Goggles should be comfortable and must not fog or leak.

WHAT THEY COST: Clear, comfortable vision during training and racing is the most important thing. It is worthy paying more for goggles that fit and perform flawlessly. That said, you can expect to pay anywhere from $10 to $30.

WHAT I RECOMMEND: There are some fabulous goggles out there now. If you want a no-frills, high-performing goggle, look no further than the Finis Lightning. It comes with an adjustable nosepiece for the perfect fit. Aqua Sphere makes an innovative product that combines the strengths of a scuba mask with the sleekness of regular swim goggles; the result is called the Seal 2.0, a pair of extremely comfortable swim goggles that are virtually leak-proof. See them at www.sealmask.com.

Many competitive triathletes and swimmers also swear by what are called Swedish racing goggles. This minimalist product only costs about $10 a pop, and although they take a bit of getting used to, they are among the most reliable and leak-proof goggles you can wear. They're sold at www.swimoutlet.com.

ANTIFOG SOLUTION

WHAT TO LOOK FOR: Antifog solution that comes in a spray or drops. This is a must-have for training and for race day. The last thing you want is impaired vision because of fogged-up goggles, especially when swimming in open water. Before putting on the goggles, apply the solution on both the outside and inside of the lenses, rubbing it in with your fingers. Leave it on for 5 to 10 minutes and then rinse off.

WHAT IT COSTS: $5 to $10.

BEWARE THE "BUCHANAN MOMENT"

You may have experienced a "Buchanan Moment" at some point in your life—that is, a moment when you say, "Forget about price, I must have this!" The experience is named for the moment in F. Scott Fitzgerald's classic novel *The Great Gatsby,* in which heroine Daisy Buchanan is overcome with desire when shown an assortment of finely made shirts.

Often the result of such an impulse buy, especially when it comes to fitness equipment, is a purchase you use only once or twice, and then it serves no other purpose than taking up space in a closet or your garage. Thanks to a few Buchanan Moments of my own, I currently have two pairs of snowshoes, a tennis racket, basketball shoes, and—hey, look, some ice-climbing gear fossilizing under my bed!

To gain control over the Buchanan Moments in my life, I now have a 30-day wish list to which I add any item I feel inclined to purchase. After 30 days, if I still need or want the item, then I go buy it. Having such a wish list gives you a moratorium to mull over the purchase and see whether you've forgotten about it or thought about it every day. This simple strategy can help you save thousands of dollars in sportswear alone in your lifetime!

WHAT I RECOMMEND: Zero-Fog spray is a top choice. Another great product is Foggies individually wrapped towelettes, which clean your goggles as well as offer antifog protection.

BICYCLE

WHAT TO LOOK FOR: While I believe you should strive to be, and give, your best in your triathlon journey, you don't need one of those space-age bikes to do it. Your own mountain or road bike will do, depending on the bike course in your race. Even if you're a competitive triathlete, the bike's fit and your training matter more than the bike itself. That said, if you need a new set of wheels, first settle on a budget (see below for help with that), and then head to your local bike shop and start test-riding lots of bikes. I'm not talking about two-minute rides. Get out there and climb, corner, descend, play! Hop from one bike to the next. This allows more direct neuromuscular comparisons. Spend at least a week trying different bikes and researching your favorites in magazines or online at www.roadbikereview.com.

WHAT IT COSTS: In the next chapter, you'll determine your fitness level by taking a simple quiz. It's best to choose a bike to match your level. Level I: $750 max (you can get a great used bike for about $300). Level II: $1,000 for a new bike/$750 for one that's used. Level III: $2,000 new/$1,500 used. Level IV+: Don't spend more than $3,000 for a new bike or $2,000 for one that's used—returns diminish after that amount.

WHAT I RECOMMEND: Bicycle technology has progressed to a point at which almost all major-brand bikes sold today are more than sufficient for 98 percent of the cycling/triathlon population. Over my 20-year triathlon career, I've ridden most major bicycle brands. You cannot go wrong with Trek, Cannondale, Specialized, or Cervélo. If pressed for a favorite, it would be Guru (www.gurucycles.com). These bikes are beautifully built and exquisitely engineered. Guru can a build custom frame for you that feels like a tailored suit. I have found Guru's bicycles to be remarkably durable and reliable.

MOUNTAIN BIKE (OPTIONAL)

WHAT TO LOOK FOR: Mountain-bike triathlons—such as Xterra—have become increasingly popular, so if you're thinking of doing an off-road triathlon, this is for you. As with most athletic gear, I cannot decisively tell you which mountain bike is best for you. I've seen people perform their best on antediluvian steel bikes with components from the 1970s. Others get confidence and speed by spending thousands of dollars on dual-suspension carbon monocoque frames. I can tell you this: From a performance standpoint, your legs, lungs, and heart determine your success more than anything else. Ninety-eight percent of the population does not need a dual-suspension bike with all the bells and whistles.

Your goal in choosing a bike should be to find something that meets your needs and feels and looks great—to you. As I suggest when buying a road bike, take several mountain bikes out for extended test rides before deciding on the one you want. Spend at least a week trying different bikes and researching your favorites in magazines or online at www.mtbr.com.

WHAT IT COSTS: Generally speaking, $800 to $1,000 new/$500 to $800 used will buy you all the mountain bike you could ever want. Spend any more and returns start to diminish.

WHAT I RECOMMEND: Like road bikes, there is parity among the best brands. When choosing a mountain bike or a road bike, you'd do fine to get a Trek, Cannondale, or

Specialized. But my personal favorite brand is Trek (www.trekbikes.com). Trek has been honing and refining the technology for decades, and their mountain bikes are solid and sublime. Another fabulous brand, and one close to my heart (and home), is Marin (www.marinbikes.com). Some say the mountain bike was "invented" in Marin County, California. So riding a Marin is a chance to own a piece of history. And they really are terrific bicycles.

INDOOR BIKE TRAINER (OPTIONAL)

WHAT TO LOOK FOR: If you live in the northern states during the winter months, you know that Mother Nature doesn't facilitate outdoor cycling. A stationary bike trainer is the next best alternative. Because you get more benefit on an indoor trainer than on the roads (there's no coasting on an indoor trainer), your indoor workouts need only last 75 percent as long as your outdoor ones. To increase the fun factor, listen to music, read a book, or watch TV. Just be sure to maintain good pedaling form.

When choosing an indoor bicycle trainer, test a few out at the store before taking one home. Make sure it runs quietly and is of solid construction. Also be sure you can adjust the resistance for easier or tougher workouts.

WHAT IT COSTS: $50 to $1,000; used models will cost about half the retail price across the board. For now, be frugal and buy the least expensive model. If you decide to stick with this sport, you can always spend more money later.

WHAT I RECOMMEND: There are a few categories of indoor trainers: stationary, rollers, and computer-driven. For a basic indoor trainer, look no further than CycleOps (www.cycleops.com). For rollers, TruTrainer makes a stellar product (www.trutrainer.com). CompuTrainer (www.racermateinc.com) is a high-end trainer that provides motivation while riding indoors by allowing you to ride actual courses on a monitor. It provides a handlebar controller with LCD display.

HELMET

WHAT TO LOOK FOR: ANSI or SNELL certification. These are watchdog groups that set safety standards for various consumer products. Look for their stamps on the inside of your helmet. Fit is also crucial. The helmet should sit level on your head and should line up with the middle of your forehead, and the straps should be snug. While wearing your helmet, place your hands on either side of the helmet and try to slide it backward and forward on your head. If you're able to move the helmet in either direction so that the back or front of your head is exposed, then the helmet is too loose. It should be snug enough that it won't slide backward or forward on your head.

If you're ever in a crash with your helmet, no matter how minor, send it back to the manufacturer to be inspected for cracks. There could be a crack so small you can't even see it, which could render the helmet useless in a future accident. For those Level IV triathletes out there looking to shave time on the bike leg of the event, you may consider investing in an aero helmet.

WHAT IT COSTS: Regular helmet, $50 to $100; aero helmet, $100 to $250.

WHAT I RECOMMEND: Your best bets, for regular or aero, are helmets made by Giro (www.giro.com), Specialized (www.specialized.com), and Garneau (www.louisgarneau.com).

BIKE SHOES

WHAT TO LOOK FOR: You have two choices: (1) running shoes with toe-clip pedals or (2) clipless cycling shoes. I strongly suggest the latter. You will cycle with more power and

Running shoes with toe-clip pedals

Clipless cycling shoes

fluidity, and it's easier to clip out of the clipless shoe-pedal combination than to pull your foot out of toe clips. Look for comfortable cycling shoes with a stiff sole. Have an experienced bicycle expert set your cleats, preferably with a Rotational Adjustment Device (RAD). This ensures the safest and best path for your knee during the pedal stroke, which will limit the stress on your knees, joints, and back.

WHAT THEY COST: $100 to $250 new; $50 to $80 used.

WHAT I RECOMMEND: Specialized, Shimano (bike.shimano.com), and Garneau all make fabulous cycling shoes. You can get regular "road cycling" shoes with more straps (slightly tighter/better fit), or you can opt for fewer straps that allow you to speed through the bike-to-run transition more quickly.

CYCLING SHORTS

WHAT TO LOOK FOR: Bike shorts include padding designed to eliminate chafing and rubbing on sensitive areas, so don't scrimp on quality here. Besides being less comfortable, a cheap pair will begin to wear after a couple of months, rendering your backside viewable to people behind you. A good pair should last several years. Look for cycling shorts that have eight-panel design, gel or chamois padding, and are made with antibacterial fabric.

WHAT THEY COST: $50 to $125.

WHAT I RECOMMEND: There are so many great cycling-apparel companies out there. I am a fan of Garneau's cycling shorts. They limit the number of seams for better comfort. Giordana (www.giordanacycling.com) and Castelli (www.castelli-cycling.com) also produce quality products. Terry is a great women's-only brand (www.terrybicycles.com).

SPORTS TOP (OPTIONAL)

WHAT TO LOOK FOR: You will wear this during the bike and run legs of the event. For many women, their swimsuit tops simply serve as their top throughout the race. Other women may choose to wear a sports top with a bra sewn right into it for added support.

Some men prefer to compete shirtless. Others would rather pull on a tank for the bike and run. Look for a Coolmax top, which is a special lightweight fabric that wicks moisture away from your skin.

WHAT IT COSTS: $30 to $60.

WHAT I RECOMMEND: Garneau makes dynamite sports tops, especially for cycling. For running tops, I recommend Under Armour (www.underarmour.com). The company sells light, durable, and fashionable options that perform well. Athleta (www.athleta.com) makes a phenomenal line of running clothing for women.

CYCLING GLOVES (OPTIONAL)

WHAT TO LOOK FOR: A sturdy pair that inspires confidence. Most of the time, your hands hit the ground before the rest of your body when you fall, so you don't want to get these on the cheap. For shorter races, you may not need gloves, but they're helpful for longer events such as Ironman. If you train in warm weather, opt for fingerless gloves. If you live in a cooler climate, stick with full-finger gloves. Also, look for gloves that have thick pads on the palms and a sweatband woven into them near the thumb for wiping the sweat off of your brow.

WHAT THEY COST: $30 to $60.

WHAT I RECOMMEND: Giro, Garneau, and Pearl Izumi all provide excellent products.

SUNGLASSES

WHAT TO LOOK FOR: A lightweight pair of shades that stays on your face and protects you from sun and debris. You may be tempted to go with the latest, greatest model here. Don't. You can get cool-looking quality shades without spending a fortune. Look for sunglasses that have UVA and UVB protection, and make sure they're shatterproof.

WHAT THEY COST: $60 to $100 is plenty.

WHAT I RECOMMEND: For great midpriced sunglasses, check out www.rudyproject.com. If you want the absolute best optics—and you will use these sunglasses every day—spend the money on a pair of Revos (www.revo.com). They'll cost you up to $250, but they're worth it. They're made with the same lens technology that NASA uses in its satellites.

TOOL KIT

WHAT TO LOOK FOR: A basic tool kit includes a spare tube, tire irons to remove your tire, a patch kit, and a pump—everything you need for basic repairs on the road or trails. Look for a ready-made tool kit at a bike shop. Attach it under your bike seat so you have it with you at all times.

WHAT IT COSTS: $40 for everything.

WHAT I RECOMMEND: Park Tool (www.parktool.com) makes complete kits that are functional and reliable. Lezyne (www.lezyne.com) engineers absolutely beautiful products.

RUNNING SHOES

WHAT TO LOOK FOR: The bottom line with running shoes is this: Get the ones that work best *for you*, the ones that best suit your biomechanics. Go to a local running specialty store and have them observe your running style, and then ask them for their recommendations. That said, it's always wise to stick to name-brand running shoes. You'll never go wrong with New Balance, Asics, Nike, Reebok, or Saucony. (For more information on how to choose and fit running shoes, turn to pages 101–102.)

WHAT IT COSTS: Expect to spend between $80 and $150 on running shoes. More than that and you get diminishing returns.

WHAT I RECOMMEND: If you're willing to try something new, check out Newton Running (www.newtonrunning.com), which encourages better biomechanics, and Hoka One One (www.hokaoneone.com), which claims to have 50 percent more cushioning than industry standards. I have not run in either of them, but I've heard great things.

RUNNING/CYCLING SOCKS

WHAT TO LOOK FOR: Most socks that you find in running specialty stores will work. You want to get a pair that are lightweight and made of a fabric that wicks moisture, such as a nylon-cotton blend.

WHAT IT COSTS: $10 to $20 per pair.

WHAT I RECOMMEND: A small company called Injinji (www.injinji.com) has invented a revolutionary antiblister "toe sock." It works like a glove in that each toe has its own sleeve so the toes don't rub against each other. There is a large, almost cultlike following for Balega socks (www.balega.com). They are certainly worth a test-drive.

HEART RATE MONITOR

WHAT TO LOOK FOR: While power meters and GPS devices have become more popular than straight heart rate monitors, I believe heart rate monitors still have their place in intelligent training. A heart rate monitor is a simple device: A wireless strap goes around your chest and transmits a constant, accurate display of your heart rate to a watch on your wrist. Unlike power meters and GPS, heart rate monitors provide an accurate reflection of how hard your body is working. This is important to know during training—and recovery—sessions. All you need is a monitor that displays a continuous heart rate and is EKG accurate. The bells and whistles that cost extra are optional.

    WHAT IT COSTS: $60 and up.

    WHAT I RECOMMEND: Polar (www.polar.com) makes excellent products. This company invented personal heart rate monitor technology more than 30 years ago and is the leading manufacturer of heart monitors in the world today. Garmin (www.garmin.com) also makes great products that integrate GPS and heart rate.

COLD-WEATHER GEAR (OPTIONAL)

If you train in weather colder than 50 degrees, you will need to use some of the following cold-weather gear, particularly while bicycling, because wind chill can cool things off an additional 20 to 30 degrees or more.

    LEG WARMERS: Made of Lycra or fleece, leg warmers slip onto your legs to keep them warm and dry. They run about $40 to $80 and can be purchased from www.performancebike.com.

    ARM WARMERS: These are easy slip-on sleeves made of Lycra that cover your arms and can be removed as things heat up. They cost $20 to $50. If you want to save a few

THE POWER OF MUSIC

One day while training in Lanzarote, which is in the Canary Islands off the Moroccan coast, I ran across 1996 200-meter Olympic gold medalist and world record holder Michael Johnson on the track. Okay, I didn't run across him—he ran by me at a pace that was embarrassingly much faster than mine. (I'm a triathlete, not a sprinter!) What struck me, other than his divine stride and motionless upper body, was the heavy bass of rap music pouring out of his Walkman. Between intervals I asked him about it, and he told me he uses it before important competitions. The music stirs his passion up to a boiling frenzy, which he then releases in training and competition.

What music really moves you? What makes you want to jump out the door and exercise? *That's* the music you need to listen to before and, if appropriate, during workouts. For me, it's either "The Olympic Hymn" or anything by The Crystal Method.

Create your own playlist on iTunes or channels on Pandora or Spotify. Because your body will generally follow the intensity level of the music, be sure that the first 10 minutes of your tapes consist of easy music. For the main part of your workout, choose music that makes you want to be in motion and helps you keep a strong, steady pace. Some researchers have found that music running at 60 to 90 cycles per minute induces alpha waves in the brain. That simply means it helps put you in "the zone" where what you're doing seems effortless.

During your musically enhanced workouts, focus on the music, your technique, and your breathing—and watch your passion and performance soar.

---

dollars, cut the toes off Wigwam wool socks and pull them over your arms! For a nice selection of arm warmers, visit www.coloradocyclist.com.

FULL-LENGTH GLOVES: The first thing to get cold on a bike ride or run are your fingers. If you consistently train in cool or cold weather, invest in a high-quality pair of full-length gloves, meaning they cover your fingers. Make sure they have a wind-resistant shell. They run $30 to $50. For really cold temps, get "lobster" gloves, which have three finger holes. Assos (www.assos.com) makes phenomenal full-length gloves.

BOOTIES: If you're one of the brave few who ride on cold, windy, or rainy days, then a pair of waterproof booties (or overshoes) that you pull over your cycling shoes are a must. They run $20 to $40. Again, I would point you to Assos.

RAIN OUTFIT: I do not recommend that you ride your bike in the rain, because doing so significantly increases the danger of crashing. Running in the rain, however, can be a wonderful, cathartic experience—unless you're soggy and cold! Running-specific rain outfits work well to keep out the rain while allowing your body heat to escape. These items must be breathable and waterproof (not merely water resistant). They range from $100 to $175. You can find the widest variety of lightweight, functional, and affordable rain outfits at www.amazon.com.

WARM HAT: You lose roughly 30 percent of your body heat through your head, so one of the quickest ways to warm up on a cold workout day is to don a warm hat. A basic tight-fitting hat made of polyester or wool will do. Try not to get something too bulky. They cost between $10 and $20.

WET SUIT: You may need a wet suit if you train in cold open water (below 75 degrees) or in an outdoor pool during cold weather. A high-quality, properly fitting wet suit will not only shield you from the elements but also help you swim faster and easier. Choose a swimming-specific wet suit (as opposed to a scuba or surfing one). They're built to have maximum buoyancy and arm flexibility, and they are easy to put on and take off (for speedy transitions during your triathlon). They range from $150 to more than $400.

I have trained and raced in almost every major brand of wet suit in existence, and the three best are Blueseventy (www.blueseventy.com), Xterra (xterrawetsuits.com), and Orca (www.orca.com).

OTHER OPTIONAL ITEMS

SPORTS BRA: Women who are looking for extra comfort and support should look into Athleta products. Athleta makes arguably the best sports apparel for women.

CAP: You may want to wear a lightweight baseball cap to shield the sun when running.

MUSIC: If you train alone, listening to music can help keep your workouts fun and motivating. I like to use my iPhone so that I have music and a phone with me in case of emergency. It's important to keep the volume down so you can hear what's going on around you. While it's tempting during the long miles, I do not recommend listening to music while you ride. It is simply too dangerous when dealing with cars on the road.

SPORTS BELT: Tune Belt makes a lightweight neoprene belt that holds your phone in place as you exercise. You'll find one for $20 to $25 at www.tunebelt.com.

4
YOUR TRAINING PROGRAM: AN OVERVIEW

"Well begun is half done."

—ARISTOTLE

Imagine that you're standing at the starting line of your triathlon event. While that moment is some six weeks away, it actually all starts here. This chapter will begin to lay the foundation of your training program so that you'll be off and running in no time. It begins by helping you determine your current Fitness Level, which will allow you to design your individualized training program later on in Chapter 9. Here, you'll also learn some general guidelines that will help you get the most out of your training time.

Now let's take the first step in this process by figuring out where you're starting from.

WHAT FITNESS LEVEL ARE YOU AT?

Not every person reading this book is at the same Fitness Level. For that reason, the book includes four different training programs designed with four different types of Triathletes-in-Training in mind. That way you're sure to find a program to fit your needs. And as you grow fitter and pursue grander goals, you can up it a notch and graduate to the next level.

To find out which Fitness Level you're at right now, answer the following questions and then add up your score.

1. Have you exercised consistently (three or more times per week) for more than four months over the past year? Yes _____ (10 points) No _____ (0 points)

2. Have you ever done a triathlon before? Yes _____ (15 points) No _____ (0 points)

3. Have you ever done a single-sport event before, such as a 5-K run, a bike event, or a swim event? Yes _____ (10 points) No _____ (0 points)

4. Have you suffered any acute or chronic exercise-related injuries over the past 12 months? Yes _____ (0 points) No _____ (10 points)

5. Do you have trouble staying motivated to exercise?
   Yes _____ (0 points) No _____ (5 points)

6. What would you rather do: go for a nice trail run or go for a nice beer run?
   Trail _____ (10 points) Beer _____ (0 points)

7. Were you a competitive runner, cyclist, or swimmer in high school or college?
   Yes _____ (10 points) No _____ (0 points)

8. Do you currently work 50 hours or more per week (including your commute time)? Yes _____ (0 points) No _____ (10 points)

9. If you had the ability, training, and finances to allow it, would you compete as a professional triathlete for one year?
   Yes _____ (10 points) No way, José _____ (0 points)

10. What's more important to you on event day: performance or enjoyment?
    Performance _____ (10 points) Enjoyment _____ (0 points)

Translating your score:
Add together the points from all 10 questions above and see where you fall.

0–40: Fitness Level I

41–60: Fitness Level II

61–80: Fitness Level III

81–100: Fitness Level IV

FITNESS LEVEL I: SLICE ABOVE COUCH POTATO

First, let me congratulate you for considering this challenge. Of all the people reading this book, *you* stand to benefit the most from this program, because you will improve by leaps and bounds in how you look and feel. You likely have not been exercising consistently for more than one year or have little or no background in the three sports of triathlon. Your program is designed to help you simply *finish* one sprint-distance triathlon with a focus on enjoyment, weight loss, a better body, and enhanced health.

FITNESS LEVEL II: NEOPHYTE

You have a strong interest in improving your health and fitness and have recently begun to exercise more regularly. Your training program will help you increase your fitness, tone your body, and allow you to complete a triathlon in a respectable time, with a smile on your face.

FITNESS LEVEL III: FITNESS ENTHUSIAST

You have been exercising consistently at least two days a week for four months or more and want to challenge yourself by doing a triathlon. Your program takes into consideration that you can already cover 12 lengths in a 25-yard pool without stopping, run 3 to 5 miles twice a week, and cycle at least 10 miles (about 45 minutes) without stopping.

FITNESS LEVEL IV: SINGLE-SPORTER ON A MISSION

You are a serious fitness enthusiast or experienced single-sporter. You're already aerobically fit and want to take your performance to the next level by competing in a triathlon—whether it's your first or your fifteenth. Your training program and the principles in this book will give you a serious competitive edge in your age group. You'll learn an array of strategies that will allow you to train and race as fast and as strong as you want.

GET THE MOST OUT OF YOUR TRAINING

No matter which Fitness Level you start out at, you likely struggle to find enough time to work out. As our daily schedules grow increasingly frenzied—what with work, family, friends, household chores, and hobbies—even the most well-intentioned of us have trouble fitting exercise into our lives. The trick is not to exercise *more* but to *get more* from your exercise. The following guidelines show you how to get the greatest possible benefit from your individual training program—so you'll be putting those four hours each week to good use! These guidelines will form a foundation upon which the following chapters will build.

A SEVEN-PHASE WORKOUT

Breaking down your workouts into the following seven phases will make your training feel easier and help you achieve better results.

1. PREWORKOUT PREPARATION. You may not regard what you do in the hour or two before a workout as part of that workout, but it is. It determines, in large part, how much benefit you're going to get from your workout and how easy your exercise feels. About two hours before your workout, drink three eight-ounce glasses of water to hydrate your body. Drink two more glasses 10 to 15 minutes before you exercise. And one to two hours beforehand, munch on a snack that contains carbohydrates along with some quality protein or fat. This will stabilize your insulin levels and provide you with longer-lasting energy. My favorite preworkout snack is a peanut butter sandwich and a protein drink. (For more on preworkout nutrition, see Chapter 10.)

2. WARMUP. This often gets short shrift, but it's an essential part of your workout, setting the tone for your entire exercise session. You may feel that you simply don't have time to warm up. ("I only have 30 minutes to exercise, so outta my way. I have to start pounding that bench press!")

In reality, you don't have time *not* to warm up. Doing light activity raises your body temperature and literally warms your muscles, making them more flexible and resilient. This increases your range of motion and boosts your performance. In addition, nerve messages travel faster at higher temperatures, speeding muscle reactions and reflexes and thereby reducing risk of injury.

A warmup also makes exercise feel easier by preoxygenating your body. When most people begin an aerobic workout such as running, cycling, or swimming, they start out too strenuously. Have you ever done this? You start your run at a moderately hard effort, but you feel uncomfortable and out of breath. The entire workout becomes a painful struggle. Had you only preoxygenated your body before exercising at a high intensity, you would have avoided that struggle.

By starting out slowly with a proper warmup, you ensure that your muscles are well-oxygenated before you call on them to do strenuous work. Because oxygen is an ingredient necessary for your body to produce energy, the more that is present, the more effectively and powerfully your muscles function. (Think about what happens when your heart muscle is starved of oxygen. It can't function, and you have a heart attack! That's how important oxygen is to your muscles.)

With all the benefits a proper warmup provides—preventing injury, increasing athletic performance, and making exercise feel easier—it's more than worth 10 minutes of your time.

Your warmup need not be complex. If you're warming up before a strength-training session, take a brisk 10-minute walk, take an easy 10-minute jog, or do a series of jumping jacks. Try to vary your warmups somewhat, so you're not always doing the same thing. When warming up for your aerobic exercise, simply do the activity at a slow, easy pace for 5 to 10 minutes. At the end of your warmup, you should just be breaking a sweat. If you start to get a bit winded, you're going too hard.

You can also experiment with a stop-and-go warmup: Begin your aerobic activity easily for a few minutes, then stop for 10 to 20 seconds and gently shake out your muscles. Start up for another three minutes and then take another 20-second rest. Continue this process through the 10-minute warmup, going a little harder during each three-minute effort. This gradual ramping up allows your body to pump blood more efficiently to the right places, with minimal stress, oxygenating your muscles better than if you were to dive right in to your workout.

3. STRETCH. After your warmup, spend two to three minutes stretching your legs, your lower back, and your arms, giving extra attention to any areas of your body that are particularly tight or sore. This will further increase performance and reduce your risk of injury. (For stretches for specific muscle groups, see Chapter 8.)

4. LISTENING PHASE. Few people know about this phase, but it's actually the most important part of your workout. Spend five minutes taking a few deep breaths and tuning in to the signals your body is sending you. "Become sensitized to exactly how much exercise is beneficial for you," writes John Douillard, DC, former director of player development for the New Jersey (now Brooklyn) Nets, in his book *Body, Mind, and Sport.*

Based on what you "hear" during the listening phase, you can either make your workout longer and harder or cut it short. On some days, your body and mind will be raring to go. Your movement will feel smooth and come easily. You'll have a positive attitude. That's when you should open up the throttle and have a passionate workout. You're only scheduled for an easy 20-minute run? Bump it up to a more intense 45 minutes.

On the other hand, if your legs feel heavy, your movement or breath is labored, or you feel a sharp pain anywhere, your body is telling you to tone it down. Change your workout accordingly by switching to a lower intensity, cutting it short or skipping it altogether.

Your body sends you vitally important messages. Trust it. Doing so ensures against burnout and even prevents injury. If you push through workouts when your body isn't up to it, you begin to associate exercise with pain—and nothing is more detrimental to your long-term fitness.

There is, however, a crucially important caveat to this concept: You must be able to make the distinction between listening to your *body* and listening to your *mind.* Even when your body is ready to exercise, your mind can argue you into a corner and convince you not to work out.

YOU: Time for a run!

YOUR MIND: No, wait a second. It's getting dark. We've had a long day. We deserve a break. Don't you think we should table this discussion until tomorrow morning?

YOU: In*deed*—where's that terrific bottle of wine?

Your mind will give you every reason not to get out there. You have to be able to determine whether your body is truly exhausted or your mind is just weary. I've invariably had my best workouts when I was convinced I couldn't get off the couch but got out there anyway.

Here's an effective strategy for getting out the door and circumventing the mental debate: Commit to working out for just five minutes. If at the end of those five minutes, your body has gotten into the exercise groove, you'll know it was just your mind that was dragging, and you can extend those five minutes to a full workout. However, if you're still struggling and getting negative signals from your body after five minutes, scale back your workout or head home.

5. WORKOUT. Chapters 5, 6, and 7 describe specific swim, bike, and run workouts that you can incorporate into your training program. Each workout allows you to focus on a different aspect of your fitness in that sport. Some zero in on improving your speed, for example, while others focus on endurance, power, or form. In order for your body to make all the physiological adaptations necessary to excel in every one of these areas, you need to train at varying intensities. Training at different intensities also produces different changes in your body. Endurance exercise, for example, which is performed at a longer duration and a lower intensity, helps you burn more fat and lose more weight. Later on in this chapter, I'll explain how to go about training at these different intensities.

Speaking of exercise intensity, when you turn to Chapter 9, you'll find that the workouts scheduled in your training program are based on time and intensity rather than distance—in other words, 40 minutes at a certain intensity instead of "five miles." While this may seem to be a small point, in fact it's not. Training by time is how most top endurance athletes work out. Here's why: Your body doesn't understand distance, because it's not the most accurate gauge of how tough a workout can be. A seven-mile run in the mountains on a 90-degree day, for example, is far more stressful to your system than a seven-mile run on flat terrain in 65-degree weather.

In the sport of triathlon, it's easy to get obsessed with logging certain distances per workout or mileage per week, but that can lead to overtraining. Training based on time and intensity will liberate you from the constraints of trying to fit in the miles, which will make your workouts more enjoyable and bring you more long-term progress.

What this means for your workouts is that you'll need to time each one and track your intensity, or effort level, throughout your workout by wearing a heart rate monitor. You'll learn how to use your heart rate to gauge your intensity level in the section ahead called "Train in the Zone." (For more information on what to look for when purchasing a heart rate monitor, turn to Chapter 3.)

6. COOLDOWN. This is an essential part of your workout because it brings you back to mental and physical balance. It's also important for recovery and injury prevention, because it loosens your muscles and gradually lowers your blood pressure and heart rate. The ideal cooldown is 5 to 10 minutes of easy walking, swimming, or cycling. Focus on relaxing your body and breathing slowly and deeply.

7. POSTWORKOUT MEAL. One reason people feel fatigued after a workout is that they fail to refuel their bodies. During exertion, your muscles use carbohydrate fuel called glycogen. So after moderate or strenuous exercise, your blood sugar levels have bottomed out, leaving you feeling wasted.

The trick is to get 30 to 60 grams of carbohydrates (depending on your body weight and exercise intensity) into your body within 30 minutes of exercising; that's roughly one bagel, two bananas, or an energy bar. Wash it down with 16 ounces of water, and you'll recover faster and feel less fatigued throughout the day. (For more on nutrition, see Chapter 10.)

TRAIN IN THE ZONE

One of the biggest myths in the fitness world is that you have to work hard and be out of breath to boost your fitness. Although it may seem counterintuitive, it is almost always better to stay below the point where you lose control of your breath; that is, below your maximum heart rate. When you work out this way, you burn more fat and exercise feels easier, so you're inclined to do it more often. Over time, you become more aerobically fit, meaning your body becomes more efficient at working out because it's more efficient at using oxygen.

The top triathletes rarely exceed their maximum heart rate, which helps them get fit without fatigue. That leads to faster progress, increased confidence, greater energy, and a desire for still more exercise. This is known as the aerobic cycle. When you work out at easier effort levels—below your maximum heart rate—you feel good during your workouts and finish them feeling invigorated. On the other hand, if you work out at your maximum heart rate, your body cannot breathe fast enough for you to continue at that pace. You're out of breath, your lungs burn, and you finish your workout feeling ready for a two-hour nap.

So rather than exercising at your maximum heart rate, you should train at your ideal Training Zones (also called target heart rate zones). In order to train in the zone,

INTERVAL TRAINING

Competitive athletes incorporate interval training into their exercise programs to boost their performance. Intervals can help you, too. An interval is a period of higher intensity during a workout. For example, in a 40-minute swim, you might do a series of five to fifteen 50-yard intervals in which you swim fast but under control, with a recovery period in between.

Intervals are a very effective part of your training program. Just be judicious with interval training, since it is stressful on your body. Limit yourself to one cycling and one run interval per week, regardless of your Fitness Level. However, you can get away with more interval work in the water than in other sports, because swimming is easier on the body than weight-bearing activities such as running. For that reason, you can do up to two swim interval sessions per week.

---

so to speak, you need to know your maximum heart rate. A number of factors influence your maximum heart rate, including your age, genetics, Fitness Level, and overall health. You can find your true maximum heart rate by exercising to exhaustion and recording what your heart rate is at that point. This can be dangerous, however, and should only be done under the watchful eye of a physician. According to the American Heart Association, you can determine your approximate maximum heart rate by subtracting your age from 220. Write that number here:

Maximum heart rate _____

You will use this number as the basis for your workouts. Think of your maximum heart rate as a speed limit of sorts. Sure, you can exercise at your speed limit, but doing so makes your engine consume more fuel, which means you'll run out of gas more quickly.

You can use your maximum heart rate to determine your ideal Training Zones, which essentially are the different levels of exercise intensity I talked about earlier in this chapter. The four different Training Zones are described below in detail. Which Fitness Level you are will determine how much time you spend exercising in each Training Zone. Each zone corresponds to a different target heart rate range. When exercising in Training Zone I, for example, you should be at 50 to 60 percent of your maximum heart rate. So if your maximum heart rate is, say, 185 beats per minute, your heart rate should be between 92 and 111 beats per minute during a Training Zone I workout (185 x 0.5 = 92.5 and 185 x 0.6 = 111).

Your target heart rate is an objective measurement of how hard your body is working, but it's important to monitor your subjective exercise intensity as well. In 1982, Gunnar Borg developed a scale for monitoring intensity based on how hard you feel you are working. The rate of perceived exertion, or RPE, scale provides a quantitative rating of exercise effort. To determine your RPE, just do a brief mental scan of your body while working out. How labored is your breathing? How hard are your muscles working? Are they burning? Then use the following scale to give your "exercise effort" a number.

RPE SCALE

6 **No exertion**

7 Very, very light exertion (This is a feeling similar to that of getting up from the couch to get a beer.)

8

9 Very light exertion (You barely feel like you're exercising.)

10

11 Fairly light exertion (You're just starting to break a sweat.)

12

13 Somewhat hard exertion (Your breathing is becoming pretty labored.)

14

15 Hard exertion (You begin to feel a lactic acid sensation in your muscles.)

16

17 Very hard exertion (You cannot speak one sentence without running out of breath.)

18

19 Very, very hard exertion (You cannot speak.)

20 **Maximal exertion**

Each of the four Training Zones below corresponds to both a target heart rate range and a range from the RPE scale. Together these two numbers help you to accurately gauge your exercise intensity so that you know you're exercising "in the zone." (In your training program schedule in Chapter 9, the ideal Training Zone for each workout is indicated as Zone I, Zone II, and so on.)

TRAINING ZONE I—RECOVERY/ENDURANCE: These workouts are conducted at a nice, easy pace. Your heart rate should be at 50 to 60 percent of your maximum heart rate and should not exceed 130 beats per minute. Your RPE score should be 10 to 12. This zone builds aerobic fitness, strengthens immunity, and uses your body fat as the primary source of fuel. The purpose of these workouts is to get out there, have fun, and gain aerobic fitness without fatigue. This Training Zone is where you will spend the majority of your training time, especially in the beginning of your program.

TRAINING ZONE II—LONG INTERVALS/TEMPO: When you are exercising in this zone, your subjective feeling is "comfortably challenging" (RPE of 13 to 15). In other words, you're working, but you're not out of control. Your heart rate should be at 60 to 70 percent of your maximum heart rate. These workouts build excellent fitness for the sport of triathlon, since you will likely spend most of your time on race day in this zone. Tempo workouts are designed to help you keep a strong pace throughout your race. These workouts are done at a steady state over a longer duration (10 to 40 minutes). Long intervals serve the same purpose but are performed as a series of short bouts (three to eight minutes) at a slightly higher intensity than the tempo workouts.

TRAINING ZONE III—SHORT INTERVALS/SPEED: When your aerobic fitness begins to plateau, it's time to sprinkle some Training Zone III work into your program. These intervals can last anywhere from 30 seconds to two minutes and should only be performed after at least four weeks of consistent, injury-free exercise. They help you focus on increasing your speed. When doing a Level III workout, your heart rate should be at 70 to 80 percent of your maximum heart rate and your RPE should be 16 to 17.

TRAINING ZONE IV—EXPLOSIVE POWER: These sessions are reserved for Fitness Level IVs who want higher-end fitness, particularly competitive athletes. Efforts should be from 10 to 30 seconds in duration and should build into an all-out effort. These sessions will dramatically improve your maximal oxygen-carrying capacity and your biomechanical technique. Your RPE should be 18 to 20, and your heart rate should be at 80 to 90 percent of your maximum. It may be difficult, however, to determine your heart rate during exertion, because an explosive-power effort lasts only 30 seconds or less, so your heart rate may not jump up until after the burst of power is over. Such a session is best done on feel. Go as hard as you can while maintaining good form.

Regardless of your Fitness Level or goals, you should spend the vast majority of your training time in Zones I and II. (This is indicated in the training schedules in Chapter 9.) Training in these zones helps you become more aerobically fit without fatigue. Mark Allen, one of the greatest triathletes of all time, was religious about sticking to Training Zone I and II workouts.

RACE TO TRAIN

Nothing is more effective at breaking through a fitness plateau than entering a short race, such as a 5-K run, bike race, or swim event. I suggest you choose a couple of short events to do over your six-week training program. These races will sharpen your skills, boost your fitness, and provide a healthy dose of motivation during your training.

There are a couple of things to consider when racing to train:

- Be sure you are well rested going into the race. You don't ever want to race in a state of fatigue. That is neither fun nor productive. When you're tired, your body is not in an optimal state to reap the fitness benefits of an activity. So for the last few days going into the race, either rest or exercise very lightly.

- Dig deep. One key benefit of doing competitive events is to redefine your limits, strengthen your body, and sharpen your mind. Depending on your level of fitness, don't be afraid to go out there and give it everything you've got. When doing races to train, I like to negative-split my events. That means pushing the second half harder than the first half. This does two things: (1) You tend to hold back a little in the first half, which gives you the energy and confidence to finish strong, and (2) it provides a better training effect, because you remain strong and in control.

- Recover from your event. After a race, particularly if you push yourself hard, you should always take a few days to recover. When you compete, you tend to push yourself harder than in training (which is the point!). But that also makes you more susceptible to injury in the days after the event. So listen to your body and rest after your race.

POWER BREATHE

Serious athletes use a technique called *power breathing* to boost the amount of oxygen their bodies can process. This helps them take advantage of a number of positive effects that oxygen has on the body. Researchers at the University of Pavia in Italy found that people who underwent focused deep-breathing exercises before and during physical exertion had higher levels of blood oxygen and were able to perform far better on exercise tests.

More simply put, increased oxygen intake makes exercise feel easier, improves circulation, lowers your pulse rate, and enhances your fat-burning metabolism. And perhaps most importantly for your overall health, it lowers stress levels and blood pressure. These health and fitness benefits are why I remind you throughout this book to focus on your breathing during your training.

On the flip side, when you exercise too strenuously and begin to lose your breath, the physical stress causes your body to release the hormone adrenaline. This makes your blood pressure rise and, over time, can result in physical fatigue, sometimes known as chronic fatigue syndrome. Not a happy condition—I've had it.

By helping to deliver more oxygen throughout your body, which keeps you in a more relaxed rather than fight-or-flight state, power breathing may help reduce the amount of adrenaline released by your body and the negative effects that come with it.

Here's how to power breathe.

1. Sit erect and place your hands lightly over your stomach. Close your eyes and clear your mind.

2. Breathe in through your nose, pushing the lower part of your lungs downward and outward (called diaphragmatic breathing). You should feel your stomach move outward. (Yes, aim for Buddha belly. Nobody's watching!) The full inhalation should take three to five seconds. Visualize the fresh, healing oxygen swirling into your bloodstream and to every corner of your body.

3. When you feel as though you've fully inhaled, breathe in a little more. Then a little more. Go on, challenge yourself. This will expand your lung capacity dramatically. Hold that full inhalation for three seconds.

4. Exhale slowly out of your mouth, with a slight "Ahh" sound. Visualize every bit of your mental and physical stress dissolving with that breath. The exhalation should last a couple of seconds longer than the inhalation.

During exercise, you won't be able to breathe this slowly, but the idea is the same: Keep your breath rate deep, relaxed, and rhythmical. (If to power breathe properly you need to expand your nasal passages, use Breathe-Right strips. They're not just NFL fashion statements; they really work.) Remember that when you start to get out of breath, you likely are approaching your maximum heart rate, which is not an efficient way to work out and will leave you feeling fatigued rather than invigorated.

TECHNIQUE FIRST

To become a better athlete, it's important to learn proper technique and then apply that over and over again in your training. Always put technique first in your training, even at higher intensities.

When you exercise, you are "grooving" neuromuscular pathways. You want to develop the most efficient technique so that you are applying your power in the most productive way. In other words, you want your effort to give you the most results. That happens when you apply your strength and power in the most economical and technically sound manner.

I like to focus on three things when I am working out.

1. Keeping my breathing nice and steady, with full inhalations and complete exhalations

2. Staying relaxed, no matter how hard I am going

3. Doing a "head-to-toe" check to ensure that I am using the best technique I can

Putting technique first will also reduce your risk of injury, because you will not start flailing about as the intensity rises.

ACTION ITEM: The next time you exercise, concentrate on breathing in through your nose and into your belly, not into your chest. As you gradually increase your exercise effort, focus on maintaining a slow, steady breath rate. Use power breathing not only to improve your workouts but also to reduce stress in your daily life.

TRAIN WITH OTHERS

In your quest to get fitter, having someone there beside you can be motivating, not to mention it can make your workouts more enjoyable. That is why I encourage you throughout this book to train with others whenever you can. According to Dariusz Nowicki, a sports psychologist for Olympic teams, people are, in fact, 47 percent more motivated to exercise consistently when they involve their family and friends.

"Studies have shown time and again that when people know others are watching them, they perform very differently than when they know they are alone," writes Nowicki in his book *Gold Medal Mental Workout*. "This powerful trait is so deeply ingrained, it's almost automated. The good news is that this quality can be used to increase one's exercise motivation. If you enter an athletic event and tell everyone you know that you are going to finish it, you've engaged this 'accountability' factor. The more involved those around you become in your event, the higher your motivation becomes to do the daily workouts."

A survey of 100 Olympic medalists asked this question: What one thing is most directly responsible for your Olympic medal? More than 75 percent pointed to their support networks. World-class athletes have such strong support structures in place that even during times of extreme demotivation and despair, they can remain on their training programs. Their support networks tighten and keep them propped up and working out through the tough times. Personally, my mom and dad are the only two reasons why I stuck with it in the first year of my professional triathlete career.

In addition to having supporters on the sidelines cheering you on, you should also work out with encouraging people who challenge you to improve at the three sports in triathlon. I cannot say enough about the power of surrounding yourself with passionate, fun, dedicated workout buddies and scheduling time to train with them each week. These exercise buddies ought to fit six criteria. They should:

1. Be at a similar Fitness Level. (If they're two levels below you, they'll slow you down; if they're significantly more advanced, you'll slow them down.)

2. Have a similar approach to training. (You don't want to be forced to change your training program to fit their needs.)

3. Be fun to hang out with.

4. Offer encouragement and be quick to affirm your progress.

5. Be reliable.

6. Challenge you. (You should feel compelled to push yourself in some small way each time you work out with them.)

When you train with people who have those six qualities, you will miss far fewer workouts and get more benefit and enjoyment from each one.

ACTION ITEM: Create a mini-community of triathlon buddies who commit to exercising together every week. Ask that each person sign a Fitness-for-Life Contract like the one on page 65. Revel in the competition, the camaraderie, and the thrill of the group dynamic. Keep a list of contact information handy. When your motivation is down or your training needs a lift, give your buddies a call and get out that door.

SOCIALIZE YOUR TRAINING

Some say social media is terrible for your fitness. After all, according to a study by the Ipsos Open Thinking Exchange, the average online American spends roughly two hours a day social networking. Perhaps we can use some of that time in a healthier way!

There is a community-driven technology called Strava that you ought to explore. Strava allows you to record the duration and speed of your workouts using GPS and then post your workouts to your social networks. There you can connect with others, compare times, and even set challenges. This can boost motivation and show the world what you've got!

You can purchase a device for running or cycling, or simply download the free Strava app to your smartphone. To learn more, visit www.strava.com.

FITNESS-FOR-LIFE CONTRACT

Name: _____

Contact Information: _____

_____

_____

_____

I, _____ , commit to _____ that I will be available for _____ workouts per week, from _____ to _____ , on the following days and times and at the following locations.

	Day	Time	Location
1.			
2.			
3.			

I also commit to being there to support _____ through the entire 6- to 8-week Triathlon Training Program.

Finally, and most importantly, I promise _____ that I will do my best to live a healthier lifestyle—not for a month or a year but for life.

_____   _____

Signature   Date

5
SWIM EASIER

"To plunge into water, to move one's whole body, from head to toe,
in its wild and graceful beauty; to twist about in its pure depths,
this is for me a delight only comparable to love."

—PAUL VALÉRY, FRENCH POET AND CRITIC

Many people enjoy a rather uneasy love-hate relationship with the sport of swimming. Those, like Valéry, who love to swim, see it as a total mind-body-spirit release and arguably the best total-body exercise around. A good swim reduces stress and leaves you feeling energized and healthy. It improves your range of motion and joint health and is the ideal adjunct to any workout program, because it improves aerobic capacity and cardiovascular fitness without impact. Injuries are practically nonexistent in this sport.

People who hate swimming say that decoding the swim stroke can be as confusing as unraveling the Gordian knot and that staring at that torturous black line at the bottom of the pool will put you directly into a straitjacket.

Whatever your swim disposition, this chapter will help you maximize your efficiency and enjoyment in the water in a short period of time—and get you out of the water in your triathlon event feeling fresh, strong, and ready to sail off on your bike.

There are four learning stages in swimming, according to Terry Laughlin, founder of Total Immersion in New Paltz, New York, a training program that teaches stroke technique to both professional athletes and beginning swimmers. First is the period of water orientation, which involves learning to be comfortable in the water. It's vital that beginners establish an early, easy relationship with the water, or they may never enjoy it. Swimming in open water—an ocean, lake, or river—is different from the confines of a pool. Getting familiar with the body of water before the event by checking tides, currents, and temperatures as well as clarity and cleanliness is prudent.

The second and third stages involve learning the basic elements of the swim stroke and then improving them to make the stroke more efficient. Finally, there is the advanced learning phase, when you focus on refining motor coordination and learning to swim stronger and faster.

HONE YOUR TECHNIQUE

Let's assume you've already familiarized yourself with the water. (If you haven't, spend two to three 30-minute sessions in the pool simply feeling the water and how your body moves in it.) Now it's time to tackle learning and polishing your technique, which is the foundation of swimming both for pleasure and performance.

Any local pool can provide a striking lesson in the importance of good technique. Look closely and you'll see swimmers flailing across the water like madpeople, as well as others gliding along the lanes effortlessly—fishlike. The difference isn't in fitness level but technique. The best swimmers have near-flawless technique, which allows them to use less energy to swim across the pool.

I once attended a training camp in Florida with four-time Olympic champion Alexander Popov, regarded as one of the top swim technicians in the world. But Popov had been ill, and we were watching his first workout in almost a month. We assumed he would have trouble even getting across the pool.

Not Popov. He dove in and cut a swath through the pool, stroking up and down the lanes as if he had been training twice a day for the past month. Onlookers were amazed. I asked his coach, the legendary Gennadi Touretsky, how Popov did this.

"Alexander has never practiced anything but perfect, flawless technique in the pool," Touretsky said. "He doesn't know any differently. He may be out of shape right now, but his body remembers the perfect technique. He has perfect body position and perfect application of strength. That is why he can swim so well even when he is out of shape—and it's why he beats the best swimmers in the world."

Honing your technique is the best way to reach your potential in any sport, but it's particularly important in swimming. That's because swimming is a technical sport similar to golf or tennis, rather than a power sport like cycling or weight lifting. Improving your swimming technique will benefit your training in three key ways.

YOUR PERFORMANCE WILL SOAR. By learning how to execute the swim stroke with greater efficiency, you'll produce more results with the same effort. In other words, if you improve your swim stroke by just 5 percent, you can increase your speed noticeably without trying harder.

YOU'LL EXPERIENCE FEWER EXERCISE-INDUCED INJURIES OR PAIN. If you swim in a more relaxed and natural way, you'll place less stress on your muscles, joints, and tendons. This applies to other sports as well: Learn to run more smoothly and you'll experience less impact stress on your body every time your foot hits the ground.

YOU'LL ENJOY YOURSELF MORE. By moving your body more efficiently through the water, swimming will feel more comfortable. You will begin to flow smoothly through swim workouts, rather than fight through them.

POSITION YOURSELF

Because water is roughly a thousand times denser than air, how your body is shaped as you propel it through the water is paramount. The easiest way to improve your body position is to refine the "hull" of your ship. Try this experiment: Push off the wall of the pool underwater, with your arms held straight out from your sides. You won't go very far, of course. But try to push off while you hold your body in a streamlined position, with your hands clasped over your head, and see how much farther you go. Swim in a streamlined position and you'll instantly increase your efficiency.

Proper Body Position

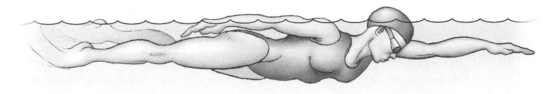

SHROUDED IN MISERY

One of the more frustrating things that can happen during your triathlon is having your goggles fog up. Sounds trivial, I know, but it makes swimming a lot more difficult, especially in open water where vision is paramount.

To prevent the fog from setting in, get some antifog solution and use it in training and on event day. You can't go wrong with Speedo brand. It's available at sporting goods stores and specialty swim shops.

Apply the drops or spray on both the outside and inside of the lenses of your goggles, and rub in the solution with your fingers. Leave it on for a couple of minutes and then rinse it off.

The next step is to balance your body. A good swimmer seems to float almost perfectly flat on the water's surface and to remain horizontal with little effort. Practice swimming flat by pushing your chest into the water. This slight action will make your hips rise in a seesaw fashion and significantly reduce your frontal drag. Because the position of your head influences the position of the rest of your body, keep your head relaxed, looking down and slightly ahead of you.

Now that you're positioned well in the water, you'll want to focus on propulsion. Swimming "from your hips" is perhaps the most important element of the swim stroke. Most people swim with their arms, which is a natural tendency, but using your hips generates power more efficiently. Picture yourself throwing a football or baseball. You rotate your hips as part of that throwing motion, right? Now picture yourself throwing the ball while buried waist-deep in sand. The ball won't go very far because you have no rotational application of power.

Swimming from the hips will also teach you to roll your body, which is the final element of better swimming technique. Rolling your body allows you to glide through the water with the ease of an ice-skater in a rink. Visualize yourself pushing off on a skate and gliding on that skate for a few seconds, rather than taking a series of choppy steps. By taking a nice, strong swim stroke and gliding on your side, you maximize efficiency and minimize drag.

That's what you want to feel in the water: a series of powerful, efficient strokes, generated through your hips into long, balanced, streamlined glides.

BREAK DOWN THE STROKE

Let's take a close look at the five basic components of the freestyle swim stroke—plus when and how to breathe to boost your efficiency in the water.

ENTRY/EXTENSION

The correct entry of your hand into the water sets up your stroke. Your thumb and index finger enter the water first, your hand slicing into the water at a 45-degree angle. Your hand should enter the water a few inches to a foot in front of your head.

Entry

Once your hand is in, roll your body downward to the same side and simply extend your hand in front as far as you can. Stretch as if you're reaching for something just beyond your grasp.

CATCH

Now "grab hold" of the water with your hand as you extend it forward and down into the catch position. The primary purpose of the catch is to prevent you from inefficiently tearing your hand through the water like many novices do. Instead, "grab" the water so you can pull yourself forward in a strong and efficient manner. Keep your elbow high to maintain your leverage and power. Your hand should remain relaxed as you grab the water to get a good hold that will set you up for the pull phase.

Catch

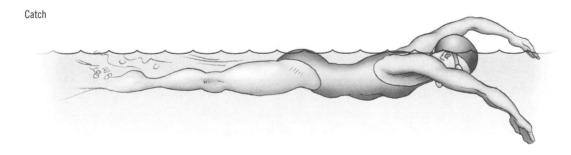

PULL

The pull is the most important part of your propulsion. Once you have a good hold on the water, apply power from your hips by rotating them as you pull yourself through the water with your hand *and* your forearm—that's a much larger "paddle." Don't allow your elbow to drop in the water or pull through the water before your hand; that will reduce your power appreciably. When your hand travels beneath your body, there should be about a 90-degree angle between your bicep and forearm.

The elbow remains straight during extension, forms a 90-degree angle beneath your body, and straightens out again as your hand passes your hip during the pull.

Use an accelerated pull to keep a good hold on the water. Gradually accelerate your hand speed as it travels from the catch under your belly past your hips to your thigh. Apply the bulk of your power as your hand passes your belly button. Then, snap your hand past your hip to the middle of the thigh.

Pull (side view)

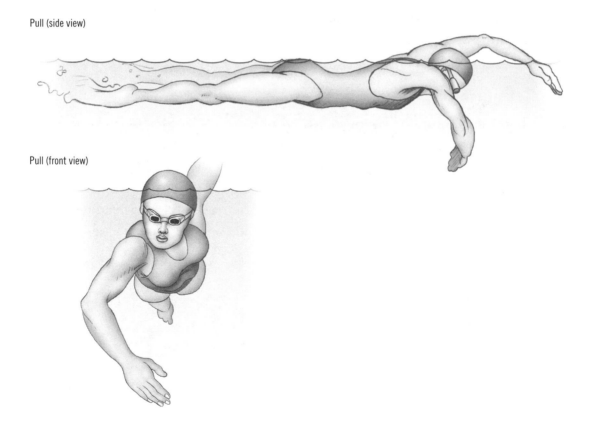

Pull (front view)

(Still with me? Hang in there: This is the most technical discussion in the entire book. I know this is a lot of information and it may appear a bit convoluted, but it's like riding a bike—once you "get it," you have it—and swimming well is a thrilling feeling. To do so, however, you need to understand the mechanics behind it.)

A good pull depends on proper hand acceleration. Too much power early in the stroke will cause you to lose hold on the water. Let your body travel over your hand as opposed to pulling your hand under your body. Rest your arm until the next pull. Avoid the tendency to push the water directly up toward the surface.

When you're pulling your body through the water with your arms, you want to maximize the amount of water pulled. Because the shortest distance between two points is a straight line, the last thing you want to do when swimming is pull your arm through the water in a straight line. Instead, practice an S shape (a longer way of completing each stroke) so that if you were to pull both arms together simultaneously, the resulting path would resemble an hourglass silhouette.

PUSH

Even some of the world's best swimmers shorten their strokes when they get tired by pulling their hands out of the water prematurely at their waist rather than at their upper thigh. You should always strive to finish your stroke with a strong push.

Push

As you complete your underwater hourglass pull, your arm should fully extend behind you, by your side, so that your thumb grazes the side of your thigh. Many swimmers begin bending their elbows toward the end of their stroke and pull their arms out of the water before allowing them to finish their path. By shortening their stroke, these swimmers lose efficiency and expend more energy, because they're taking more strokes per lap (essentially spinning their wheels).

RECOVERY

This is your chance to give your arm a break and allow the blood to flow back in. After your hand finishes its pull, relax your muscles and release your hold on the water. Lift your elbow up to the sky, allowing your hand to sweep freely under your elbow. Extend your hand to its fullest extension. It should feel as if your hand is making a straight-line recovery from the rear to the front of the stroke.

For the entire recovery portion of the stroke, keep your elbow higher than your hand. Rotate your shoulders as your elbow rises to its highest point. It's vital during this phase to keep your back and arm muscles relaxed so that you can give your muscles a break.

Recovery

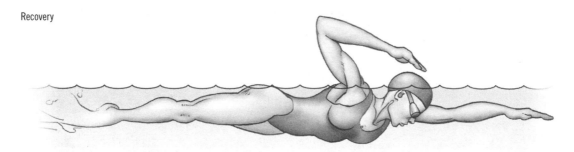

BREATHE

Because air isn't always accessible while swimming in the way that it is while cycling or running, breathing in the water requires special focus. It's easy to build up an oxygen debt while swimming if you don't breathe properly. As you push your hand past your thigh and roll your body to the side at the end of the push phase, take a deep breath through your mouth. With each stroke as you complete your arm pull, exhale forcefully and completely under the water, then roll your body and draw in a nice deep breath of fresh air. Breathing this way increases your confidence in the water, because it puts you in control of your body and mind.

SWIM IN OPEN WATER

You may never have considered venturing into open water for your training, but it's one of the most beautiful and invigorating workouts you can do. It's also a nice way to escape the chlorine and the crowds of your local pool—plus it's essential to triathlon preparation.

BE SAFE

Although it can be an exhilarating experience, you must exercise extreme care when swimming in open water. First and foremost, never, ever swim alone. Either swim with a buddy or have someone watch from shore. Next, be sure your swimming spot is free from boating traffic. Beware local marine life—schools of running bluefish are brutal, as are bites from water lice, stings from jellyfish, and pricks from sea urchins. Rashes, abrasions, and stings are sometimes par for the course. Finally, you may want to look into getting a wet suit, which will provide you with protection against the cold and other elements and make you more buoyant in the water.

SWIM STRAIGHT

The shortest distance between two points is a straight line, but swimming straight in open water is easier said than done. Many new triathletes aren't used to navigating without that omnipresent black line to guide them. (You hate that black line in the pool, but you'll miss "trusty black" when you hit the open water!) You need to learn how to sight on a distant stationary object such as a building or dock, and really zero in on that object. Because doing this can place very different demands on your body, it's vital that you practice it.

If you normally train in a pool, practice sighting by raising your head and picking a spot at poolside such as your gym bag. You must learn to lift your head out of the water and look ahead during your pool training (one sighting per lap during training is ideal). Once you learn to sight, you'll feel more confident in the open water.

PREPARE FOR THE MASS START

Swimming in the open water during your event can feel like frothing mayhem with myriad arms and legs flailing around you. That can cause you to lose your focus and feel panicked. This response is entirely natural; it happens to the best triathletes in the world. That's why I want you to do the following:

PRACTICE. The more you train in the open water, the more comfortable you'll become with it.

BE AN OUTSIDER. At your event, start on the outside and at the back of the pack with the other people who may be more timid of the water. Team up with these people and swim with them—it will provide camaraderie and safety.

LEARN TO RESET. If you start to feel panicked, recapture your focus by immediately performing what is known as a reset. Stop swimming, do a couple of relaxed breast strokes, take some deep breaths, look around you, get your bearings, clean your goggles if you need to, and then continue on. You'll feel significantly better after doing this.

It's also a good idea during your reset to remind yourself why you're doing the triathlon in the first place: to have fun, to challenge yourself, and to seize the day. This clears your mind and keeps you focused on the positives, which will increase your enjoyment and your performance.

PACE YOURSELF

The swim is the first leg of a triathlon, and it sets the stage for the next two legs of the event both mentally and physically. Beginner triathletes tend to get caught up in the excitement and go too fast, which can ruin their race. That's why establishing a strong sense of pace in your training—and sticking with that pace on race day—is so critical. You want to come out of the water feeling strong, confident, and relaxed, ready to begin the bike leg of the event—not exhausted and spent.

MASTER THE SPORT OF SWIMMING

Whatever your fitness level or background, swimming with a team of people under the guidance of a knowledgeable, effective coach will help you tremendously. You can watch the better swimmers underwater and have the coach watch you from above the water. Masters programs of all levels exist around the country. Seek one out at your local pool, YMCA, or nearby college. You can also contact the U.S. Masters Swimming national office by calling (800) 550-SWIM, or check out their Web site, www.usms.org.

WORK OUT

Swim training has the potential to be a lot of fun but can also be a boring grind. The following workouts are designed to give you the most possible benefit in the least amount of time and in the most enjoyable way.

Pools come in four standard sizes: 25 yard, 25 meter, 50 yard, and 50 meter. Yards and meters are so similar in distance (1 meter = 1.1 yards) that most swimmers consider them about equal. For the purposes of this book, I'll use yards. The following workouts are designed around training in a 25-yard pool, where one lap equals two lengths of the pool. Here are some common distances in your standard 25-yard pool.

50 yards = 1 lap

100 yards = 2 laps

Sprint triathlon swim distance = ¼ mile = 400 meters = roughly 450 yards = 9 laps

1 mile = 35 laps

Your swim training will be slightly different than your training for the other two triathlon sports. That's because when it comes to cycling and running, it's essential to wear a heart monitor as a training tool. But it isn't very practical to wear one during swimming, plus your heart rate is naturally higher in this sport. So you need to train more on feel.

To get the greatest benefit from your swim training, you need to vary the intensity of your workouts. To make this simple for you, the workouts below are divided by intensity levels, or Training Zones, with Training Zone I being the easiest and Training Zone IV the most challenging. Turn to pages 58 through 60 for more information about the four Training Zones and their benefits.

One type of training that competitive athletes incorporate into their exercise programs is called interval training; intervals can help boost your performance, too. An interval is a period of higher intensity during a workout. For example, in a 40-minute swim, you might do a series of five to fifteen 50-yard intervals in which you swim fast, but under control, and then recover in between. Intervals are an effective part of swim training; just be judicious with this type of training because it's stressful on your body. Never do more than two swim interval training sessions per week. You can, however, get away with more interval work in the water than in other sports (for which you should limit yourself to one interval workout per week), because swimming takes less out of your body than a weight-bearing activity such as running.

Swimming is different in another way: It's the most technical of the three sports in a triathlon. For this reason, you should begin all swim sessions with at least a five-minute warmup and five minutes of drill work to hone your stroke, using one of the following drills.

PRESS THE BUOY: This drill is the brainchild of swim guru Laughlin and is one of the best for improving your body position in the water. The idea is that the most common and frustrating swimming handicap occurs when you drag your hips and legs.

The human body is essentially a teeter-totter in the water, with the fulcrum somewhere between the waist and sternum. The longer, heavier end (your legs and hips) naturally sinks. During these swims, you'll work on pressing your chest into the water, which will allow your hips to rise to the surface.

Picture a beach ball or something similarly buoyant. If you push it into the water, what happens? The water pushes it back out. We have only one place in our body that is similarly buoyant—our chest, because like a beach ball, the lungs within our chest wall are filled with air. Most everything else on your body (except for body fat wherever you may have it) tends to sink. So let's call this area in your chest your buoy.

If you press your buoy into the water, the water will respond by trying to push it back out. Rather than allowing your chest to rise out of the water, let your hips release to the surface instead. Then keep your head down and straight with your eyes focused on the bottom of the pool. The weight of your head will add the counterweight that completes the teeter-totter.

Do six to ten 50-yard swims in which you work on keeping a perfectly flat position on the water going down the pool, and then swim normally coming back.

CATCH UP: Watch great long-distance swimmers and you'll notice how they hold their glides for as long as possible. This drill will ensure a long, balanced swim stroke and a long body position. Swim regular freestyle, but keep one arm stationary and extended forward in front of you, while you stroke with the other arm. When the working arm moves forward and catches up with the stationary arm, swap the working and stationary arms and continue the drill. This may feel awkward at first, but once you get the hang of it, you'll know your swim stroke is improving. Do four to eight laps of this drill.

PUNCH IT: This promotes "feel" for the water. Swim normally except for one small detail: Hold one or both of your hands in a fist. Sounds like a small variation, but what you'll immediately notice is that you barely move through the water! This teaches you to keep a high elbow position, which is essential to efficient swimming. Swimming with fists will also help you become more sensitive to using your forearm as a paddle, so when you unclench your fists, you should feel as though you have a much stronger, more efficient paddle than when using fists.

Do fist swims going down the pool and regular swims coming back, focusing on that larger surface area of the hand and forearm.

BUDDY UP: Two swimmers of near-equal ability start swimming freestyle simultaneously in the same lane from opposite ends of the pool. Both swim continuously (in circles or on either side of the lane) until one swimmer catches the other. This drill teaches you to become fast and efficient, because if you sprint all out, you'll run out of air. The swimmer who has been caught must swim one length of butterfly as a punishment lap, and the winner takes a rewarding rest. Because this is a fairly rigorous session, you need only do it once before beginning your regular workout session.

TRAINING ZONE I

R&R

SUBJECTIVE EFFORT LEVEL: Nice, steady pace; 10 to 12 on the Borg Rate of Perceived Exertion (RPE) scale. (For an explanation of the RPE scale, see Chapter 4.)
DURATION/DISTANCE: 10 to 30 minutes

Just getting into the pool and moving your body will provide you with physiological benefits. How? Swimming is all about feel for the water. Each session is also wonderful recuperation from your running, cycling, and strength training—you are washing the stress of gravity from your joints and muscles. That weightlessness is very therapeutic and provides excellent recovery from more strenuous exercise. During this session, just swim entirely based on what feels good. Do any strokes you want, or simply float, tread water, or bob up and down by pushing off the floor of the pool with your feet and taking a breath of air as your head comes out of the water. There are no rules here. The goal is to recover mentally and physically and to get a feel for the water. Nothing more. You should finish this session feeling relaxed and fantastic.

TECHNIQUE WORK

SUBJECTIVE EFFORT LEVEL: Nice, steady pace; 10 to 12 on the Borg RPE scale
DURATION/DISTANCE: Six to twelve 50-yard swims

As you read earlier in this chapter, swimming is a highly technical sport. Therefore, nothing will net bigger strides in swimming than improving your technique. After a 5- to 10-minute warmup, do six to twelve 50-yard swims (depending on your fitness and comfort level) as follows: Do one of the above drills for one length of the pool, and then do the freestyle stroke coming back. During the freestyle portion, focus on imprinting the technique from your drill into your swim stroke. For example, if you do the "catch up" drill (see page 78), then accentuate your glide as you swim back. Take a nice long break between each 50—you want to be very well rested for these swims. Cool down with 200 yards of easy swimming, focusing on perfect technique.

ENDURANCE

SUBJECTIVE EFFORT LEVEL: Nice, steady pace; 10 to 12 on the Borg RPE scale
DURATION/DISTANCE: Estimated length of time of the swim leg

As with all endurance sessions, this will ensure that you can finish the swim comfortably, with plenty of energy left for the bike and run. Regard these workouts as your insurance policies. Determine how long the swim leg will take in your event; let's use 15 minutes as an example. After a nice, easy five-minute warmup, swim 15 minutes without stopping. Of course, you can work up to this, beginning with a five-minute swim and building from there. If you can extend your endurance session to 30 percent beyond your projected swim time in your event, in this case to 20 minutes, then you'll be fully ready for the swim. This session can also be performed in open water, which I encourage you to do at least once every few weeks.

TRAINING ZONE II

LONG INTERVALS

SUBJECTIVE EFFORT LEVEL: Comfortably challenging; RPE: 13 to 15
DURATION/DISTANCE: Two to eight 200-yard swims

This session will boost your fitness in the water without undue fatigue. After an easy five-minute warmup and five minutes of drills, do between two and eight (depending on your fitness and comfort level) 200-yard swims. Within each 200-yard interval, swim the first 100 slower than the second. This is called negative-splitting your swims and is a very effective way to build fitness. Be sure to recover completely between each 200-yard swim by allowing your breathing and heart rate to return to a comfortable level. Finish the workout with a five-minute cooldown.

STRENGTH

SUBJECTIVE EFFORT LEVEL: Comfortably challenging; RPE: 13 to 15
DURATION/DISTANCE: Five to fifteen 50-yard swims with paddles

This workout will develop your swim-specific strength so that you can apply more force to your stroke. Perform a longer warmup than usual (10 to 15 minutes), and do five to fifteen 50-yard swims with paddles strapped onto your hands. (Most pools provide paddles, but if you wish to buy your own, look for Speedo brand paddles at sporting goods stores.) Increasing the surface area of your hand by wearing paddles is one of the best ways to build strength in the water. Don't pull too hard; just focus on taking long, perfect strokes, and rest about 15 to 45 seconds between each swim. Finish with a 10-minute cooldown.

TRAINING ZONE III

SHORT INTERVALS

SUBJECTIVE EFFORT LEVEL: Difficult; RPE: 16 to 17
DURATION/DISTANCE: Four to eight 50-yard swims

This session is similar to Long Intervals, but the swims are shorter and are performed quite a bit faster. When you are swimming, cycling, or running at faster paces, it's important to spend more time warming up to boost performance and decrease the risk of injury. That is why you'll see the pros warming up for an hour or two before sprint-distance triathlons but only 20 to 30 minutes before an Ironman! After a nice, long 20-minute warmup, do between four and eight 50-yard fast swims, always maintaining proper technique. You want to feel like you are pushing yourself but never to the point that you are flailing in the water. That just ingrains poor technique, which is the death knell to efficient swimming. Recover completely between each interval so that your breathing and heart rate return to normal. Finish with a five- to 10-minute cooldown.

TRAINING ZONE IV

EXPLOSIVE POWER

SUBJECTIVE EFFORT LEVEL: Maximum effort; RPE: 18 to 20
DURATION/DISTANCE: Four to eight 75-yard swims

Perform these workouts only if you are a Level III or IV Triathlete-in-Training—and only after you have put in two to three weeks of consistent swim training. These sessions will develop the explosive power you need to get out in front of the swim and recover into a nice, steady pace. Start with a 10-minute warmup and a little extra drill work. The extra drill work is important, because when you go all out, you tend to forget about technique. The additional drill work will reinforce good technique, which you'll take into your workout session. After the drill work, do four to eight 25-yard "blasts" right into 50 yards of steady swimming, so each swim is actually 75 yards. Swim all out for the first 25 yards, and then ease into a strong pace that you want to hold for the swim leg in your event. Finish with a 10-minute cooldown . . . and go have some Ben & Jerry's. You deserve it!

6
CYCLE STRONGER

"I thought of that while riding my bike."

—ALBERT EINSTEIN, ON THE THEORY OF RELATIVITY

Some of us, like Einstein, find riding a bike can clear our heads, allowing us to hatch our best ideas. Whether or not you've had a lightbulb experience while riding your bike, you no doubt find that as each pedal stroke thrusts you forward to your destination, it also sends you back to the innocence of your childhood.

We all rode bikes as kids—blissfully snaking in and out of our backyards or the local playground, limited only by our legs and the daylight. Based on such experiences, most of us know how to ride a bike. If you're new to cycling, this chapter will enhance your knowledge and familiarity with the sport. If you're more experienced, this chapter will show you how to ride stronger, better, and more comfortably so that ultimately you can excel in the triathlon.

GET A GOOD FIT

In a one-hour ride, you'll likely pedal between 3,000 and 5,500 times. Ideally, your bike should feel like an extension of your body rather than an alien mass of metal beneath you. Watch top-level cyclists on their bikes and you'll notice how at ease they are. Much of that has to do with their position. If you aren't properly positioned on your bicycle, your body will sustain stress with every pedal stroke. A seat set just three centimeters too high, for example, will force your hamstrings to hyperextend and pull on your lower back. So before you even take to the road or trail, find an expert to properly fit you on your bike. A few simple changes to your bike position can dramatically boost your performance, increase your comfort, and reduce your risk of injury.

One of the nation's leading authorities on bicycle positioning is Andy Pruitt, EdD, director of the Boulder Center for Sports Medicine in Boulder, Colorado. He describes proper bike fit as "a marriage between the human body, which is somewhat adaptable, and a machine that is somewhat adjustable."

Experts agree that the ultimate goal in proper bicycle fit is to achieve what is known as biomechanical synchronicity: the point at which all muscle groups of your lower body—your quadriceps, your hamstrings, your calves, and your gluteus maximus—are working together fluidly to move your bike forward. You'll be amazed at how far, how fast, and how comfortably you can ride your bicycle once you achieve biomechanical synchronicity.

STEP ONE: FRAME SIZE

"The first step to proper bike positioning is to make sure you have the right bike frame size," says Paul Swift, eight-time U.S. National Cycling Champion and master bike-fitting technician. "Stand over your bicycle's top tube (the piece between the seat and the handlebar). The general rule of thumb for road or triathlon bikes is roughly one inch of clearance between your crotch and the frame. For a mountain bike, aim for two to six inches."

STEP TWO: SADDLE POSITION

Seat position will vary based on personal preference, riding style, and physiology. Finding the correct saddle position depends on how high the saddle is and how far forward or backward it's set on the seat post (called its fore/aft position in cyclist lingo).

"Correct saddle height—the distance from the pedal axle to the top of the seat—is one of the most important factors in bike positioning," says John Howard, former Olympian and seven-time National Cycling Champion. According to Howard, your saddle height should be set so your legs almost fully extend at the bottom of each pedal stroke.

Check for correct let extension.

Find your setback measurement.

To check for correct leg extension, sit on your bike and pedal to the 12 o'clock and 6 o'clock positions. Your bottom leg (6 o'clock position) should bend roughly 30 degrees at the knee. "Your hips should not rock back and forth when you pedal—that means your legs have to stretch too far to reach the bottom of the pedal stroke. If your hips rock, lower your saddle," Howard advises.

"The fore/aft position of your saddle can have a significant effect on your body position while you ride," says Joe Friel, masters athlete, fitness expert, coach with more than 30 years of personal and team experience, and author of *The Cyclist's Training Bible*. With your bike fixed in a bicycle trainer or leaning straight up against a wall, kneel down beside the bike. You'll need a piece of string roughly 40 inches long with a weighted object (like a pencil) tied to one end. Pinch the top of the string and place your fingers at the "nose," or front, of your seat. Let the string dangle straight down under the weight of the pencil. Now measure the distance that the string lies relative to the bottom bracket, which is the bolt that runs through the middle of your cranks. That is your true setback measurement. Although these machinations may sound tricky, they're well worth the time and energy in achieving perfect biomechanical synchronicity on the bike!

STEP THREE: HANDLEBAR POSITION

Handlebar position will determine the comfort level of your back and upper body. Handlebars that are too low force you to bend down too far, placing unnecessary stress on your back and neck. Competitive triathletes looking for less aerodynamic drag typically lower the handlebar as far as possible. But everyone else can find the best height by first setting the handlebar at the same height as the saddle, then testing it out to see how that feels. Raise the bar slightly if your lower back starts to hurt.

STEP FOUR: SHOE/CLEAT ALIGNMENT

You can ride your bike using toe clips with running shoes. But if you ride with clipless pedals, take heed: Cleat position on your cycling shoes determines the comfort of your feet, ankles, knees, hips, and back. Once you clip in to your pedals, the path your leg follows during the pedal stroke is locked in. Misaligned cleats will send stress from your foot to your lower back with every pedal stroke.

"When mounting cleats, you want your feet to feel straight when clipped into the pedals," says Sean Drake, an exercise physiologist who works with the U.S. National Triathlon and Cycling Teams. "When setting fore-aft cleat position, the ball of your foot should be directly over the pedal axle. Side-to-side adjustment is based on personal preference—usually, the narrower stance, the better. Start somewhere in the middle and see what feels right." It may take some time to find the ideal cleat position. Continue adjusting your cleats until you feel no torsion, or twisting, stress in your leg as you pedal.

DO AN ABOUT-FACE

Seasoned cyclists and triathletes use a common tactic called reverse loop to keep workouts fresh. This change in direction is one of the simplest ways to alter the scenery of your workouts without finding a new route. Say you ride your bike in a 15-mile loop around your town or a park. The next time you ride, flip it—do that loop in the opposite direction. It will look and feel like an entirely different cycling experience.

For optimum cleat positioning, visit a bicycle shop that uses a Rotational Adjustment Device. This tool is widely regarded as one of the most reliable methods for setting cleat position that allows for the rider's natural gait.

STEP FIVE: SEASONAL CHANGES

Your bicycle is an unyielding piece of machinery; your body is not. In fact, your muscle elasticity changes all the time. A bike position that feels right in summer when your muscles are elongated from the warmer weather may feel uncomfortable during winter when the colder air contracts, or shortens, your muscles. Set up your bike according to the tips above, but let your body guide you in making small, subtle changes.

MASTER THE ART AND SCIENCE OF PEDALING

Just as important as having proper bike fit is using proper pedaling technique. Master the technique and you'll cycle not only faster but also with greater ease. Just a 5 percent improvement in your technique can make a big difference over a two-hour ride.

To improve your technique, focus on smoothing out your stroke by pedaling with relaxed strength in smooth circles. In other words, rather than mashing down on your pedals like an overzealous child, let gravity help your foot naturally perform the push-down portion of the pedal motion. Think about kicking across the top of the pedal circle and dragging your foot along the bottom. Once you've felt that perfect pedal motion, even just once, work on repeating it during your training.

One of the best ways to both smooth out your pedal motion and balance your leg strength is to allow one leg to dangle free as you pedal with the other. You'll likely find that you can only pedal with one leg for 10 to 15 seconds when you first do this drill. When you can pedal this way for one minute and not lose control of your pedal stroke, you have reached a solid level of cycling technique.

POSITION YOURSELF

You may elect to train and race in the "aero position" in which you attach a set of padded aero bars to your handlebar and ride with your elbows resting on the pads. This reduces frontal drag and can save you time in the bike leg of the triathlon. Use caution when riding downhill and while cornering because the aero position doesn't give you as much control over your bike. You also may notice some stress on your lower back when first riding in this position, but with practice and a good lower-back stretching routine, your back should become acclimated. When I'm riding, I take a stretch break every half hour or whenever I feel any soreness or

Aero Position

stress in my back. Doing so helps me ride more comfortably and perform better. I simply hop off my bike, lie down on the grass, and do the stretch shown on page 115.

PUT SAFETY FIRST

Cycling is potentially the most dangerous of the three sports in a triathlon because you travel at higher speeds and deal with multiple variables, including the powerful piece of machinery that is your bike—which is why you must set yourself up for maximum safety. Here's how.

CHOOSE SMART ROUTES. Spend a little time mapping out your routes. Some roads have less car or truck traffic than others. Always choose the roads with the lightest traffic and stick to bike paths whenever possible.

WATCH YOUR BACK. Scanning in front and to the sides of you is easy when you're on a bike; knowing what's happening behind you is the problem. A product called the

Third Eye is one of the best rearview mirrors for cycling. Choose a model that attaches to your sunglasses or one that hooks on to your helmet. Each costs around $15. Look for them at your local bike shop, or read about them on the Web site www.3rd-eye.com.

MAKE EYE CONTACT. Assume that drivers don't see you until you're certain they do.

RIDE WITH TRAFFIC. State laws and common sense require that, like other vehicles, cyclists travel on the right side of the road.

OBEY TRAFFIC SIGNS AND SIGNALS. Cyclists must follow all traffic laws to ensure their safety on the road—and to avoid getting ticketed by police. (Yes, they will ticket you. I'm living proof. I've received three stop-sign violations, totaling $345.)

USE HAND SIGNALS. Use the standard hand signals to tell motorists and pedestrians what you intend to do. Signal as a matter of law, courtesy, and self-protection.

Stop or Slow Down   Right Turn   Left Turn

FOLLOW LANE MARKINGS. For example, don't turn left from the right lane and don't go straight in a lane marked "Right Turn Only." These faulty moves lead to more accidents than you might imagine.

DON'T PASS ON THE RIGHT. If you're riding in slow or stopped traffic and absolutely need to pass a car, do so only on the left, where you have a better view of oncoming traffic. Motorists often don't pay attention to things passing on the right, and they can suddenly turn into your path.

AVOID ROAD HAZARDS. Watch out for sewer grates, gravel, large potholes, ice, and debris. Ride over railroad tracks at right angles, otherwise you risk getting your tire stuck in a rut, which could lead to a dangerous crash.

BE READY TO BRAKE. Although you don't need to remain white-knuckled on your brakes, you should always be ready to stop if need be. Allow extra distance for stopping in the rain, because wet brakes are less efficient.

ALWAYS WEAR A HELMET. Some experienced cyclists don't wear helmets because they believe going without proclaims, "I'm so good, I don't need to wear a helmet." These people follow the examples set by some professional riders who forgo helmets. I don't care how cool or fast you think you are, it's never cool to suffer brain damage from a bike crash. I've seen too many tragedies that could have been avoided with the simple click of a helmet buckle. Never ride your bike anywhere without wearing a helmet.

And if you do crash, send your helmet back to the manufacturer to have it checked out—even if it appears fine. I know a man whose helmet had an internal crack he couldn't see, and his helmet later split in half like a cracked egg. Had he been in a crash, the helmet would have offered zero protection. If, when you send the helmet back to the manufacturer, any damage is found, they'll likely replace the helmet for free or else charge you a nominal fee.

KEEP YOUR EQUIPMENT IN GOOD WORKING ORDER. Equipment failures like flat tires or broken components can cause accidents and leave you at the side of the road in heavy traffic—or, worse, stranded in the middle of nowhere. To avoid such mishaps, keep your gear in tip-top shape. Get your bicycle tuned up by a trained mechanic every six months, clean and oil your chain every eight to ten hours of cycling, and check your tire pressure before every ride. Always carry a basic tool kit that contains a spare tube, tire irons, and a pump, and learn basic bike maintenance, including how to change a flat tire. (For step-by-step instructions, see "How to Fix a Flat" on page 91.)

READ UP. For more information on bike safety, log on to www.nhtsa.gov. Run by the National Highway Traffic Safety Administration, this site includes federal, state, and local rules and is *the* definitive guide to bicycle safety.

HOW TO FIX A FLAT

If you get a flat tire, your first order of business is to get off the road and park yourself in a safe, comfortable location. Don't panic or feel anxious; everyone gets flat tires. Take a deep breath and a drink of water.

Now remove the wheel with the flat tire. Using your tire irons, loosen one side of your tire and remove the tube. Check to see what caused the flat by inspecting the tire: Use your fingers to carefully feel the inside of the tire casing for any sharp object that may have punctured the tube. If you miss any such object, it will quickly puncture the new tube, so take your time here!

Once you're sure the tire is clear, partially inflate your fresh tube and carefully insert it back into the tire. Then roll the tire back onto the rim, making absolutely sure not to pinch the tube inside. Now make sure the tire bead (that thing that lines the outside of your tire and hooks it into the rim) is securely fastened into the rim all the way around the wheel on both sides by pumping the tire up a little. Then inflate the tire to its recommended pressure—and you're on your way.

It's important to note that your newly installed tire is a little more susceptible to flats (you may not have reinstalled it perfectly), so pay extra attention to it until you arrive home. Then have an expert mechanic reinstall the tire. (It's well worth the expense.)

Investing in high-quality name-brand tubes and tires—such as Panaracer, Vittoria, or Specialized—will dramatically reduce the frequency of flats. You can also investigate air-free tires that allege flat-free performance for life. Visit www.airfreetires.com for more information.

MAKE IT A GROUP EFFORT

I cannot overemphasize how valuable it is to routinely ride with a group of experienced cyclists. Here are three good reasons.

- **SAFETY.** Riding with other cyclists is safer because a larger group of cyclists commands more respect from motorists—and, should an emergency or bike malfunction arise, there are others around to help you.
- **FUN.** Hours can fly by when you're out with other people.
- **SKILL DEVELOPMENT.** If you ride with cyclists who challenge you in some way, you'll naturally elevate to their level. Talented and skilled bikers can teach you a lot in a short period of time.

Riding with a group certainly has its advantages, but it takes some extra care. Keep these things in mind when riding in a pack.

- **BE ONE WITH YOUR BIKE.** Before you join the group, make sure you've mastered the essential skills of cornering, climbing, shifting, and descending so that you feel as though your bike is an extension of your body, rather than a mass of metal beneath you.
- **GO WITH THE FLOW.** Just like when you drive your car in traffic, you should blend into the pace and rhythm of the group so that you're part of the traffic flow. Keep your movements as smooth and predictable as possible. It's when you suddenly slam on the brakes that things go wrong.
- **STAY ALERT.** Just like when you're driving in traffic, remain acutely aware of everything going on around you. When driving a car, you don't fixate on the car in front of you; you constantly scan to the side and up ahead several cars. Do the same when you're on your bike.

It shouldn't be difficult to find a group with which to ride—thousands of group rides take place regularly around the country. They're composed of cyclists at all skill levels and break up into smaller groups as the ride progresses. Start with a group in which you feel comfortable and keep challenging yourself to move up. During these rides, ask the more experienced cyclists lots of questions. Take my word for it: They love to showcase their cycling acumen. Watch them corner and descend. Ask them about equipment issues. Find out how much Ben & Jerry's Chunky Monkey they eat before big training days and events.

Riding with cyclists who aren't triathletes is actually a plus. Pure cyclists know a lot more about cycling, so training with them is one of the best ways to elevate your bike-riding performance. That's why many professional triathletes train with single-sporters: When they go back to their triathlon events, they kick butt.

HIT THE TRAIL

With the popularity of mountain biking, you may decide to train for your triathlon on the trails rather than on the road. Mountain biking is the perfect outdoor sport for forging high levels of fitness while enjoying the great outdoors. The sport not only sends your aerobic fitness, coordination, balance, and strength into the stratosphere but also allows you the freedom to explore new and beautiful places.

To discover great trails you can conquer, visit your local bike shops and talk to other mountain bikers. There are some excellent sources online as well. My personal favorite is www.trails.com. It lists and reviews more than 20,000 trails across the United States. For a great guide to mountain bike training, check out *The Mountain Biker's Training Bible* by Joel Friel or *Mountain Bike Magazine's Complete Guide to Mountain Biking Skills*.

When taking your triathlon training off-road, remember that mountain bikers share trails with hikers, joggers, and wildlife. So always stay in control of your bike and review the "Rules of the Trail" established by the International Mountain Bicycling Association and posted on its Web site, www.imba.com. As with road biking, keep your bike and gear in good repair, and always take a repair kit with a spare tire and pump with you on your rides. If you have a cell phone, take that as well. It may come in handy if you're ever hurt, lost, or broken down somewhere in the woods. It's also wise to take some extra food and water (besides the 12 ounces of water you need to drink each hour when mountain biking). That way you won't go hungry or risk becoming dehydrated if you ever find yourself stranded or having to hike out of the woods.

I've seen (and been involved in) some pretty unsightly mountain bike mishaps. With the varying terrain and obstacles, mountain biking can send you sailing over the handlebar if you aren't careful. These basic tips will help you "keep the rubber side down."

SCOUT IT OUT. To be on the safe side, scout any unfamiliar terrain on foot before biking over it.

RESPECT YOUR LIMITS. Most accidents occur when people ride beyond their abilities. It's always good to challenge yourself. Just be smart. Trust your instincts and make it a rule to go a bit slower than you think you should. Especially make sure to err on the side of caution when riding through windy passes and on steep descents.

GET OFF YOUR DUFF. If you're at all unsure about whether you can make it through an area safely, get off your bike and walk. Even pros will get off their bikes and hike through really rough terrain. You're still mountain-biking when you're walking, plus you're getting a great cross-training workout.

STAY FOCUSED. Mountain biking requires an entirely different level of focus than road riding. Because of constant terrain changes and surprising obstacles, you need to keep your eyes and mind focused on what's ahead on the trail—and try not to get distracted by the scenery. When you want to check out the view, stop your bike for a few minutes and take it all in.

As you ride, scan to your sides as well as straight ahead, looking for potential obstacles, such as falling tree branches or rocks or animals, that could move into your path. Use your ears along with your eyes to listen for anything that could signal a problem with your bike, such as a broken spoke or shocks that have gone out.

BIKE TO WORK

Commuting to work on your bike is a great way to boost your fitness, increase your mental clarity, lose weight, reduce stress, save time and money, and spare the environment—not to mention train for your triathlon! When the weather allows, give it a try. It's a way to sneak in training time that just may change your life. It did mine. When I first thought about biking to work, I had all the typical doubts: I didn't have enough time. It was too much hassle. I was still too out of shape. All of those reservations vanished after the first week.

Take the time issue, for instance. When I began my bike commute, riding 45 minutes to and from work three days a week, I didn't need additional cycling workouts! And once I streamlined my routine, which took only four or five rides, biking to work became not a hassle but an essential part of my day. The ride cleared my head and mentally centered me for a more productive workday. It helped control my appetite all day, inspiring me to make better food choices. I was less inclined to eat an extra-large piece of cheese pizza when I knew I'd have to drag it up that hill on the way home.

That's another benefit of cycling to work: It requires you to ride home! The evening commute aids in the digestion of the food eaten during the day and creates a healthy appetite for your evening meal.

Last but not least, it relieves work-related stress. Cycling has a way of putting life into perspective. It's satisfying to watch a car-traffic jam while you stream past on your bike, your legs pumping, your whole being fully alive. I guarantee that the argument with your coworker will seem far less earth-shattering after your ride home. These reasons are why I fell in love with cycling and what eventually led me to become a professional triathlete. The bike made me a stronger, healthier, happier human being.

Plus, bicycle commuting is easier than you think. It just takes some intelligent planning and a willingness to break out of your rut. Besides your regular bike gear, the only other stuff you'll need is a lock and a well-fitting backpack, such as a Timbuk2 bag, to hold your work clothes and toiletries.

Remember to go easy for the last 10 minutes of each ride to cool your body temperature. I made the rookie bike-commuting mistake of riding hard all the way to work. I became so superheated that for the first hour at my desk, I sweated like a farm animal. Trust me, you don't want your cubicle smelling like a pig sty!

WORK OUT

As I have explained before, I don't advocate training by logging 10 miles your first week, 15 your second, 20 your third, and so on. Mileage is not an accurate measurement tool, because riding 10 miles on flat land on a sunny day is infinitely different than riding 10 miles over hilly terrain on a windy, cold day. For this reason, training simply by tracking your mileage inevitably leads to overtraining.

That said, it's still a good idea on certain days to keep track of how many miles you ride and at what pace, because this information can show you how much you're progressing over time.

The training tool I prefer to use is exercise intensity, as measured by target heart rate. As you read in Chapter 4, the most important consideration during exercise—whether you're a first-time triathlete or seasoned veteran—is exercise intensity. Because training at different intensities produces very different results in your body, it's important to vary your exercise intensity throughout the week. That way you'll enjoy steady progress with a minimum amount of fatigue.

Each intensity level, or Training Zone, below corresponds to a specific target heart rate. Training this way requires you to know your own maximum heart rate. For instructions on how to find your maximum heart rate, see pages 56 and 57. For more information about the four Training Zones and their benefits, see pages 59 and 60.

TRAINING ZONE I

THE SOFT-PEDAL

HEART RATE/INTENSITY: 50 to 60 percent of maximum heart rate
DURATION: 20 minutes
SUBJECTIVE EFFORT LEVEL: Nice, steady pace; 10 to 12 on the Borg Rate of Perceived Exertion (RPE) scale. (For an explanation of the RPE scale, see page 58.)

This workout serves as active recovery, helping you spin out sore or tired legs. For that reason, this workout is ideal for rest days that follow heavy workouts. It will help speed your recovery by moving your muscles without placing significant stress on them. Focus on pedaling in nice, smooth circles with minimum pressure on the pedals. If you're doing it right, it will literally feel like a massage on your legs. Perform this ride only on flat terrain or on an indoor trainer with almost no resistance.

ENDURANCE

HEART RATE/INTENSITY: 50 to 60 percent of maximum heart rate
DURATION: Duration of bike leg plus 15 to 20 percent
SUBJECTIVE EFFORT LEVEL: Nice, steady pace; RPE: 10 to 12

Your endurance workouts are the most important in your triathlon training program. They build tremendous aerobic fitness with a minimum of residual fatigue. Perform these workouts at a moderate intensity, well within your comfort level.

Determine how long it will take you to complete the bike leg of your event and work up to that duration of nonstop riding—plus an additional 15 to 20 percent. So if you estimate that it will take you an hour to do the bike leg, work up to a ride that's about an hour and 20 minutes long. That gives you extra insurance that you won't be too tapped out partway into the bike leg of the event.

During your entire workout, keep your heart rate below 120 to 130 beats per minute. (Yes, that low.) For example, on a one-hour bike ride, set your upper heart rate limit on your heart monitor at 130 beats and do not exceed that number for the entire workout.

TRAINING ZONE II

HILLS

HEART RATE/INTENSITY: 60 to 70 percent of maximum heart rate
DURATION: Depends on your fitness level
SUBJECTIVE EFFORT LEVEL: Comfortably challenging; RPE: 13 to 15

In this session, ride your bike over a nice hilly route. For Levels I and II Triathletes-in-Training, that may mean 20 minutes of climbing; Level III Triathletes should climb half the time over the duration of their ride; and Level IV Triathletes and the more technical riders who measure their climbs using an altimeter (a device that measures elevation gained) should shoot for doing over 1,000 feet of climbing.

No need to focus on going too hard or too fast; the hills will provide all the resistance you need. Instead, focus on pedaling in complete, smooth circles when climbing and keeping your breathing under control. For maximum efficiency, time your breathing with your pedal strokes. Inhale for two pedal strokes and then exhale for three. On really tough rides when you need even more air, inhale for three pedal strokes and exhale for five. (This may seem counterintuitive, but it prevents you from panting.)

Try to remain seated on your bike as much as possible to build extra cycling-specific strength. Cycling in a seated position works your legs much more than when you ride out of the saddle, because you aren't able to use your body weight to aid in pedaling and pushing the bike forward. Although you may notice that pros frequently ride out of the saddle during races, they train by riding almost entirely in a seated position to build up pedaling strength.

When you do need to ride out of the saddle, position your body directly over or in front of the pedals. Keep your upper body muscles loose and relaxed as you use your arms to push the handlebars left and right in sync with your pedal rhythm.

TEMPO

HEART RATE/INTENSITY: 60 to 70 percent of maximum heart rate
DURATION: Half the duration of the bike leg
SUBJECTIVE EFFORT LEVEL: Comfortably challenging; RPE: 13 to 15

Tempo workouts will help you ride at a strong pace through the bike leg of your triathlon. After a 10-minute warmup, ride at a pace you want to maintain for the bike portion of your event. Determine your pace based on heart rate rather than speed. In other words, if you feel comfortable riding the bike leg of your triathlon at a pace that keeps your heart rate at 145 beats per minute, then that should be your goal. Your tempo workouts only need to last half as long as your projected bike time in the event. So if you think your time will be 50 minutes, your tempo ride should last 25 minutes.

TRAINING ZONE III

SHORT INTERVALS

HEART RATE/INTENSITY: 70 to 80 percent of maximum heart rate
DURATION: Five to eight 1-minute intervals
SUBJECTIVE EFFORT LEVEL: Difficult; RPE: 16 to 17

Sprint intervals are effective at breaking through frustrating plateaus. Start with a thorough 20-minute warmup that isn't too hard but is more intense than your typical warmup. You should definitely be breaking a sweat when you're through. Then take a few minutes to stretch or shake out any areas that may feel sore or tight. Once you're warm and limber, sprint hard for one minute five to eight times with complete recovery between each interval. As with all interval sessions, you want the last to be as strong as the first, so be a bit conservative in the first couple of intervals. Be sure to cool down completely after this workout by ramping down your intensity for 15 minutes. At the end of your workout, you want your heart rate to be below 100, and, though you may be tired, you should feel completely at ease (rather than keyed up).

INDOOR TRAINER

HEART RATE/INTENSITY: 70 to 80 percent of maximum heart rate
DURATION: Four to eight 45-second intervals
SUBJECTIVE EFFORT LEVEL: Difficult; RPE: 16 to 17

Rollers or an indoor bike trainer offer you more benefit in less time, because they don't allow you to coast downhill. As a result, your indoor workouts need only last 75 percent as long as your outdoor ones. To make your indoor ride more fun, listen to music, read a book, or watch inspiring videos. Just be sure to maintain good pedaling form.

Start with a 10-minute warmup. Then do between four and eight 45-second intervals in which you feel like you're pushing hard but are under control. Recover fully between each interval.

TRAINING ZONE IV

ROLLING SPRINTS

HEART RATE/INTENSITY: 80 to 90 percent of maximum heart rate; it may be difficult to determine your heart rate during exertion because of lag time between effort and heart rate response
DURATION: Four to eight 20-second sprints
SUBJECTIVE EFFORT LEVEL: Maximum effort; RPE: 18 to 20

Perform these sprints only if you are a Level IV/Single-Sporter on a Mission Triathlete-in-Training. After a 20-minute warmup, do four to eight 20-second all-out sprints from a rolling start. In other words, get going at a nice speed and then begin your 20-second effort. These workouts will develop power and leg speed at the same time. Remember to maintain perfect pedaling form during this workout. Cool down for 10 minutes at the end of your rolling sprints. And yes, then go have some Ben & Jerry's!

7
RUN FASTER

"I always loved running . . . it was something you could do by yourself,
and under your own power. You could go in any direction, fast or slow
as you wanted, fighting the wind if you felt like it, seeking out new sights
just on the strength of your feet and the courage of your lungs."

—JESSE OWENS

Outside of soccer, running is the most popular participatory sport in the world, and for good reasons.

IT'S AN EFFICIENT WORKOUT. Running is the most effective way to boost cardiovascular fitness and burn body fat in the shortest time. If you run at a pace of six miles per hour for one hour, you will burn roughly 700 calories. That's roughly one-fifth of a pound of pure body fat in one workout.

IT'S CHEAP. You don't have to join a gym or buy fancy gear. The only equipment you need is a good pair of shoes, socks, shorts, and a T-shirt. You can jog in a local park or on a high school track—or better yet, just lace up and step out your front door.

IT MELTS AWAY STRESS. Running is just you, the terrain, your breathing, and the sound of your feet. After about 20 minutes of steady running, the pressure of everyday life gives way to a clearer perspective. Running also releases endorphins, those "feel-good" natural chemicals your body produces that ease pain and elevate mood. That's where the term *runner's high* comes from.

IT'S GOOD FOR YOUR HEALTH. As a weight-bearing exercise, running strengthens your bones and helps prevent osteoporosis—particularly important to women as they age. It also works wonders on your heart, dramatically reducing your risk for heart disease. That's because running is an aerobic form of exercise. All that huff-and-puff work helps to improve the condition of your cardiovascular system, lowers your blood pressure, and helps to keep your arteries clear.

Still, running carries the highest incidence of pain and injury of any physical activity. Serious runners often suffer through every tendinitis known to humankind. They've even discovered some new ones. And unless you're a very experienced runner, the run is likely the toughest part of the triathlon. Because it's the last leg of the race, you start off the run already feeling fatigued from the swim and the bike portions. That's where proper training comes in. With the tips and workouts in this chapter, you'll be running fleet of foot and pain free in no time—and crossing the finish line with energy to spare.

MAN'S BEST TRAINING BUDDY

His name is Owen, and of all the champion athletes around the world with whom I have trained, he's top dog.

Owen is my Labrador-greyhound, and he runs like the wind. We've spent many fog-laden Northern California mornings running across mountain trails together, gliding in a harmony of strides—for no other reason than the sheer pleasure of running. Owen's unqualified love of physical activity has reminded me that every exercise session can and should be fun and in the moment. Running with Owen doesn't feel like training. When I sprint with him on the beach, I'll try to outrun him for 20 seconds at a time. It's a phenomenal workout that doesn't feel like work. (Oh, and I never make it the full 20 seconds before he catches me.)

Since Owen has come into my life, my workouts have taken on a new level of excitement and performance. Owen has greyhound genetics, and therefore, he can outrun me with nary a pant. On our last workout together, in fact, I was completing a series of running intervals. After sprinting at full speed for three minutes, I stopped for the rest portion of the interval. Owen stopped, too, then turned around and had the audacity to *yawn* at me (and Lab-greyhound yawns are wider and held longer than most dogs'). I have a steelier resolve in my training now, so that that never happens again!

Owen also motivates my wife, who jogs just for general health. Every morning at precisely 7:52 a.m., Owen begins gazing at her—with a blinkless stare—to take him for a run or walk, even when that's the last thing my wife wants to do. The message is clear: "What? You're actually thinking of *not* taking me for a walk? You're a horrible person!"

Dogs can be fantastic motivators, and sometimes their subtle (and not-so-subtle!) nudges are all we need to get out the door for a workout. I urge you to add some dog days to your training schedule. The workout involves no rules beyond just getting out and running with your dog. Don't have a furry friend? Then borrow a neighbor's dog for a run—or take a shelter dog out for some much-needed exercise.

CHOOSE THE RIGHT GEAR

Your running shoes determine how much impact and stress your body absorbs, because each time you take a step, force travels from the ground up through your body. Running shoes protect your feet, ankles, knees, hips, and even your back from this stress.

"The most important step in choosing the right running shoe is to determine your individual biomechanics or, in other words, how you move," says Sam A. Labib, MD, an associate professor of orthopedic surgery at Emory University and a specialist in foot, ankle, and sports medicine. When you run, observe how you land on your shoes. If you land on your heel and roll to the outside edge of your shoes, you are a supinator. If you roll to the inside edge, you are a pronator. If you roll gracefully up the middle to your toes, you are gifted with being neutral. No matter how your foot rolls, if you weigh more than 180 pounds, you need extra cushioning.

Knowing your personal running style is important when shopping for running shoes. It's best to go to a running specialty store where the salespeople are trained to determine which shoes suit your individual biomechanics. No matter which shoes fit your needs, the best values range from $60 to $80, although running shoes are not something to scrimp on or buy off-brand. Along with spending millions of dollars on slick marketing, the name brands spend millions of dollars perfecting shoe design. New Balance, Nike, Saucony, Asics, and Reebok are (in that order) your best bets.

When shopping for your shoes, here are a few additional things to keep in mind from the American Podiatric Medical Association.

- Visit the shoe store when your feet are largest in size (at the end of a day or after a workout).

- Wear the socks you normally wear when running.

- The best-designed shoes will not do their job if they don't fit properly. As I've already mentioned, it's ideal to get fit by a running-shoe specialist. When you try on shoes, make sure to stand, bend, and even run in them to see how they feel. They should have adequate arch support and must not feel tight, since they will not stretch. As a rule of thumb, so to speak, press down on your shoe above your big toe with your thumb. The distance between your big toe and the tip of the shoe should be a bit shorter than the width of your thumb.

When buying running shoes, consider purchasing two pairs at a time. Here's why: To absorb the impact between the ground and your body, shoe manufacturers use a special material in most running shoes called ethylene vinyl acetate (EVA). When you run, the EVA compacts and requires about 24 hours to regain its shape. So rotating shoes every other run maintains maximum protection against pain and injury.

While shoes are the most important equipment in running, you also need to put thought into what you wear above your ankles. "Running increases your core body temperature by up to 20 degrees above the ambient temperature," says Timothy Noakes, MD, professor of exercise and sports science at the University of Cape Town Medical School in South Africa and author of *Lore of Running*. That means you need to dress according to the weather. When running on hot days, you need to protect against overheating. If it's 70°F or above, you're better off wearing as little as possible, such as a tank top and shorts.

When running in cold temperatures, dress in layers so that you can peel them off as you go along. Thin layers are more efficient at keeping you warm and are easier to run in than thick layers. Wear a thin long-sleeve base shirt, for example, under a long-sleeve race-type shirt with a lightweight fleece or waterproof jacket. You should feel a bit cool as you start out on your run, since your body will quickly warm up. As things heat up, take off your top layers and tie them around your waist. (See Chapter 3 for more specific information on what types of clothing to look for.)

CHOOSE THE RIGHT VENUE

Where you run is almost as important as the shoes you wear. Here are your choices, from best to worst.

SMOOTH, EVEN TRAILS. Hiking trails in parks or in the country offer scenic beauty and the best running terrain. One reason the Kenyans are such phenomenal runners is that their training grounds are the soft-soiled hills of Kenya—easy on the bones. This develops tremendous aerobic strength and power while minimizing the risk of injury. And because trails usually snake across undulating terrain, running them boosts your fitness by forcing your body to work different muscle groups. Plus the calming effect of jogging through nature cannot be matched by running along the side of a busy highway. The next time you have the option, head for soft, even trails.

YOUR LOCAL TRACK. A track is one of the most effective and convenient places to run. Most towns have a local school track that's about a quarter of a mile around. One caveat: Always running in the same direction places more strain on your outer leg, because it has to extend a bit more than the inner leg. Walk or run the first half of your workout in one direction around the track, then head in the other direction for the second half. Tracks also usually have stadium steps that can provide a fantastic strength workout. Walking or running up and down these steps builds aerobic and muscular strength at the same time.

THE BEACH. If you live near a beach, work out there as often as once a week but at least once a month. The fresh ocean air and the rhythmic sounds of the waves will provide a nice break from your routine. Stick to the compressed sand near the water break. While soft, deep sand is a good strength builder, it can stress your ligaments and tendons, because with each step, your feet and legs have to work harder.

THE TREADMILL. While many treadmills have some shock absorption, this advantage is negated by the tendency to slam your foot down harder than when running on other surfaces. Doing so increases the impact stress on your body and can make treadmill running about as bad as running on asphalt. If you choose to use a treadmill, seek out one with extra cushioning and pay special attention to how hard you put your feet down with each step.

THE ROAD OR SIDEWALK. Concrete and asphalt are simply the worst surfaces on which to run. Studies have shown that people who consistently run on cement suffer a higher incidence of injuries such as shin splints and a type of arch pain known as plantar fasciitis.

While an asphalt road is a softer surface than a concrete sidewalk, the natural slope along a road's shoulder forces your body into an uneven position. If you're running against traffic on the left side of the road, for example, your left leg must extend farther downward than your right. That can lead to muscle soreness and injuries. For this reason, I'd rather run on an even sidewalk than an uneven road.

HONE YOUR TECHNIQUE

Most injuries stem from bad running technique. Good form starts with the following principles.

- Maintain an upright, balanced, and relaxed posture with hips, shoulders, and torso aligned. Lean forward slightly from the ankles, not the waist. Relax your shoulders so they're not up by your ears.

- Keep your arms, wrists, and hands relaxed and moving in a natural path, with your elbows bent about 90 degrees. Your arms should not cross the midline of your torso—keep them moving forward.

- As for your hands, visualize carrying a potato chip in each hand—palms facing in, thumbs on top. This is a natural position, but it may not feel right to you. However you hold your hands, they should feel natural and relaxed, not clenched or forced.

- Don't overstride. Your foot should land underneath your knee easily with each stride, not out in front of your body.

- Relax. Be sure not to tense your muscles or force your stride. The motion should feel smooth and fluid, with light steps rather than heavy ones.

TIPS FROM THE PROS

To simulate race conditions while training, many professional triathletes run after they ride their bikes (these sessions are known as *bricks*). To prepare for your event, it's a good idea to work bricks into your training program periodically.

A different approach to training comes from Simon Lessing, one of the top runners in the sport of triathlon, whom I met at a race in Bath, England. Lessing says he only runs when he feels great, and he focuses on perfect biomechanical technique. If he's having a slightly off day, he skips his run entirely. This way he trains like a pure runner and beats all the triathlete runners at races. Maybe his training style will work for you.

Another tip from the pros is to run in groups. This is one of the best ways to learn how to improve your running. Just don't fall prey to the tendency to push too hard. While you want to push yourself and learn from better runners, ultimately you need to stick to your triathlon program and not let anyone alter your training. Use a heart rate monitor to keep yourself in aerobic check during group runs. It will serve as a personal coach on your wrist and keep you exercising smart no matter what level athlete you train with.

STRENGTHEN YOUR WEAKNESSES

To become a better runner—and to feel strong and confident in your triathlon—you must address your weaknesses as part of your training. To figure out which areas need your extra attention in the next six weeks, answer the following questions.

DO YOU SAIL ALONG FLATS ONLY TO CRAWL UP HILLS? If so, you may lack strength. Running well in a triathlon requires more strength than speed—you lose your speed from the fatigue accumulated from the swim and bike legs. Strength helps you finish and helps you win. To improve running strength, head for the hills.

No hills in your area? Then do some additional strength training on the muscles you use in running. Pay extra attention to strengthening your quadriceps, hamstrings, and calves. This will not only help you finish strong but also protect you from injuries. Most running injuries are caused by muscular imbalances. The strength-training program in Chapter 8 is designed to help you build balanced muscle strength while increasing your flexibility.

DO YOU FADE NOTICEABLY IN LONGER RUNS (MORE THAN 45 MINUTES)? The ability to go the distance is known as endurance. It's your insurance policy in the triathlon—have enough of it and you will finish. To improve your endurance, add some 90-minute or longer runs to your training schedule.

WHEN YOU RUN, DO YOU TAKE FEWER THAN 60 STRIDE CYCLES A MINUTE? (ONE FULL STRIDE CYCLE IS ONE STEP OF EACH FOOT.) If so, you lack leg speed. A few workouts in which you focus on your leg speed will go a long way to improving your running. The Training Zone IV stride-outs workout on page 111 is specifically designed to help you increase your leg speed.

CAN YOU MAINTAIN A STRONG, STEADY PACE FOR 20 MINUTES OR LONGER? Power is the hallmark of professional triathletes and top runners. They can hold a strong pace over longer distances. To improve your power, focus more attention on your Training Zone II tempo runs (see page 110).

KNOW WHEN TO SAY WHEN

You rise at first light, ready to work out and take one more step toward triathlon greatness. You lace up your running shoes and knock back your preworkout smoothie, all while humming the theme to *Rocky*. You bolt out your front door and brace yourself for a record-breaking run.

It hits you immediately. You feel sluggish, heavy, and slow. You won't be breaking any records today. In fact, you wonder if you'll even make it around the block. Your drive lessens with each step, because while your mind is raring to go, your body just won't listen.

What's going on?

You're having an off day. And it's frustrating. Have enough of them and you might even think about throwing in the towel on your triathlon-training program.

Rest easy. Bad days are normal—and they can provide you with an opportunity to pull back, reassess your training program, and even take some needed time off.

It's helpful to understand what's going on with your body when you feel less than stellar during exercise. Ask yourself if you're hydrated and if you've been eating and sleeping well lately. Are you under unusually intense pressure at work? If the answer to those questions is "no" or "not really," then your body is likely in the midst of a low cycle.

"The human body goes through distinct physiological changes over the course of each month, often referred to as circatrigintan rhythms," says Murray Mittleman, MD, associate professor of medicine at Harvard University and former board member of the American Association of Medical Chronobiology and Chronotherapeutics. "These physical highs and lows are perfectly natural. Listen to your body and modify your fitness program accordingly day to day."

Sound advice, sure. But most of us don't follow it. We push through when our bodies don't respond to our commands during exercise. No pain, no gain, right?

Wrong. While it's important to positively stress your body during exercise, fighting a physical low can lead to fitness regression, loss of motivation, illness, and even injury. Just as you should heed a twinge in your Achilles or hamstring, you should also listen to your body when it says, "Not today!"

These are some signs that you need to take a few days off, especially if they occur over three or more workouts.

HEAVY LEGS/GENERAL SLUGGISHNESS. This indicates that your muscles are overworked or your body is undergoing a low physical cycle.

EXTREME MUSCLE SORENESS. As you run, your muscles should loosen up and become less sore. If your muscle soreness doesn't improve or gets worse during your run, that's a sign to take a break.

RUN SAFE

One of the unfortunate realities of life is that personal safety is not always guaranteed, especially for women. That doesn't mean you should run in fear, but it does mean you'd be wise to take some precautions.

When you head out the door, make sure you have your ID, take a cell phone (with a charged battery!), and consider carrying mace—and not just to use against a human perpetrator. If you run on trails, it may come in handy to ward off wild animals as well. Wear brightly colored clothes that have reflective material so you don't blend in with your surroundings and can be easily spotted.

Avoid running alone or at night in isolated areas. Only run routes with which you are familiar. Be aware of your surroundings at all times. If you listen to music, keep one ear free to hear everything around you. Also, let someone know where you're going and when you'll be back. Better yet, drag your loved ones with you and get them running, too! Or run with a different buddy—your dog!

ELEVATED HEART RATE. An unusually high heart rate is a signal that your body is under negative stress. If at a certain workout pace your heart rate is normally around 110 but on this occasion it's 140, that may mean you're tired or getting sick.

SUGAR CRAVINGS. When you crave sugary foods, your body may be in a state of glycogen depletion. You may be exercising at too high an intensity level (burning sugar). Either tone down your workouts or take a few days off.

ANXIETY/FRUSTRATION. It's natural to not always want to exercise. But if you approach workouts with more anxiety and negativity than excitement and motivation, things need to change in your fitness program. Make your run workouts more enjoyable by running on scenic trails, teaming up with a buddy, or listening to music or comedy tapes. Or enter a local 5-K charity run to increase your motivation.

When you experience an off day (or two or three) in your training program, you have two choices. Of course, you can turn around and head home. And yes, that's perfectly okay. Perhaps even smart. I've seen world-class swimmers leave the pool after 10 minutes and call it quits. They know their bodies simply are not receptive to training, and forcing the exercise would be detrimental to their long-term motivation and progress.

The other option is to continue your workout but abandon your expectations. In other words, ditch the watch, heart monitor, and rules. Let your body guide you. Relax and work out based entirely on what feels right to you on that day. You'll be amazed at how much pressure this removes.

Work on developing an inner coach that guides you through workouts. Many professional triathletes often rely on this coach more than they rely on their real-world coaches. Your inner coach will help you distinguish between those days when your body is not ready to exercise and when you're simply feeling lazy. Your inner coach will also guide you through more effective and more comfortable workouts—which will lead you to long-term motivation and progress.

RUNNING WORKOUTS

As I explained in Chapter 4, when it comes to running, mileage is not the most accurate measurement tool, because running five miles on a flat trail on a comfortably cool day is far different from running five miles over hilly terrain on a blustery, cold day. Because of this, you'll tend to overtrain if you train simply by tracking your mileage.

It's still a good idea to keep track of how many miles you run and at what pace on certain days, because this information can help you monitor your progress over time. The training tool I prefer to use, however, is exercise intensity as measured by target heart rate. Exercise intensity is the most important consideration during exercise, whether you're a first-time triathlete or a seasoned veteran. Training at different intensities produces a more powerful and efficient athlete, which is why it's important to vary the exercise intensities of your workouts throughout the week. That way you'll also make steady progress and minimize fatigue.

Each intensity level, or Training Zone, indicated before the workouts ahead corresponds to a specific target heart rate. Training this way requires you to know your maximum heart rate. For instructions on how to find your maximum heart rate, see pages 56 and 57. For more information about the four Training Zones and their benefits, see pages 59 and 60.

Begin each workout with at least a 10-minute warmup in which you run at roughly 50 percent of your maximum effort. At the end of the 10 minutes, you should just be breaking a sweat. Then take another 5 minutes to slowly increase your pace to the prescribed intensity for that day's training. Doing this will reduce your chance of injury by gradually elevating your body's temperature and circulation.

After each run workout, slowly cool down by walking for about 5 minutes. Then stretch and shake out any muscles that feel particularly tight. Pay special attention to your hamstrings, quadriceps, calves, and lower back. (For specific stretches for these muscle groups, see Chapter 8.)

TRAINING ZONE I

WALK

HEART RATE/INTENSITY: 50 to 60 percent of maximum heart rate
DURATION: 10 to 20 minutes
SUBJECTIVE EFFORT LEVEL: Nice, steady pace; 10 to 12 on the Borg Rate of Perceived Exertion (RPE) scale. (For an explanation of the RPE scale, see page 58.)

Brisk walking is a great active recovery workout. It provides an important mental and physical break (and, hey, most professional triathletes have walked portions of the run leg). Take a nice 10- to 20-minute walk and stretch out any muscles that feel sore or tight. Do light stretches throughout the walk and/or when you're finished. Because this is an easy workout, there's no need for a warmup or cooldown.

ENDURANCE

HEART RATE/INTENSITY: 50 to 60 percent of maximum heart rate
DURATION: Work up to the projected time of the run leg in your triathlon event
SUBJECTIVE EFFORT LEVEL: Nice, steady pace; RPE: 10 to 12

Long runs are the most important workouts in your entire triathlon training program. Why? Because more people quit during the run than any other leg of the race. They simply run out of gas. If you do your longer runs consistently, you will have the mental and physical edge you need to get through the final triathlon minutes. These long training runs need only last as long as your projected run time in your event. Build up slowly over the weeks (by no more than 10 percent a week) and keep your heart rate under control to avoid injury or fatigue.

TRAINING ZONE II

TEMPO

HEART RATE/INTENSITY: 60 to 70 percent of maximum heart rate
DURATION: 5 to 20 minutes
SUBJECTIVE EFFORT LEVEL: Comfortably challenging; RPE: 13 to 15

After a 10-minute warmup, settle into a pace that feels comfortably challenging to you. Run anywhere from 5 to 20 minutes at this pace. Keep your rhythm steady through the entire run. Cool down for 5 to 10 minutes by walking or jogging, and finish up with some stretches.

LONG INTERVALS

HEART RATE/INTENSITY: 60 to 70 percent of maximum heart rate
DURATION: Two to six 800-yard intervals
SUBJECTIVE EFFORT LEVEL: Comfortably challenging; RPE: 13 to 15

Use your local track or a flat, even trail for this workout. After a 10-minute warmup, do two to six 800-yard (or two-lap) runs with a complete recovery between each one, so that your heart rate comes back down and your breathing is under control. (If you're running on trails, cover a fixed distance in three minutes.) Note your times and heart rates and record them in your Success Journal. (See Chapter 9 for more on keeping a Success Journal.) Cool down and stretch well after this session.

TRAINING ZONE III

SHORT INTERVALS

HEART RATE/INTENSITY: 70 to 80 percent of maximum heart rate
DURATION: Three to six 1-minute intervals
SUBJECTIVE EFFORT LEVEL: Difficult; RPE: 16 to 17

After a thorough 20-minute warmup and some light, easy stretches, do three to six 1-minute relatively hard efforts with complete recovery between each. These are essentially controlled sprints in which you run as hard as you can while maintaining good form. Focus on driving forward with your legs and keeping your arm swing in the same plane as your body. (In other words, don't swing them wildly out at your sides.) Build up your speed over the 1-minute interval so that 30 seconds into it, you're at full effort and you finish stronger than you started. Be sure to cool down completely after this workout.

TREADMILL

HEART RATE/INTENSITY: 70 to 80 percent of maximum heart rate
DURATION: 5 minutes
SUBJECTIVE EFFORT LEVEL: Difficult; RPE: 16 to 17

A treadmill will improve your running because you can focus on maintaining proper running form; you can even analyze your form in a mirror. After a 10-minute warmup, set the treadmill to your favorite preprogrammed course and run hard for about 5 minutes. Try to maintain an even pace throughout, and when things get tough, focus on keeping your breathing calm and steady. Cool down thoroughly.

TRAINING ZONE IV

STRIDE-OUTS

HEART RATE/INTENSITY: 80 to 90 percent of maximum heart rate; it may be difficult to determine your heart rate during exertion because of lag time between effort and heart rate response
DURATION: Five to ten 15-second stride-outs
SUBJECTIVE EFFORT LEVEL: Maximum effort; RPE: 18 to 20

Warm up for a minimum of 15 minutes and do some easy stretching. During each 15-second stride-out, you want to maintain absolutely flawless running form and build your speed to maximum by the end of the workout. The point of these stride-outs is to run your fastest 15-second sprint by focusing on quick leg speed. Keep your legs moving fast with short strides and light steps off the ground. (No heavy foot slamming. That will slow you down.) Do between 5 and 10 stride-outs once every two weeks and watch your run performance soar. Only Level IVs and those with a solid running background should attempt these, because fast, ballistic sprinting stresses ligaments, tendons, and muscles—and they must be well trained from running to safely endure these workouts. (And after this workout, no Ben & Jerry's for you this time; you've had enough already!)

8
STRETCH AND STRENGTHEN YOUR BODY

"Prepare yourself for the world, as the athletes . . . do for their exercise;
oil your mind and your manners, to give them the necessary suppleness
and flexibility; strength alone will not do."

**—PHILIP DORMER STANHOPE,
FOURTH EARL OF CHESTERFIELD, ESSAYIST, AND ORATOR**

Our daily lives often place physical stress on our bodies that they aren't physiologically equipped to handle. Over time, this stress can really take its toll.

Ever wonder, for example, why so many Americans suffer from lower back pain? The answer is simple: The majority of us spend eight-plus hours a day sitting in an unnatural position that is very hard on our bodies, especially our lower backs.

By stretching and strengthening your body using the strategies in this chapter, you will counteract the stressors of daily life so you'll be able to function more efficiently and with less day-to-day pain. You'll also perform at a higher level during your workouts and recover more quickly from exercise.

STRETCHING

Researchers, coaches, and sports therapists are on an unending quest to maximize performance. Their clients—many of them world-class athletes—depend on it.

One of the best discoveries in the upper echelon of the sporting world might also be the best-kept fitness secret for the rest of us. It's an effective yet simple technique called *active-isolated stretching* that has boosted many athletes' performance. It can help you become less prone to injuries, feel more comfortable in your body, and perform better in exercise and in daily activities.

The goal of stretching is to provide the means for muscle and tendon fibers to gradually relax and lengthen, allowing for a full range of unencumbered movement. The stretches people perform to achieve this vary greatly. Some athletes, for example, bounce like ballerinas before runs, whereas others contort their bodies into bizarre positions. Still, most people perform the classic "hold for 30 seconds" static stretch. The jury is still out on the benefits of static stretching, and some experts believe it can lead to muscle damage and soreness. One study of college-age men published in *Research Quarterly for Exercise and Sport* found that those who did a series of 17 static stretches actually had more soreness and higher levels of creatine kinase, an enzyme associated with muscle injury, than those who didn't stretch at all.

How could this be? Your muscles have a built-in stretch reflex that's engaged after a rapid movement or after three seconds in a stretched position. When a muscle is statically stretched, it has a natural tendency to protect itself from this motion by contracting back to its normal range. If you continue stretching while your muscle is trying to contract, you're in a tug-of-war that invites damage.

Only a warm, relaxed muscle can be stretched effectively. That's why many experts believe that active-isolated stretching, or AIS, is one of the most promising ways to get the benefits of stretching while minimizing its risks. In AIS, you hold each stretch for just two to three seconds, and then you return to the starting position and relax. After resting for a few seconds, you ease into the stretch again, progressively warming and elongating the muscle in more of a gentle pumping action. In this way, AIS works with your physiology, not against it.

Since I began using the AIS technique, my body has never felt looser, and my athletic performance has skyrocketed. A few minor injuries also went away. World-champion runner Steve Spence agrees: "I always hated to stretch because it didn't seem to make a difference," he told me. "But now I use this program every day, and I haven't been injured." The definitive guide to AIS is *The Whartons' Stretch Book* by Jim and Phil Wharton. It will show you step-by-step how to reap the rewards of this remarkable stretching technique in just minutes a day.

What follows are two exercises for stretching two common problem areas—your lower back and shoulders—using AIS. Most people will suffer lower back pain at some point in their lives. This stretch sequence, done twice a day, can reduce the amount of back pain you experience. (Important note: Stretching can actually worsen certain back injuries, so consult your doctor before beginning a stretching routine.)

A few things to keep in mind to achieve the benefits of AIS: Don't force yourself beyond the point of gentle discomfort. Take your time. The best results come when you are relaxed and breathing deeply. Hold the full stretch for two to three seconds, and then return to the starting position. At this point, your blood is flowing into your muscles, which are now a little warmer. Do the move again, trying to increase the depth of the stretch by 5 percent. Repeat six to eight times. Each time you should be able to go a little deeper into the stretch.

Lying Back Stretch

On a carpeted floor or exercise mat, lie flat on your back with your knees bent and your feet flat on the floor. Use your abdominal muscles to bring your knees toward your chest. Keep the small of your back pressed firmly into the floor while lifting your butt and hips slightly off the floor. When you can't bring your knees any closer to your chest on their own, wrap your arms or hands around the backs of your upper thighs and gently pull them deeper into your chest while exhaling fully. Physiology dictates that when you contract a muscle group (in this case, your abdominals), the antagonistic, or opposite, muscle group (your back) must relax.

Shoulder Stretch

Stand with your feet shoulder-width apart, your arms down at your sides, and your abdominal muscles tucked in. Keeping your left arm straight, bring it up and across your chest toward your right shoulder as far as it will go. Then place your right hand on your upper left arm just above your elbow. Without twisting your upper body—in other words, keep your shoulders square—gently push your left arm toward your right shoulder a few inches more while exhaling. Hold for two to three seconds, and then drop your left arm down and shake it out. Repeat six to eight times. When you're finished—if you've done it correctly—your left shoulder should feel noticeably looser and warmer than your right. Now repeat the stretch sequence with your right arm.

STRENGTH TRAINING

The body of a Triathlete-in-Training must be as strong as it is loose. Strength training is arguably the most beneficial exercise there is, and it's a must for all triathletes. Strength training reverses the trend of muscle loss that occurs at a rate of roughly half a pound per year, every year after age 30. It also burns body fat, increases bone density, and improves posture. To reap these benefits, you must strength train twice a week, but the results are well worth it.

Using flawless technique is paramount when strength training. If you plan to do your workout at a gym, it's wise to get some personal attention if you don't know how to use the machines. Whether you're lifting at Gold's Gym or in your basement, here's some general advice to follow.

ISOLATE. When performing a lift, focus on the specific muscle you're using. In other words, don't throw your back into your bench press by arching it and bouncing the weight off your chest. That works your back, not your chest. It's also important to go through your full range of motion to improve your flexibility. And don't hold your breath. Remember this rule of thumb: Exhale during a two-second lift and inhale on a three-second recovery.

USE RELAXED STRENGTH. When you learn to put forth great effort with a calm, loose body, your physical and mental fitness will skyrocket. Here's a tip: While strength training, your facial expressions reflect your perception of effort. Aim for Buddha, not Schwarzenegger. Keep your movements and your breathing smooth and rhythmical.

USE DUMBBELLS WHENEVER POSSIBLE. Because they force you to balance the free weight, which increases the benefit of the workout, dumbbells give you more value from the same lift than Nautilus-type machines. Dumbbells can also prevent injury, because they build your muscles symmetrically, and many soft-tissue injuries are caused by muscular *imbalance* rather than muscular *weakness*.

ALWAYS VARY YOUR WORKOUTS. You will experience noticeable improvements in how you look and feel after about four weeks on this strength-training program, but after that, your results will begin to plateau as your muscles adapt to their new workload. To continue seeing and feeling results at the same rate, you must keep your muscles guessing by varying your routine. One way to do that is to use different exercises to work the same muscle groups in back-to-back workouts. So, for example, if on Monday you used the leg curl machine to work your hamstrings, on Wednesday do the stability ball leg curl. As you'll see in the strength-training program that begins on page 119, there are several different exercises to work each muscle group. Make it your goal to never do the exact same workout in a single month.

KEEP YOUR SPORT IN MIND. The strength program that follows is fairly general in that it will help you get stronger no matter what your sport. But if you want to *really* boost your performance in triathlon, you must lift to meet the specific demands of swimming, cycling, and running. Here's one variation you may want to try, for example: When doing a lat pulldown, stand and push the bar down to your waist with your arms straight out in front of you, in a swim-stroke motion, rather than doing the traditional seated lat pulldown where you pull the bar down to your upper chest.

WATCH YOUR WEIGHT. If you lift weights that are too light, you won't get the maximum benefit from the exercise. On the other hand, if you lift weights that are too heavy, you risk getting injured. As a rule of thumb, you should use weights you can lift with proper form for two sets and still comfortably challenge yourself. If you feel like you could do a complete third set, you know your weight is too light. It's too heavy if you can't complete your two sets or if you begin compromising your form so you can lift the weight.

If you've never lifted weights or haven't done so for three months or more, it's vital that you ease into it. If you don't, your muscles will become very sore and you'll risk getting injured. The first four to six strength-training sessions should be easy. This period

THE FAB FIVE: FOR DAYS WHEN YOU DON'T HAVE TIME FOR THE FULL 40

Sometimes we run short on time. On those days, the biggest mistake you can make is to skip your workout entirely. Don't. Although you should always strive to make time for the Full 40, if you absolutely, positively can't fit it in, then simply do this abbreviated Fab Five routine at home. It's a simple, 20-minute stretch-and-strength workout consisting of five exercises and five stretches you can do while watching the evening news. The only pieces of equipment you need are three sets of dumbbells and a stability ball. If you have hardwood floors, you may also want to use a foam exercise mat for the floor exercises and stretches.

Begin with a two- to three-minute warmup by completing three sets of 25 jumping jacks or by jogging in place. This may sound militaristic, but these two methods are highly efficient at warming up your body in a short period of time. After this warmup, spend a few moments stretching any areas of your body that feel tight using the stretches shown on the following pages of this chapter. Then go right into your workout.

LUNGE. Do one set of 8 repetitions stepping forward with your left leg, and then do a set with your right leg. Now stretch your quadriceps (front thigh muscles) by performing the Standing Quad Stretch (page 121).

CHEST PRESS. Do two sets of 8 to 10 repetitions, and then do the Chest Stretch (page 140).

ONE-ARM ROW. Do two sets of 8 repetitions with your left arm and two with your right, and then finish up with the Upper-Back Stretch (page 130).

AB CRUNCH. Two sets of 20 high-intensity crunches will provide you with all the abdominal work you need. Top that off with either the Ball Drape (page 147) or Cobra (page 147) ab stretch.

SUPERMAN. Do two sets of this exercise sequence, holding each move for 10 seconds. Take a 30-second rest after the first set to stretch using the Lying Back Stretch (page 115). Repeat the stretch after the second set.

of *anatomical adaptation* trains your body to more fully absorb the effects of strength training later. In these sessions, lift lighter weights more times. This strength program calls for one set of 12 repetitions followed by another set of 8 repetitions. If you're new to this, start with lighter weights and do one set of 20 repetitions and a second set of 15 repetitions. After about six sessions, switch to heavier weights and the 12-and-8 sequence.

LIFT TO FAILURE. An important secret of strength training is to put some extra oomph into the last few repetitions of each set. Really push yourself to maintain your form and to go through the full range of motion for those last few repetitions. By exerting yourself at this high level, your pituitary gland releases a substance known as growth hormone—a highly potent fat-burner, health promoter, and the most anabolic (muscle-building) substance known to humankind. To reap the benefits of naturally produced growth hormone, you should lift almost to the point of failure at the end of your final set—meaning the muscles you're working become so fatigued you feel as though you couldn't lift that weight one more time with proper form. This is where most people fall short in their strength-training routines. Lifting to failure will help you make the most muscle gains in the least amount of time.

KEEP IT SIMPLE. You don't need to join a gym to lift weights. In fact, you don't even need to set up an elaborate home gym. All you need to buy are three pieces of equipment: a set of dumbbells, a stability ball, and a resistance band. I recommend that women get pairs of 5-, 8-, and 15-pound dumbbells and men buy pairs of 10-, 20-, and 30-pounders. If you have hard flooring, you may also want to get a foam exercise mat for the floor exercises and stretches. That's all you need to create the ultimate home gym! Purchase used items to save money. Go online (ebay.com will likely net the best deals) or to local yard sales.

THE FULL 40: THE ULTIMATE 40-MINUTE STRETCH AND STRENGTH ROUTINE

What follows is a simple, total-body circuit program that will stretch and strengthen almost every area of your body in just 40 minutes. It's like nothing you've ever done before.

PHASE I: WARMUP (FIVE MINUTES). Begin with a gradual five-minute aerobic warmup so that by the end of the five minutes, you just begin to break a sweat. If you're working out at home, head out your front door and go for a brisk walk around the block. If the weather is nasty, stay inside and warm up with three sets of 25 jumping jacks. At the gym, vary the machines on which you warm up: stairclimber, treadmill, stationary bike. You can even play a little basketball or racquetball as a warmup—think outside the box. Anything that increases your heart rate and warms your muscles will do, so have some fun with it!

PHASE II: INITIAL STRETCH (FIVE MINUTES). Spend a few moments doing the following total body stretches and focusing on any areas that feel particularly sore or tight to you. This is important to reduce your risk of injury when lifting weights and to get you in tune with your body. Focus on breathing deeply and rhythmically as you stretch.

Overhead Stretch

Stand with your feet shoulder-width apart and reach both arms straight over your head with your hands flat against one another and both palms facing forward. Fully extend your arms, point your fingers, and reach as high as you can straight up over your head, making your body as long as possible. Hold for two to three seconds and then relax. Repeat six to eight times, deepening the stretch and elongating your body even more with each repetition.

Lying Back Stretch

Do this stretch as described on page 115.

Arm Swings

To loosen and warm up your shoulders, swing your left arm in large circles like a windmill. Swing your arm forward five times and then backward five times. Repeat six to eight times, and then do the same with your right arm.

Standing Quad Stretch

To loosen your quadriceps—the muscles along the front of your thighs—stand with your feet slightly apart. Keeping your thighs still and your knees slightly apart but next to each other, raise your lower left leg behind you, lifting the heel of your foot toward your butt. Grab the ankle of your left foot with your left hand, and gently pull your heel closer to your butt. If you have trouble keeping your balance, you can hold on to the back of a chair with your free hand. Hold for two to three seconds and repeat six to eight times, deepening the stretch with each repetition. Then do the stretch sequence on your right leg.

Upper-Body Rotation

To loosen and warm up your midsection, stand with your feet shoulder-width apart and your knees soft, not locked. Hold your arms in front of you with your elbows bent and your forearms at about ribcage height. Rotate your upper body to the right as far as you comfortably can. Pause slightly and then rotate to the left. Repeat this fluid movement six to eight times, each time attempting to rotate farther to each side.

Neck Rolls

Many of us carry a great deal of tension in our necks. To relieve that tension—and to avoid taking it into your workout—gently drop your head forward so your chin is close to your chest. Place your fingertips on the back of your head and gently push your head down to deepen the stretch slightly. Hold for about three seconds. Then repeat the stretch six to eight times, each time making the stretch a bit deeper. Now drop your head to the right so that your ear is close to your shoulder. Place the fingertips of your right hand on your head and gently press your head down toward your shoulder to deepen the stretch. Hold for about three seconds. Then repeat the stretch six to eight times, each time making the stretch a bit deeper. Now drop your head to the left and repeat the stretch sequence on that side.

PHASE III: MAIN SET (25 MINUTES). In this program, you'll alternate between stretching and strengthening. For example, you'll begin by stretching your quadriceps muscles for about one minute using the Standing Quad Stretch (page 121), and then you'll strengthen those muscles with one of the quadriceps exercises on page 124. For each exercise, do one set of 12 lifts (called repetitions) followed by a 30-second rest while you stretch the muscle you're working. Then do a second set of eight repetitions followed by a 1-minute rest before moving on to another exercise. During that rest, you again stretch the muscle you just worked. Boston researchers found that men who stretched a muscle group for 20 to 30 seconds after lifting with that muscle actually increased their strength by 20 percent. Plus, this alternating approach of stretch and strengthen will elongate and build your muscles concurrently, saving you time and increasing the efficiency of your workout.

Cover the seven main muscle groups and stretch-strengthen in this order: quadriceps, upper back, hamstrings, chest, calves, abs, lower back. After this main workout, I've also included a few exercises that work the arms, although doing these exercises is not an essential part of your Triathlete-in-Training program. Note that for each muscle group, I've included several different exercises to prevent boredom and to help make it easy for you to vary your workouts from week to week. For your workout, choose just one exercise for each of the seven muscle groups.

PHASE IV: COOLDOWN (FIVE MINUTES). Spend a few minutes at the end of your workout walking easily on a treadmill or around the block or pedaling lightly on a stationary bike. This will help your muscles recover better by returning your body to homeostasis, or balance, after a tough workout. Round out your workout with a couple of your favorite stretches, and you're all finished.

Head-to-toe stretching and strengthening in 40 minutes flat!

WILL I BULK UP?

Some people worry that lifting weights will expand their muscles, making them look like a bodybuilder. Sure, if you spend five hours a week in the gym and lift very heavy weights, then, yes, your muscles will grow. But you rarely see bulky triathletes, because endurance exercise—that is, long bouts of aerobic exercise—tends to break down muscle mass. That's why professional bodybuilders avoid endurance exercise.

If you're worried about adding too much muscle bulk to your frame, stick to more repetitions and lighter weights in your strength workouts and stay true to the aerobic bike, swim, and run workouts in your triathlon training program.

QUADRICEPS EXERCISES

Standing Quad Stretch: Do this stretch as described on page 121.

AT HOME
Dumbbell Squat

1. Stand holding two dumbbells at your sides at arm's length, your feet shoulder-width apart. Keep your shoulder blades back and your toes pointed straight ahead.

2. Initiating your descent at the hips, not the knees, lower yourself as though sitting back into a chair. Stop when the tops of your thighs are parallel to the floor. Keep your lower back in its natural alignment and avoid moving your knees forward past your toes. (If you have trouble keeping your heels on the floor or feel like you're rocking forward on your feet, place weight plates or a thin book under your heels to raise them one to two inches off the floor.) Return to the starting position by standing as you push down through your heels. Do one set of 12 repetitions and then rest for 30 seconds while stretching your quadriceps. Do a second set—this time of 8 repetitions—and then take a minute to stretch your quads before moving on to your upper back.

Lunge

1. Stand holding two dumbbells at your sides, your feet shoulder-width apart and your toes pointing straight ahead.

2. Take a large stride forward, far enough so that your front thigh ends up parallel to the floor with your knee over (not past) your toes. Push back up to the starting position by bringing your front leg to your back leg. This motion strengthens your entire leg—and your butt—while increasing the range of motion in your hips. Do a set of 12 repetitions with the first leg and then 12 with the other leg. Rest for 30 seconds after your first set while stretching your quadriceps. Then do a second set with each leg, this time of 8 repetitions. End the sequence by stretching your quads for about 1 minute before moving on to your upper back.

DOUBLE UP TO BURN MORE FAT

Generally speaking, strength training is fueled by sugar that's stored in your muscles (called glycogen). Aerobic exercise, on the other hand, uses both sugar and fat as its fuel sources. If losing weight is one of your goals, you should add 20 to 30 minutes of aerobic work after your strength training (such as running, cycling, or stairclimbing). That way, lifting weights uses up the sugar stores in your muscles, leaving you to burn more body fat with your aerobic workout.

Step Up

1. Stand in front of a sturdy chair or bench holding dumbbells in both hands, your arms down at your sides. Make sure the chair or bench is on a nonskid surface so it won't slide out from under you when you step up onto it. If you're using a chair, the seat back should be to one side of you (not in front of you). Put your left foot flat near the center of the bench or chair seat—that's the leg that's going to do the work. Keep your lower back in its natural alignment, your shoulders pulled back, and your eyes facing forward.

2. Push down through your left heel to lift your right leg off the floor. Plant your right foot on the bench or chair next to your left foot, and then step down with your right to return to the starting position. Make sure to keep all of your weight on the left foot throughout the move and not to push off with your back foot. Do one set of 12 repetitions and then do a set with your right foot on the chair. Rest for 30 seconds while stretching your quadriceps. Then do a second set with each leg, this time of 8 repetitions. End by taking a minute to stretch your quads before moving on to your upper back.

AT THE GYM
Cable Squat

1. Set the bar on the peg of a Smith-type machine so you have to bend your knees slightly to step under it, and set it on your shoulders. After adding the weights to the bar, position yourself under it with your feet at least shoulder-width apart and knees slightly bent. Rest the bar on the back of your shoulders and your upper back, not on your neck. (If you experience pain, that's a sign that you have the bar in the wrong place.) Grab the bar with a wide, overhand grip and straighten your legs to lift it straight up off the pegs. Then rotate the bar backward slightly with your hands to keep the hook from catching on the lower pegs on your way down. Keep your elbows pointing straight down to the floor, your wrists straight (not bent back), and your knees soft (not locked).

2. Initiating the descent at the hips, not the knees, lower yourself as though sitting in a chair behind you. Lower yourself until your thighs are parallel to the floor, pause, and then push through your heels back up to the starting position. Throughout the movement, keep your chest up, your elbows pointing straight down (not back), and your knees in line with your feet—they shouldn't go forward past your toes or be off to one side or the other. Do one set of 12 repetitions and then rest for 30 seconds while stretching your quadriceps. Do a second set—this time of 8 repetitions—and then take 1 minute to stretch your quads before moving on to your upper back.

Back Squat

1. If you use a squat rack, set the barbell on the squat supports so you have to bend your knees slightly to step under it and set the bar on your shoulders. (That way the supports are below you and you can lower the barbell to the supports when your muscles are tired after the set, rather than having to lift the bar up onto the supports.) Position the bar so it rests on the back of your shoulders and your upper back, not on your neck. (If you experience pain, that's a sign that you have the bar in the wrong place.) Hold the bar with a wide, overhand grip. Keep your elbows pointing straight down to the floor and set your feet shoulder-width apart with soft knees (not locked).

2. Initiating the descent at the hips, not the knees, lower yourself as though sitting in a chair behind you. Lower yourself until your thighs are parallel to the floor, pause, and then push through your heels back up to the starting position. Throughout the movement, keep your chest up, your elbows pointing straight down (not back), and your knees in line with your feet—they shouldn't go forward past your toes or be off to one side or the other. Do one set of 12 repetitions and then rest for 30 seconds while stretching your quadriceps. Do a second set—this time of 8 repetitions—and then take 1 minute to stretch your quads before moving on to your upper back.

Leg Press

1. Sit in a leg press machine with your feet flat against the foot plate. Adjust the seat so your knees are bent at about a 90-degree angle or slightly less to start. Hold on to the handlebars at your sides, and keep your back flat against the backrest and your upper body relaxed.

2. Push up through the foot plate and straighten your legs until they're almost fully extended. Keep your legs slightly flexed so that your knees aren't locked. Lower the foot plate to the starting position and repeat. Do one set of 12 repetitions, then rest for 30 seconds while stretching your quadriceps. Do a second set—this time of 8 repetitions—and then take 1 minute to stretch your quads before moving on to your upper back.

UPPER-BACK EXERCISES

Upper-Back Stretch

Stand about two feet away from a wall, with your feet about hip-width apart and your toes pointing toward the wall. With straight arms, place the palms of your hands flat on the wall slightly above eye level. Lower your head so your ears are by your upper arms. Your back may arch slightly. Squeeze your shoulder blades together. You should feel a good stretch in the muscles of your upper back. Hold for three seconds and repeat at least six times, deepening the stretch with each repetition.

AT HOME
One-Arm Row

1. Holding a dumbbell in your right hand, place your left hand and knee on a workout bench or the seat of a chair. Keep your back flat and let the dumbbell hang down at your side so that it's just in front of your shoulder.

2. Focus on using your upper-back muscles as you pull the dumbbell up and back toward your hip, keeping your arm close to your body. Do not lift the dumbbell higher than hip level. Pause at the top of the move and then slowly lower the dumbbell to the starting position. Do 12 reps with your right arm and 12 with your left. Follow the set by stretching your upper-back muscles with the Upper-Back Stretch (see above). Then do a set of 8 reps with each arm and stretch the upper-back muscles once again.

Seated Overhead Press

1. Sit in a chair with good posture, so that you aren't slouching and your abdominal and back muscles are supporting your trunk. Your feet should be flat on the floor, toes pointing straight ahead. Hold a pair of dumbbells above each shoulder at about jaw level with your palms facing forward. Your elbows should point straight down and your wrists should be straight, not bent back.

2. Press the dumbbells straight up and in toward each other slightly so that they're about three to six inches apart at the top of the move. Avoid shrugging your shoulders up by your ears and keep your elbows soft, not locked. Do 12 reps followed by stretching your upper-back muscles with the Upper-Back Stretch (page 130). Then do a set of 8 reps, followed by stretching the upper-back muscles once again.

Pullover

1. Lie on your back on a stability ball so that your head, neck, and upper back are supported by the ball. Keep your hips and butt lifted so your thighs are parallel to the floor and your knees are bent at a 90-degree angle. Hold two dumbbells over your midchest with an overhand grip and straight arms. Don't lock your elbows.

2. Keeping your head and upper body still and your arms straight with soft elbows, slowly lower the dumbbells behind your head until your upper arms are slightly below your ears. Pause and then pull the dumbbells back up to the starting position. Do 12 reps followed by stretching your upper-back muscles with the Upper-Back Stretch (page 130). Then do a set of 8 reps, followed by stretching the upper-back muscles once again.

AT THE GYM
Lat Pulldown

1. Sit directly in front of the lat pulldown machine with your feet flat on the floor and grab the bar with a false (thumb on the same side as your fingers) overhand and a shoulder-width grip. Keep your arms straight and your torso upright or leaning back slightly. Your back should remain straight, not arched.

2. Pull your shoulder blades together and down, stick out your chest, and pull the bar down toward your chest. Pause with the bar just past your chin, about an inch or two off your chest, and then slowly let it rise to the starting position. Do 12 reps followed by stretching your upper-back muscles with the Upper-Back Stretch (page 130). Then do a set of 8 reps, followed by stretching the upper-back muscles once again.

Seated Cable Row

1. Sit in the seat of a cable row machine with your knees slightly bent and your feet flat against the foot plates, and lean back slightly with a straight back. Grab the handle with your palms facing in toward each other and your arms fully extended.

2. Squeeze your shoulder blades together as you pull the handle to the lower part of your sternum. Pause and then slowly return to the starting position. Do 12 reps followed by stretching your upper-back muscles with the Upper-Back Stretch (page 130). Then do a set of 8 reps, followed by stretching the upper-back muscles once again.

One-Arm Row

Perform the exercise as described on page 130 while leaning over a workout bench for support.

HAMSTRING EXERCISES

STRETCHES
Lying Hamstring Stretch

Lie on your back on a carpeted floor or exercise mat. Raise your right leg straight up and bend your knee slightly so it isn't locked. Keep your left leg bent with your foot flat on the floor. Wrap a rope, belt, or towel around the arch of your right foot and gently pull your leg toward your right shoulder to deepen the stretch. Hold for three seconds and repeat six to eight times, deepening the stretch with each repetition. Repeat with the other leg.

Standing Hamstring Stretch

Place the heel of one foot up on a chair or bench at about waist height. Keeping your back straight, bend at the waist and press down with your hand on your upper thigh just above your knee. Be sure to keep your hips facing forward, not turned, with your toes pointing straight up and your knee soft (not locked). You should feel a good stretch along the back of your upper thigh. Hold for three to five seconds and repeat six to eight times, deepening the stretch with each repetition. Repeat with the other leg.

Hip Lift

1. Lie on your back on a carpeted floor or exercise mat with your knees bent and your feet hip-width apart. Your toes should point straight ahead and your arms should be straight out at your sides, palms up.

2. Press down through the heels of your feet to lift your hips and buttocks off the floor. Your body should form a bridge from your shoulder blades to your knees, and you should feel the exertion in the muscles along the backs of your thighs. Squeeze your gluteal (butt) muscles at the end of the move. Then lower yourself back to the starting position. Do 12 repetitions and then pause for 30 seconds to stretch your hamstrings using either the Lying Hamstring Stretch (page 135) or the Standing Hamstring Stretch (page 135). Now do a set of 8 repetitions, followed by another hamstring stretch.

Stability Ball Leg Curl

1. Lie on your back on a carpeted floor or exercise mat with your legs extended and your heels up on a stability ball. Keep your arms straight out at your sides with your palms down. Press down through your heels on the ball to lift your pelvis, butt, and most of your back off the floor. Your body should form a bridge from your shoulder blades to your feet, and you should feel the exertion in the muscles along the backs of your thighs.

2. Keeping your body lifted, squeeze your gluteal muscles and press your feet flat into the ball as you bend your knees and roll the ball in toward you. Pause and then roll the ball back out to the bridge position. Roll the ball in and out 12 times before taking 30 seconds to stretch your hamstrings using either the Lying Hamstring Stretch (page 135) or the Standing Hamstring Stretch (page 135). Then do another 8 repetitions, followed by a 1-minute stretch of your hamstrings.

Standing Leg Curl

1. Place one end of an elastic Resist-A-Band under your left heel and hook the other end around your right heel. Stand straight with your abs tight, looking straight ahead as you hold on to the back of a chair for support. Keep the toes on your left foot pointed straight ahead. Your feet should be a few inches apart, with the toes on your right foot on the floor a few inches behind your left foot.

2. Keeping your knees and thighs in line with each other, bend your right knee and lift your foot behind you until your lower leg is parallel with the floor. Pause and then lower your foot back to the starting position. Although this move may look easy, it's quite tough. You may not be able to lift your leg to parallel at first, but try to work toward that. Do 12 repetitions with your right leg and then 12 with your left. Stretch your hamstrings for 30 seconds using either the Lying Hamstring Stretch (page 135) or the Standing Hamstring Stretch (page 135). Then do a set of 8 repetitions with each leg and stretch your hamstrings again for a minute.

Single-Leg Hamstring Curl

1. Lie facedown on the bench of a leg curl machine, with your feet hooked behind the lifting pads and your knees just over the bench's edge. For support, hold on to the bench or the machine's handlebars, if available. Your legs should be fully extended, with some flex at the knee and your toes pointing down.

2. Keep your pelvis pressed against the bench as you raise one heel up toward your butt so that your leg bends to a 90-degree angle. Keep your toes pointing out away from your body. The other leg should remain in the extended position. Slowly lower the raised leg back to the starting position. Do 12 repetitions with your left leg and then 12 with your right. Follow that set with a 30-second rest to stretch your hamstrings using either the Lying Hamstring Stretch (page 135) or the Standing Hamstring Stretch (page 135). Then do 8 more repetitions on each leg before stretching your hamstrings again for another minute.

Standing Hamstring Curl

1. Stand facing a low cable machine with the cable strap wrapped around your left ankle. Stand straight with your abs tight, looking straight ahead as you hold on to the handlebar for support. Keep the toes of both feet pointed straight ahead. Your feet should be a few inches apart.

2. Keeping your knees and thighs in line with one another, bend your left knee and lift your foot behind you until your lower leg is parallel with the floor. Pause and then lower your foot back to the starting position. Do 12 repetitions with your left leg and then 12 with your right. Stretch your hamstrings for 30 seconds using either the Lying Hamstring Stretch (page 135) or the Standing Hamstring Stretch (page 135). Then do a set of 8 repetitions with each leg, stretching your hamstrings again for a minute.

CHEST EXERCISES

Chest Stretch

Stand next to a wall so that you're just a few inches away with your arm. Place your hand palm down on the wall straight behind you so that your hand lines up with your shoulder. Keep your hips and shoulders squared and your free hand down at your side. Hold for two to three seconds. Repeat the stretch six to eight times. Then repeat the entire sequence with your other arm.

AT HOME
Chest Press

1. Lie on your back on a stability ball so that the ball is supporting your head, neck, and upper back. Keep your feet shoulder-width apart and your hips and butt lifted so your thighs are parallel to the floor and your knees are bent at a 90-degree angle. Hold two dumbbells over your midchest with an overhand grip and straight arms. Your palms should face your feet and your elbows should be slightly bent, not locked.

2. Pinch your shoulder blades together as you bend your elbows and slowly lower the dumbbells until they're by your armpits, just higher than chest level. Pause and then press the dumbbells back up to the starting position, bringing your hands close together without clanking the weights. Do 12 repetitions and then take a 30-second rest, stretching your chest muscles with the Chest Stretch (see above). Now do another set of 8 repetitions, followed by stretching your chest muscles for 1 minute.

Chest Fly

1. Set up on the stability ball exactly as you would for the Chest Press (page 140), with your head, neck, and upper back supported by the ball and your hips lifted. Hold the dumbbells straight over your midchest as with the chest press.

2. Leading with your elbows, which should remain slightly bent, move your arms out and down in a wide arc until your upper arms are parallel to the floor. Use your chest muscles to pull the weights back up to the starting position, moving in the same arc motion, only in reverse. Do 12 repetitions and then take a 30-second rest, stretching your chest muscles with the Chest Stretch (page 140). Now do another set of 8 repetitions, followed by stretching your chest muscles for 1 minute.

Pushup

1. Support your body with the balls of your feet and your hands, positioning your hands about three inches wider than shoulder-width on either side, palms flat on the floor. Straighten your arms without locking your elbows. Your butt should be slightly above the line of your body so your back doesn't sag.

2. Lower your torso until your chest is almost to the floor. Push yourself up to the starting position. Do 12 repetitions and then take a 30-second rest, stretching your chest muscles with the Chest Stretch (page 140). Now do another set of 8 repetitions, followed by stretching your chest muscles for 1 minute.

Bent-Knee Pushup

Assume the standard pushup position, except instead of having your legs out straight, keep your knees bent and your feet up off the ground. You may want to do this exercise on a well-padded floor or exercise mat to cushion your knees. Lower your torso until your chest is almost to the floor. Push yourself up to the starting position. Do 12 repetitions and then take a 30-second rest, stretching your chest muscles with the Chest Stretch (page 140). Now do another set of 8 repetitions, followed by stretching your chest muscles for 1 minute.

AT THE GYM
Chest Press

Do the Chest Press as described on page 140 on a workout bench instead of a stability ball.

Chest Fly

1. Sit in a chest fly machine with your feet a comfortable distance apart and flat on the floor. Grab the handles with a false grip (thumb on the same side as your fingers). Your elbows should be at shoulder height resting on the pads.

2. Keeping your back and shoulder blades against the backrest, use your chest muscles to squeeze the pads together in front of your chest. Pause before returning to the starting position. Do 12 repetitions and then take a 30-second rest, stretching your chest muscles with the Chest Stretch (page 140). Now do another set of 8 repetitions, followed by stretching your chest muscles for 1 minute.

CALF EXERCISES

Lying Calf Stretch

Lie on your back on a carpeted floor or exercise mat. Raise one leg straight up with a soft knee (not locked), keeping the other bent with your foot flat on the floor. Flex the foot of the raised leg so your toes point toward your head. Wrap a rope, belt, or towel around the ball of your raised foot and gently pull your toes straight down to deepen the stretch. Hold for three seconds and repeat six to eight times, deepening the stretch with each repetition. Repeat with the other leg.

Standing Calf Stretch

Stand on the bottom step of a staircase, holding on to the railing with one hand to keep your balance. If your home doesn't have a staircase, you can stand on an aerobic step or thick phone book and hold on to the back of a chair for support. Place your left foot on the step so that the ball of your foot is at the step's edge and your heel hangs off the back. Hook your right foot behind your left heel and stand with good posture (don't lean backward or forward). With both knees slightly bent, drop your left heel below the level of the step and shift your weight so it's over that heel. Hold for three seconds. Repeat the stretch six to eight times, deepening the stretch with each repetition. Then repeat to stretch your right calf.

AT HOME
Floor Calf Raise

1. Stand with your feet no wider than hip-width apart. Hold dumbbells in both hands, with your arms down at your sides.

2. Stand up on your toes and focus on keeping your feet straight—don't turn your ankles outward or inward as you raise up. Pause in the raised position and then lower your feet so they're flat on the floor once again. Do 12 repetitions and then rest for 30 seconds while doing either the Lying Calf Stretch (page 144) or the Standing Calf Stretch (page 144). Then do 8 more repetitions and end by stretching your calves again.

Stair Calf Raise

1. Stand on the bottom step of a staircase, holding a dumbbell in one hand. Hold on to the railing with your free hand for support. If your home doesn't have a staircase, you can stand on an aerobic step or thick phone book and hold on to the back of a chair at your side. Place the front of both feet on the step so that the balls of your feet are on the step's edge and your heels hang off the back, below the level of the step.

2. Keeping your body in a straight line with your toes, lift up onto your toes as high as you can, making sure not to turn your ankles out as you raise up. Keep your knees soft (not locked) and avoid leaning forward. Pause in the raised position and then slowly lower your heels below the level of the step. Do 12 reps and then pause to stretch your calves using either the Lying Calf Stretch (page 144) or the Standing Calf Stretch (page 144). Then do a set of 8 calf raises and end by stretching your calves again.

Seated Calf Raise

1. Sit upright on the bench facing a seated calf raise machine, with your abs and back muscles supporting your trunk. Place the balls of your feet on the foot bar with your heels below the level of the bar. Rest the weight pad on your thighs, a few inches back from your knees. Hold on to the bench or weight pad for support and look straight ahead.

2. Lift your heels above the level of the metal foot bar, as high as you comfortably can. Pause and then lower back to the starting position. Do 12 reps and then rest for 30 seconds while stretching your calves using either the Lying Calf Stretch (page 144) or the Standing Calf Stretch (page 144). Then do a set of 8 more repetitions and end by stretching your calves again.

ABDOMINAL EXERCISES

STRETCHES
Ball Drape

Lying on your back on a stability ball, drape yourself over the ball so that your pelvis opens up and you feel a good stretch in your abs. Keep your feet flat on the floor as you allow the pressure of the ball to run up through your hips and the small of your back. Your head and neck should fall down the back of the ball while you hold your arms outstretched in a natural position with your fingertips grazing the floor for balance. Hold for two to three seconds and then repeat six to eight times, deepening the stretch with each repetition.

Cobra

Lie facedown on a carpeted floor or exercise mat with your feet wider than shoulder-width apart. Place your palms down on the mat directly under your shoulders. Now push up with your arms to lift your torso off the floor, making sure to keep your pelvis pressed into the floor. Keep your elbows bent and your shoulders relaxed (not shrugged up by your ears), and focus your gaze slightly higher than the horizon. Hold for two to three seconds and then repeat six to eight times, deepening the stretch with each repetition.

Ab Crunch

1. To perform the perfect crunch, lie on your back with your knees bent and your feet flat on the floor about hip-width apart. Place your fingertips lightly behind your ears to gently support your head.

2. Use your abs to lift your head and shoulder blades four to six inches off the floor. Keep your lower back pressed firmly against the floor and your elbows pointing straight out (not forward). Hold a tight crunch for 10 to 15 seconds as you exhale, then slowly lower back to the starting position. Rest for 15 seconds and repeat 10 times. Then stretch your abs for one minute using either the Ball Drape (page 147) or Cobra (page 147) stretch.

It's important to note that when doing ab crunches, you should never push through back pain. Stop at even the slightest twinge in your lower back.

LOOK AB-SOLUTELY GREAT

Say what you will, but nothing feels quite like showing up on race day and strutting a tight tummy in front of the crowd. Few other parts of the body are the target of more infomercials, pills, and potions as the enigmatic and revered abdominals. In our culture, the "six-pack" is a fitness status symbol. Thus, we are bombarded with ab-centric contraptions—including electrified toning belts—that profess to help us craft the perfect abs.

Sorry to disappoint, but these devices aren't worth their weight in shipping. "Ab machines offer no physiological advantage over doing crunches with good form," says John Jakicic, PhD, an exercise physiologist and professor at the University of Pittsburgh School of Medicine.

If you have a gut, you can do crunches until you're blue in the face, but that alone won't give you six-pack abs. You need to begin by burning the fat that's hiding your abs from view. The sheer act of training for a triathlon will burn gobs of body fat. Combine your swim, bike, and run training with 10 well-executed crunches, done three days a week, and your abs will make an appearance in no time. Strong, well-defined abs not only look great but also help prevent lower-back injury by supporting your spine and stabilizing your midsection, or core.

Roman Chair Run

Stand in a Roman chair with your lower back against the backrest, your arms bent at 90 degrees, and your forearms against the pads. Grab on to the handles, and hold yourself up with your arms and abs so your feet are a few inches off the floor. Allow one leg to dangle naturally as you lift the other like you're doing a high step march. Lift the leg as high as you can, and then bring it down as you lift the other leg in a fluid, running-in-slow-motion kind of movement. Breathe deeply and rhythmically as you lift each leg 10 to 20 times. Take a 30-second break to stretch your abs using either the Ball Drape (page 147) or Cobra (page 147) stretch. Then do another set, followed by stretching your abs once again for a minute.

Weighted Crunch

1. Sit in an ab crunch machine with your back against the backrest, your legs bent at a 90-degree angle, and your feet flat on the floor. Hold the straps snug to your chest and strap your thighs tightly to the seat.

2. Keep your lower back pressed into the backrest as you use your abs to curl your torso so that you shorten the distance from your bottom ribs to your hips. (Don't just bend forward at your waist.) It should feel just like a crunch you perform on the floor. Pause at the end of the move and then slowly raise your torso back up to the starting position. Do 20 repetitions and then take a 1-minute rest to stretch your abdominal muscles using either the Ball Drape (page 147) or Cobra (page 147) stretch.

LOWER-BACK EXERCISES
Lying Back Stretch

Do the stretch as described on page 115. Use the stretch before you exercise your lower back, between sets, and after your final set.

AT HOME OR THE GYM
Superman

1. Lie facedown with your legs straight and your arms stretched straight out in front of you, with your palms on the floor. Gently lift your legs, arms, head, and chest off the floor, making sure to fully squeeze the muscles of your lower back. Lift your arms and legs to the same level to where your arms are parallel to the floor, keeping them as straight as possible and reaching with both your legs and arms as far as you can. Look down at the floor so that your ears are by your upper arms. Hold the position for 10 seconds, breathing slowly and deeply. Repeat twice. Relax.

2. Raise your left hand and right leg, leaving your chest on the floor. Breathe slowly as you hold for 10 seconds and then relax. Now raise your right hand and left leg, hold for a count of 10, and relax. Next, raise your right hand and right leg, hold for 10, and relax. Lastly, raise your left hand and left leg, hold for a count of 10, and relax. Rest for 30 seconds, then do the Lying Back Stretch (page 115). Repeat the entire exercise sequence before stretching your lower back for another minute.

Bridge

Get into a position similar to a pushup, with your weight on your forearms and toes. Your body should form a straight line from head to heels with your butt lifted a bit so that your back doesn't sag. Pull in your abs and breathe steadily as you hold this position for 20 to 60 seconds. If you can maintain the position for a full 60 seconds, one rep is enough. If not, do any combination of reps that add up to 60 seconds. Then stretch your lower back for 30 seconds and do another set of reps that add up to 60 seconds. End by stretching your lower back once again for about a minute.

BICEPS EXERCISES

Biceps Stretch

Do the Chest Stretch as described on page 140. This move stretches your biceps as well as your chest.

Dumbbell Curl

1. Sit on the edge of a chair with good posture, so that you aren't slouching and your abdominal and back muscles are supporting your trunk. Plant your feet flat on the floor about hip-width apart with your legs bent at a 90-degree angle. Hold a dumbbell in each hand, keeping your elbows and upper arms pressed against the sides of your body. Your forearms should be extended straight down, with your palms facing forward.

2. Lift the dumbbells at the same time in one smooth motion, keeping your elbows pressed against your sides. Pause and then slowly lower the dumbbells back to the starting position. Do 12 repetitions and then take a 30-second rest to stretch your biceps using the Chest Stretch (page 140). Do a second set—this time of 8 repetitions—and then stretch your biceps again for about a minute.

TRICEPS EXERCISES

Triceps Stretch

Stand with a wall at your side so that you're about one foot from the wall. Set your feet slightly wider than shoulder-width apart, your toes pointing straight ahead. Bend the knee of the leg closest to the wall and shift your weight onto that leg. Place your palm on the wall above your head. Make sure your upper arm is by your ear and your arm is fully extended. Now keep your hips and torso squared as you lean toward the wall into the stretch. You should feel the stretch along the back of your upper arm. Hold for two to three seconds, then repeat the stretch six to eight times, deepening the stretch with each repetition. Repeat the entire stretch sequence with your other arm.

Overhead Triceps Press

1. Sit on the edge of a chair with good posture, so that you aren't slouching and your abdominal and back muscles are supporting your trunk. Plant your feet flat on the floor about hip-width apart with your legs bent at a 90-degree angle. Hold a dumbbell in each hand with your palms facing in toward each other. Your arms should be bent at right angles, with your upper arms next to your ears and your forearms behind your head.

2. Keeping your upper arms and elbows still, raise the dumbbells with your forearms until they're straight over your head. Pause and then slowly lower the dumbbells back to the starting position. Do a set of 12 repetitions and then rest for 30 seconds while doing the Triceps Stretch. Do a second set—this time of 8 repetitions—and then stretch your triceps again for 1 minute.

DO CORE TO BE MORE

Over the past few years, "core" has become a fitness buzzword—and for good reason. There has been a strong movement toward strengthening one's core as a way to prevent injury and improve performance. I have had direct experience with how important and effective core training can be. After a slight disc herniation prevented me from training for roughly two months, I came back stronger than ever thanks to the simple, daily core routine that follows.

Your core is composed of the muscles that stabilize your spine, mostly the abdominals and lower back. A strong core protects your spine by preventing excessive movement. But more importantly, it helps connect the movements of your lower and upper body in a more integrated and synchronous fashion. When you have a solid midsection, your body tends to work more as one unit than many disparate parts.

Specifically for triathlon, a strong core improves your swimming by solidifying your body position in the water. It also enhances rotation, which leads to better application of power in the water. On the bike, a strong core helps stabilize your position, improve power transfer, and prevent lower-back pain. Core strength improves running by elevating efficiency with a stronger midsection; you will experience less side-to-side movement, and more of your energy will go to driving you forward. You'll start to feel like you're running from your hips (good) instead of running from your arms (not good).

Having a strong core also helps you carry yourself in a more confident manner. Your posture will naturally become more upright and solid. When you have a strong and solid midsection, you will benefit from a distinct feeling of strength and centeredness. Think of yourself as a tree. A tree does not carry its strength in its limbs but rather in its trunk. Strengthen your trunk and you strengthen yourself.

THE CORE FOUR: "ANYTIME-ANYWHERE" EXERCISES

The key to developing a strong core is consistency. You needn't do a lot; you simply need to be consistent. The nice thing about the exercises that follow is you can use your own body weight, so you can do them pretty much anywhere, at any time. Much to the dismay of my wife, I have been known to slip a core workout in while waiting to board a flight!

The Plank

No, this isn't about walking the plank; it's about rocking the plank! This is the most popular and arguably most effective core exercise.

While laying facedown on the floor, bring your body up on your forearms, with your hands in fists in front of you. Bring yourself off the ground on your forearms and your toes. Hold this position for 10 to 60 seconds.

The Side Plank

As the name indicates, this is a variation of the plank. This is an excellent move to develop the stabilizing muscles of your lower back.

Lie on your side and raise your body off the ground from your elbow and the outside of your foot. Your forearm should be perpendicular to your chest. Hold this position for 5 to 30 seconds. To get added benefit, you can move your hips up and down toward the floor.

Pelvic Tilts

This is a very simple yet profound exercise that will stabilize your spine and strengthen your abdominals.

Lie flat on your back with your knees bent and your feet flat on the floor. There is a natural curvature of your lower back. You are going to flatten that out by pressing your lower back into the floor. As you do this, your hips come forward. Repeat this move 25 to 100 times.

Simple Crunches

This is one of the simplest moves to strengthen your core, which makes it one of the best.

Lie flat on your back with your knees bent and your feet flat on the floor. Interlock your hands behind your head. Engage your abdominals to bring your head three to six inches off the ground. Be sure not to pull with your hands; they're there simply to support your neck. Your abdominals should do the work. Repeat this 25 to 100 times.

PILATES

Pilates is a system of exercises invented by Joseph Pilates in the early 20th century. It has become extremely popular in the United States. With correct execution, Pilates can build strength, expand endurance, and improve flexibility.

"I must be right. Never an aspirin. Never injured a day in my life. The whole country, the whole world, should be doing my exercises. They'd be happier."
—JOSEPH HUBERTUS PILATES IN 1965, AGE 86

"It is an education in body awareness," says celebrity Pilates teacher Siri Dharma Galliano, who owns Big Bear Pilates in Big Bear Lake, California. "It changes your shape by educating you in daily life. When you're cooking, brushing your teeth—the lessons are coming home to pull your stomach in and pull your shoulders down. There is an attention required (in doing the exercises) that changes your awareness." And when preparing for, and competing in, a triathlon, body awareness is everything.

THE PILATES 3

While Pilates has many unique and creative variations, there is a generally accepted order that Joseph Pilates developed. We will stick with the three exercises that are easiest to do and provide the most benefit to you. These three exercises will give you most of the benefits of Pilates with minimal risk of injury. And if you combine these three moves with some of the core exercises above, you'll develop an epic midsection in no time.

Start with a gentle 5-minute warmup of running in place or pedaling on a stationary bike. This will improve muscle elasticity, which elevates performance and prevents injury.

The Hundred

This is the first exercise in the classical Pilates series. It's called the Hundred because you do 10 sets of 10 repetitions of breaths. You inhale for five counts and exhale for five counts. That's one set. You do that 10 times and you've got your hundred.

Lie on your back and raise your knees up so that your ankles and shins are hovering in the air, parallel to the floor. Your arms should be by your sides, palms down, with your thumbs touching your hips. Draw in a deep, empowering breath and raise your arms—keeping them straight, palms down—off the floor a couple of inches. Bring your legs out straight to 45 degrees from the floor. Keep your heels together and bring your toes out slightly. (This is known as the Pilates stance.)

As you exhale, use your abdominal muscles to elevate your head with your chin tucked into your chest. Bring your upper back off the floor two to four inches. Remain in this position and take in a deep breath. Now begins the Hundred. Inhale for a five count and exhale for a five count. As you do this, move your arms in a controlled up-and-down manner, timed with your breathing, roughly six to eight inches in height. That's 10. Repeat this sequence 10 times.

If you get tired, you can bend your knees a bit. But always keep your abdominals engaged and your hips motionless and stable on the floor. To finish, bring your knees in toward your chest, grab your knees, and bring your upper back and head down to the floor. Take a nice, full, cleansing breath out.

SUPPLEMENTARY STRETCH-STRENGTH TECHNIQUES

PILATES

This exercise system improves your flexibility, balance, and total-body strength. It's very hot right now with top athletes and many celebrities. The most important thing to remember with Pilates is to be patient: It takes a few sessions to get comfortable with the poses, but it's well worth it. *The Pilates Body* by Brooke Siler is an excellent guide to incorporating this great workout into your life.

YOGA

An increasing number of people are taking up this ancient Eastern health and fitness practice. Do yoga right and it will produce tremendous cardiovascular and strength results. It also develops a deeper body awareness.

The following tips will help you get the most out of yoga.

CHOOSE A CLASS. Yoga techniques vary. But there are benefits to be gained no matter what type you try. Before signing up, sit in on a few classes to determine if the instructor's technique and style are right for you.

DRESS APPROPRIATELY. Attire varies depending on the type of yoga. If you are practicing Bikram, for example, dress in your coolest clothes possible—say, Spandex shorts and a jog bra or shorts and a tank top. Other types of yoga are best performed in loose-fitting clothes. Follow the dress of the instructor. As for footwear, all types of yoga are performed in socks or bare feet.

BRING A TOWEL. Most yoga requires only a mat and a towel. Some studios provide these as well as blankets and blocks (used as aids in certain poses). Other studios rent these items to you. Once you decide to make the yoga commitment, you can buy your own mat if you wish.

RELAX. Don't worry about not being flexible. Remember that everyone, no matter how flexible they are now, had to start somewhere. And people who have practiced for years may not be super-flexible, but they are reaping significant benefits from their regular yoga practice. One major aim of yoga is to relax your body—and your ego. Yoga isn't a competitive sport. Most yoga environments are supportive places where you can let your guard down and be yourself.

TIME IT RIGHT

Timing when you perform yoga, Pilates, and other supplementary stretch-strength sessions is important within the context of your overall training program. It's best to do these activities on off days or in the evenings after tough workouts. Also, evenings are always better than mornings for stretching, because your muscle elasticity is greater in the evening, reducing your risk of pain and injury.

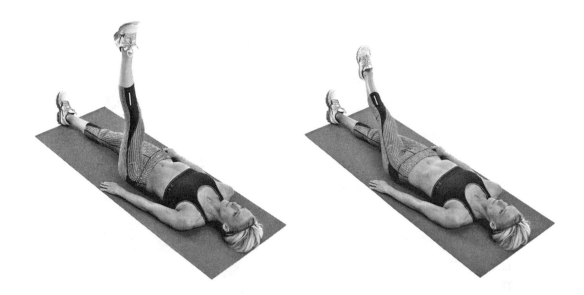

One-Leg Circle

This is a terrific exercise for triathletes because it develops core stability and strengthens the hip flexors (particularly important in cycling and running).

Focus on the stability of your pelvis. That is where your power comes from. Start by laying flat on the floor, legs straight out and arms by your sides. Bend your right knee toward your chest and extend your leg, point your toe, and turn your leg out. The foot on your mat is flexed and parallel. Circle your right thigh toward your left thigh and down, in a half circle. Then bring your leg straight back up. You do not complete a full circle, just half circles. Inhale as you do the half circle and exhale as you stop your leg at the top. Do 5 to 10 repetitions. Then switch the direction and inhale as you lower and exhale as you do the half circle.

When you finish, bring your leg back down to the mat and repeat with the other leg. As with everything in Pilates, keep your body stable and control your breathing.

Single-Leg Stretch

I prefer these over the Double-Leg Stretch because it's important to develop balanced flexibility.

Lie on your back and hold your knees to your chest. Inhale. As you exhale, bring your head, neck, and upper back up a few inches off the ground. Bring your arms and legs straight up to the ceiling. Use both hands to hold the back of your right leg. (If you are very flexible, you can grab your ankle or calf. If you need to grab behind your knee, or even bend your leg and hold your hamstring, that's fine.)

Pull your leg two times. Then switch legs and pull-pull again. The motion resembles scissors, which is why the Single-Leg Stretch is often referred to as Scissors. Keep your hips stable on the mat and find a comfortable breathing pattern— in for two stretches, out for two stretches. Repeat this 10 times and bring your legs back down to the mat. Exhale.

9
PUT IT ALL TOGETHER

"Make everything as simple as possible, but not simpler."

—ALBERT EINSTEIN

Broken down into its simplest parts, the triathlon is swimming, biking, and running. Pretty straightforward. I've already given you specific training advice for each of these three sports. It's the putting-it-all-together part that fills most people with trepidation.

Seamlessly integrating all the elements of your triathlon training is easier than you may think. The key is to keep things simple. This chapter will show you how to create the most streamlined, effective, and enjoyable training program. I'll tell you everything you need to do over the next six to eight weeks to finish your triathlon and feel great as you cross the line—all with minimum encroachment on the other important aspects of your life: family, friends, work, and leisure time.

TRAINING TIMELINE

You can refer to this pretriathlon calendar for fitting your race preparation in with your life. Here's what you have to do before your event and when you need to do it.

TWO MONTHS

CHOOSE YOUR EVENT. Since training for your triathlon will take six to eight weeks, obviously you must decide which event you'll participate in at least that far in advance, if not earlier. Picking the appropriate event can be easier said than done. In the sport of triathlon, good events are very, very good and bad events can be very, very dodgy! You don't want to show up on race day at an event with poor organization, no race support, no fans to cheer you on, and only cookies and water at the finish line.

It's best to stick to time-tested events—those that have been around for at least three years. By then, the race organizers will have worked out the bugs, such as awkward swim starts, dangerous traffic conditions on the bike course, or confusing run routes. In choosing your event, look to other participants, not the media, the sponsors, or the race directors. Talk to people who have done the event before and ask them whether they'd do it again. That usually nets the best information.

While choosing a triathlon close to home will make things easier logistically, don't be afraid to venture out. There are terrific events all across the country. You could even choose an event held overseas and turn it into a family vacation. For example, the Cayman Islands Triathlon on Grand Cayman is one of the most well-organized, enjoyable, down-to-earth, and user-friendly events in the world. This annual triathlon is held in early November.

For an extensive list of triathlons, visit www.active.com/triathlon. Active.com also offers discounts on travel, lodging, and race entry fees. (For more on that, turn to page 259.)

ASSEMBLE YOUR GEAR.

BEGIN YOUR TRAINING PROGRAM. Later in this chapter, I'll present the integrated three-sport schedules for all four Fitness Levels.

ONE MONTH

REGISTER FOR YOUR EVENT. Of course, you may need to do this sooner if you choose an out-of-town event, to make sure you reserve your spot in time to make travel arrangements.

GET DIRECTIONS TO THE RACE SITE. I cannot tell you how many times I have tried to find my way to a triathlon only to get there minutes after the start.

BEGIN POSITIVE VISUALIZATIONS. Once a week, before you go to bed, spend a few moments visualizing in full-color detail every part of your event—from when you arrive to when you cross the line. Picture yourself racing and finishing confidently. This will do wonders for your mental preparation.

ONE WEEK

RAMP DOWN YOUR TRAINING. Seven to 10 days before your event, begin taking it easy and erring on the side of doing too little. Beginners especially tend to overdo it during race week, trying to cram in extra fitness. Don't. This is not a history test. All that cramming will tire you out before your event. The training programs for all four Fitness Levels are structured to avoid hard or long workouts the week of the race. You'll stay sharp with shorter, slightly quicker workouts.

PAY EXTRA ATTENTION TO HOW MUCH YOU EAT. I once packed on three pounds of pure, visibly jiggling body fat during race week. My appetite was still elevated from the hardest week of my training schedule, so I kept eating at that pace, even though I was exercising much less. I lost a lot of confidence and was mocked (rightfully so) by the other pros.

GET YOUR BIKE TUNED UP AND TEST YOUR RACE SETUP.

WATCH FOR YOUR RACE PACKET TO ARRIVE IN THE MAIL. When you receive it, read it thoroughly.

RELAX A LITTLE. You may want to get a massage. Try to take as many naps as possible. A couple of hot baths, followed by stretching, are good, too. Also, try to eliminate as much physical labor as possible—this is the perfect excuse to have other people dote on you!

TWO DAYS

REVIEW THE COURSE. If you have the opportunity, you should definitely check out the race course in advance. It will likely be marked by now. Familiarizing yourself with the swimming, biking, and running routes will demystify the event, attenuating your race-day jitters. It will also let you take your performance up a notch or two during the event, because you'll know exactly where you're going. Of particular importance is the bike course. Know it. You don't want to head off-course into a cornfield during the cycling leg. (Yes, that has happened to me—and yes, cows looked on, befuddled.)

RACE DAY

SEIZE THE EVENT DAY! You'll find a Race Timeline on pages 237–242. Double-check it—and have fun!

START YOUR TRAINING PROGRAM

By choosing the appropriate program for your Fitness Level, as determined in Chapter 4, you can successfully blend the training for all three triathlon sports with the strength training that is integral to balanced fitness. Three aspects of training—brick workouts, benchmarks, and breakthrough sessions—apply to all Triathletes-in-Training, regardless of Fitness Level. So let's discuss them before getting into the details of the four different programs.

THE THREE BS

BRICK WORKOUTS. One of the most important ways to integrate your three triathlon sports is to do brick workouts, in which you perform two or even all three sports back-to-back, with minimal rest in between. Brick sessions are an essential part of your event preparation because they help you familiarize yourself—both mentally and physically—with the specific transitional demands of the triathlon. You don't need to go too hard during brick workouts; they're just to work on transitions.

The swim-to-bike variety is best performed from a pool. This allows you to leave your cycling gear poolside. When you finish with your swim, simply suit up, get to your bike, and ride from the pool.

The simplest way to perform a bike-to-run brick is to set up a transition area in a wide-open parking lot, park, or track, with a friend watching over your gear.

The training programs for each particular Fitness Level all include brick workouts. I've scheduled the bricks for Saturdays, as that's when you'll most likely have time to do two or three sports in a row. Not every Saturday workout needs to be a brick, however. Unless the program calls for a brick, feel free to do each sport separately, whenever you can fit it into your day.

BENCHMARKS. Measurable improvement is a great motivator. The best way to gauge your fitness progress and boost your exercise motivation over time is with benchmark workouts. Benchmarks are simply two or more workouts that you perform the exact same way—over the same distance and within the same heart rate range. You need to document your time and average heart rate for these workouts so that you have a record of your results for comparison. Benchmark workouts don't need to be long or intense, just controlled and repeatable. They can even be just a portion of a longer workout. I recommend that you perform your benchmarks as Zone II workouts, no matter what your Fitness Level. You should also make sure to warm up thoroughly before doing a benchmark workout.

An example of a benchmark swim session would be to do five 100-yard repeats with 30 seconds of rest in between each one. An ideal bike benchmark session would be to ride a 5-mile course at a specific heart rate and then ride the same course in the same heart rate range again later in your training. A run benchmark session is best performed in a controlled environment, such as at your local track. Run two 1-mile repeats at a specific heart rate and record your time. When you repeat these benchmark workouts a few weeks later, you should find that it takes you less time or that you can perform the same workout at a lower heart rate. That's because a fitter, more efficient body will run faster at the same heart rate.

The training programs for all four Fitness Levels include one pair of benchmark workouts per sport over the duration of the program. In addition to confirming your progress, benchmarks can prevent overtraining and even predict oncoming illness. Once you've established a baseline of fitness, a workout that falls below that level is usually a sign of bad things to come. It indicates that you need to rest, adjust your training schedule, or rework your nutrition. As you record more benchmarks, you will develop deeper body awareness and learn to move with greater efficiency, strength, and grace.

Most important, benchmarks build your confidence. When your workout produces improved numbers, that's proof of the positive effects of your holistic approach to exercise, rest, and nutrition. The best athletes in the world continue to improve because they constantly monitor their progress with benchmarks and modify their training programs accordingly.

There are just two caveats to doing benchmark workouts. First, you need to conduct them on days when you feel like you're performing at your peak. If there's a benchmark scheduled on a day when you're having an off day, it's best to perform the workout as a regular workout and do the benchmark on another day when you feel better. Secondly, you may have a benchmark scheduled on the same day you are also scheduled to do a strength-training workout. When this happens, make sure to do your benchmark session *before* the strength training. Lifting weights can tire out your muscles and may have a negative effect on your benchmark workout.

BREAKTHROUGH SESSIONS. As I've mentioned before, training for a triathlon is as much about redefining your limits and strengthening your self-image as it is about reshaping your body. To that end, you need to challenge yourself in some small way—and break through your perceived limits—several times over the next six weeks. You can do that by performing what I like to call breakthrough sessions. These are workout sessions that are either longer or more intense than you are accustomed to.

Breakthrough sessions can provide you with exciting mental and physical results in a very short period of time. They can also increase your daily energy levels and prevent exercise-induced injury. Exercise places a positive stress on your body: It increases the demands on your muscular and cardiovascular systems, prompting your body to grow stronger and more efficient in preparation for the next workout.

However, that same adaptability can also be your nemesis. Have you ever experienced a period in which, no matter how much you exercised or how little food you ate, your body didn't change proportionally? This is known as a plateau. It happens when your body has, in essence, grown wise to you. It has adapted to the stress of the exercise you've been doing, so unless you sufficiently increase that stress, your body will no longer change its shape.

That's where breakthrough sessions come in. By providing stress that is higher in volume or intensity, they help you overcome plateaus. They also take your confidence to the stratosphere.

You will notice that the breakthrough sessions are not scheduled into your training program. There's a reason for that. These sessions need to be done on days when you're feeling your absolute best. Only you know when those days are. On those days, you will likely need to perform a different workout than what is scheduled into your program, because breakthrough sessions need to be either longer or more intense than your typical workout.

As a general rule, long breakthroughs should be at least 60 minutes. Level Is and IIs will need to work up to this, and Level IVs will be able to go significantly longer (say 90 to 150 minutes). When you're doing a regularly scheduled workout and feel great, that's when you should break through and extend it to the 60-minute or longer mark. As for breakthroughs that are more intense rather than longer in duration, shoot for an RPE of 15 to 17, which would be a tough Zone II workout or an easier Zone III workout.

WORK WITH YOUR DOC

Before beginning any exercise program, you should consult with your physician regarding your current physical condition and the particular demands of the related program—particularly if you have any history of heart disease, pulmonary disease, diabetes, or bone/joint ailments such as osteoporosis.

Even if you are already very healthy and fit, getting regular blood work will ensure you stay that way. Be smart: Review your triathlon training program with your physician.

In addition to deciding when you do your breakthroughs, you also get to choose which sports you do your breakthrough sessions in. You can do all of your breakthroughs in one sport, two sports, or all three. You decide based on your comfort level with the various sports.

How many breakthrough sessions you should perform during your training depends on your Fitness Level. (No matter what your Fitness Level, however, you should not do any breakthrough sessions during your first week and final week of training, because this is when you are easing into exercise and ramping down for your event.) Level I Triathletes-in-Training should do one breakthrough about every two weeks for a total of two to three sessions. Level IIs should complete a breakthrough every 10 days for a total of three. Level IIIs should do one every week for a total of four. And Level IVs can perform up to two breakthrough sessions a week for a total of eight.

Regardless of your Fitness Level, make sure to rest before and after each session. A breakthrough requires a well-rested body and a sharp mind. Therefore, you do not want to perform a breakthrough on a day following a tough workout or strength-training session. Your body is still recovering from that workout, so you do not want to overstress it by performing another tough workout. When you do a breakthrough— say you go for a long, hard bike ride, for example—you should take at least one day completely off from exercise after that to allow your body to recover. That may mean dropping a workout that is scheduled in your program, which is fine. If you feel you want to exercise on your rest day to stay loose, limit yourself to a walk or an easy swim. Resting for a day will ensure that you absorb all the positive effects of the session, because it's during downtime that your body adapts and grows stronger.

You may need to take more than one day off after a particularly tough workout. If your muscles are very sore, you feel extremely fatigued, or your resting heart rate is elevated, then you should rest for another day or so until you feel better.

Let me give you a personal example about the importance of rest. In my first year as a triathlete, I achieved a good measure of success. I worked out four hours a day, four times a week. The length and difficulty of those workouts pushed me outside my comfort zone—and my body and mind adapted to those increased demands. I reached new heights, I constantly improved, and my confidence grew.

Then I made the classic rookie miscalculation: Since four days a week had made me so strong, I figured that seven days a week would make me even stronger. So I began training for six hours a day, every day of the week. The result was not what I had expected. Rather than getting more powerful, I made zero forward progress. I was in such a constant state of mental and physical fatigue that I had no energy to do breakthrough sessions. I spent two years overtrained, exhausted, and irascible—fraught with nagging injuries . . . and facial tics!

The same rules of stress and rest apply to you, a Triathlete-in-Training. For this reason, the four training programs include rest days along with the workouts.

THE FOUR TRAINING PROGRAMS

Now that you're familiar with the training elements that are common to all Fitness Levels, you can move on to the specifics of the program for your own Level, be it I, II, III, or IV.

The duration of the workouts in these programs may not perfectly match the duration of the workouts described in the single-sport chapters. That's because the sport-specific workouts are provided simply as example workouts that you may choose to use in your training. If you're scheduled to do a 45-minute run, for example, it's important that you modify the sample workout's prescribed duration to fit your individualized training program. Your program has been carefully designed to follow the basic tenets of physiology so that you balance stress and rest and get the right amount of cardiovascular and muscular stimulation.

Photocopy the appropriate training plan for your Fitness Level and post it in a highly visible place. (Mine resides on my refrigerator, a place I visit often—after all, that's where Ben & Jerry live!) Also schedule your workouts in your daily planner so that nobody can take that time from you. Try to assign actual times and locations to these workouts as well—that will keep you on track. From now on, workouts are serious appointments with yourself, investments in your quality of life. Treat them as such.

I'm assuming that the triathlon for which you're training will be held on a Sunday (since most triathlon events are on that day), so the programs are scheduled to reflect that. If your event will fall on a different day, obviously you can shift the workouts accordingly.

FITNESS LEVEL I: SLICE ABOVE COUCH POTATO

Even if you have been inactive for years, that's okay. You've dared to dream of completing a triathlon, so good for you! Remember that every year, thousands of people just like you do their first triathlons and reap huge rewards for doing so. You can, too. It's all about taking it one step at a time.

This program is very simple and progressive, with no surprises. It's about building your body and having fun doing it. Your aim is to enjoy yourself and live more fully, not win the race. Focus on making progress, feeling the new energy in your muscles, and bragging to your friends about your new endeavor.

To allow you to ease into exercise very gradually, your program will last for eight weeks, as opposed to six. This will ensure that you don't get injured or overtired by doing too much, too soon.

You likely don't want to devote an excessive amount of time to training. That's absolutely fine. In fact, in the first two weeks you'll exercise for just an hour and 45 minutes per week. Each of those two weeks, you'll do one session per sport: one 30-minute swim, one 30-minute walk/run, and one 45-minute bike ride. Begin easily, spending the first few weeks warming up to each sport. For example, you can power walk your first four or five run sessions. Then you'll slowly build up to a maximum, in week seven, of 3 hours and 45 minutes of training. In week eight, you'll ramp down again, to a total of just an hour and 20 minutes of training. This will ensure that you'll be practiced but still fresh for your triathlon on Sunday.

To keep you progressing, remember to conduct one breakthrough session about every two weeks during weeks two through five. That means you will do two or three in all.

Each week you'll need at least two days off from exercise. This will allow you to rest and recover and avoid exercise-induced pain and injury. Just as important, you can dedicate these rest days to other nonathletic activities, such as family or hobbies.

WEEK 1: ADAPTATION

Monday: Rest

Tuesday: Swim for 30 minutes in Zone I

Wednesday: Power walk/run for 30 minutes in Zone I

Thursday: Rest

Friday: Rest

Saturday: Bike for 45 minutes in Zone I

Sunday: Rest

WEEK 2: ADAPTATION

Monday: Rest

Tuesday: Swim for 30 minutes in Zone I

Wednesday: Power walk/run for 30 minutes in Zone I

Thursday: Rest

Friday: Rest

Saturday: Bike for 45 minutes in Zone I

Sunday: Rest

WEEK 3: EASY

Monday: Rest

Tuesday: Swim for 20 minutes in Zone I

Wednesday: Power walk/run for 35 minutes in Zone I

Thursday: Strength train for 20 minutes

Friday: Rest

Saturday: Bike for 45 minutes in Zone I

Sunday: Swim for 15 minutes in Zone I

WEEK 4: EASY

Monday: Rest

Tuesday: Swim for 20 minutes in Zone I

Wednesday: Power walk/run for 35 minutes in Zone I

Thursday: Strength train for 20 minutes

Friday: Rest

Saturday: Bike for 45 minutes in Zone II (Benchmark)

Sunday: Swim for 15 minutes in Zone I

WEEK 5: MODERATE

Monday: Rest

Tuesday: Swim for 30 minutes in Zone II (Benchmark)

Wednesday: Bike for 30 minutes in Zone I; run for 30 minutes in Zone II

Thursday: Swim for 20 minutes in Zone I; strength train for 20 minutes

Friday: Rest

Saturday: Brick workout: Bike for 20 minutes in Zone I and run for 15 minutes in Zone I

Sunday: Strength train for 20 minutes

WEEK 6: MODERATE

Monday: Rest

Tuesday: Swim for 30 minutes in Zone II

Wednesday: Bike for 45 minutes in Zone I; run for 30 minutes in Zone II (Benchmark)

Thursday: Swim for 20 minutes in Zone I; strength train for 20 minutes

Friday: Rest

Saturday: Brick workout: Bike for 30 minutes in Zone I and run for 20 minutes in Zone I

Sunday: Strength train for 20 minutes

WEEK 7: HARD

Monday: Rest

Tuesday: Swim for 30 minutes in Zone II (Benchmark)

Wednesday: Bike for 45 minutes in Zone II (Benchmark); run for 30 minutes in Zone II (Benchmark)

Thursday: Swim for 20 minutes in Zone I; strength train for 20 minutes

Friday: Rest

Saturday: Brick workout: Bike for 40 minutes in Zone I and run for 20 minutes in Zone I

Sunday: Strength train for 20 minutes

WEEK 8: EVENT

Monday: Rest

Tuesday: Bike for 30 minutes in Zone I

Wednesday: Swim for 15 minutes in Zone I

Thursday: Run for 15 minutes in Zone I

Friday: Rest

Saturday: Swim for 10 minutes in Zone I; bike for 10 minutes in Zone I

Sunday: Seize the race day!

FITNESS LEVEL II: NEOPHYTE

Granted, you don't have a lot of baseline fitness, but you can do more—and you likely want to. While you need to be very smart about this program and ease into it, you should also challenge yourself mentally and physically so you break through to new levels of physical and mental performance. To that end, remember to incorporate one breakthrough session about every 10 days during weeks two through five of your training. That means you should do about three breakthroughs in all.

The program is in fact designed for you to start slow, with only 2 hours and 15 minutes of training per week for the first two weeks. Your third and fourth weeks will consist of about 4 hours and 20 minutes per week. In your one hard training week, your total will rise to 4 hours and 50 minutes. The last six days before your triathlon will require just an hour and 40 minutes of training, to make sure you're sufficiently rested before your event.

Rest is so important that each week you need at least two days completely away from exercise. I've already scheduled these days off for you in the programs.

WEEK 1: ADAPTATION

Monday: Rest

Tuesday: Swim for 30 minutes in Zone I

Wednesday: Run for 30 minutes in Zone I

Thursday: Rest

Friday: Rest

Saturday: Bike for 45 minutes in Zone I

Sunday: Swim for 30 minutes in Zone I

WEEK 2: ADAPTATION

Monday: Rest

Tuesday: Swim for 30 minutes in Zone I

Wednesday: Run for 30 minutes in Zone I

Thursday: Rest

Friday: Rest

Saturday: Bike for 45 minutes in Zone I

Sunday: Swim for 30 minutes in Zone I

WEEK 3: MODERATE TRAINING

Monday: Rest

Tuesday: Swim for 35 minutes in Zone II (Benchmark); strength train for 20 minutes

Wednesday: Run for 30 minutes in Zone II; bike for 45 minutes in Zone II (Benchmark)

Thursday: Swim for 20 minutes in Zone I; strength train for 20 minutes

Friday: Rest

Saturday: Brick workout: Bike for 60 minutes in Zone I and run for 30 minutes in Zone I

Sunday: Rest

WEEK 4: MODERATE TRAINING

Monday: Rest

Tuesday: Swim for 30 minutes in Zone II; strength train for 20 minutes

Wednesday: Run for 40 minutes in Zone II (Benchmark); bike for 45 minutes in Zone II

Thursday: Swim for 20 minutes in Zone I; strength train for 20 minutes

Friday: Rest

Saturday: Brick workout: Bike for 60 minutes in Zone I and run for 30 minutes in Zone I

Sunday: Rest

WEEK 5: HARD

Monday: Rest

Tuesday: Swim for 35 minutes in Zone II (Benchmark); strength train for 40 minutes

Wednesday: Bike for 45 minutes in Zone II (Benchmark); run for 40 minutes in Zone II (Benchmark)

Thursday: Swim for 30 minutes in Zone I; strength train for 20 minutes

Friday: Rest

Saturday: Brick workout and test triathlon: Swim for 20 minutes in Zone I, bike for 40 minutes in Zone II, and run for 20 minutes in Zone I

Sunday: Rest

WEEK 6: EVENT

Monday: Rest

Tuesday: Bike for 30 minutes in Zone I

Wednesday: Swim for 20 minutes in Zone I

Thursday: Run for 20 minutes in Zone I

Friday: Rest

Saturday: Swim for 15 minutes in Zone I; bike for 15 minutes in Zone I

Sunday: Seize the race day!

FITNESS LEVEL III: FITNESS ENTHUSIAST

You likely have pretty ambitious goals: either making some serious changes in the way you look and feel or going out to push yourself and perhaps notch a respectable finishing time. Whichever goal you choose, balance it with the enjoyment factor.

Your training schedule pans out as follows: about 3 hours of exercise in the first two weeks, close to 5 hours in weeks three and four, 5 hours and 45 minutes in week five, and just one hour and 55 minutes in week six, leading up to your event. Also, remember to incorporate one breakthrough session per week in the second through fifth weeks of your training program. That means you should perform four breakthroughs in all.

You are likely aware of how important rest days are in any fitness program. Because you will be working out at higher intensities at times, you must take at least two rest days each week. On your days off, recover with a relaxing activity such as a hot bath, yoga, or, my favorite, a nap.

WEEK 1: ADAPTATION

Monday: Rest

Tuesday: Swim for 30 minutes in Zone I

Wednesday: Run for 40 minutes in Zone I; strength train for 20 minutes

Thursday: Rest

Friday: Rest

Saturday: Bike for 60 minutes in Zone I; strength train for 20 minutes

Sunday: Swim for 15 minutes in Zone I

WEEK 2: ADAPTATION

Monday: Rest

Tuesday: Swim for 30 minutes in Zone II (Benchmark)

Wednesday: Run for 40 minutes in Zone II (Benchmark); strength train for 20 minutes

Thursday: Rest

Friday: Rest

Saturday: Bike for 60 minutes in Zone II (Benchmark); strength train for 20 minutes

Sunday: Swim for 15 minutes in Zone I

WEEK 3: MODERATE

Monday: Rest

Tuesday: Swim for 30 minutes in Zone II (Benchmark)

Wednesday: Run for 30 minutes in Zone III; strength train for 40 minutes

Thursday: Swim for 30 minutes in Zone I; bike for 60 minutes in Zone III

Friday: Rest

Saturday: Brick workout: Bike for 50 minutes in Zone I and run for 20 minutes in Zone II

Sunday: Strength train for 20 minutes

WEEK 4: MODERATE

Monday: Rest

Tuesday: Swim for 30 minutes in Zone II

Wednesday: Run for 40 minutes in Zone II (Benchmark); strength train for 40 minutes

Thursday: Swim for 40 minutes in Zone II; bike for 60 minutes in Zone III

Friday: Rest

Saturday: Brick workout: Bike for 50 minutes in Zone I and run for 20 minutes in Zone II

Sunday: Strength train for 20 minutes

WEEK 5: HARD

Monday: Rest

Tuesday: Swim for 40 minutes in Zone III

Wednesday: Bike for 30 minutes in Zone I; run for 45 minutes in Zone II; strength train for 40 minutes

Thursday: Bike for 60 minutes in Zone II (Benchmark)

Friday: Rest

Saturday: Brick workout and test triathlon: Swim for 30 minutes in Zone I, bike for 50 minutes in Zone II, and run for 30 minutes in Zone I

Sunday: Strength train for 20 minutes

WEEK 6: EVENT

Monday: Rest

Tuesday: Bike for 40 minutes in Zone I

Wednesday: Swim for 25 minutes in Zone I

Thursday: Run for 20 minutes in Zone I

Friday: Rest

Saturday: Swim for 15 minutes in Zone I; bike for 15 minutes in Zone I

Sunday: Seize the race day!

FITNESS LEVEL IV: SINGLE-SPORTER ON A MISSION

Okay, hotshot, you are an experienced athlete, so one of your goals will likely be a particular finishing time or place. I strongly urge you to set challenging goals. You have the aerobic base, the intrinsic motivation, and the experience to actualize ambitious plans. Go for it!

You may even decide to do an Olympic-distance triathlon or a half-Ironman. This program template can prepare you for those distances. For the Olympic distance, increase the duration of each workout by 50 percent. For a half-Ironman, double the workout times.

While enjoying this process should always be a goal (you'll perform best when it is), you are a fit, strong person who should push your body to new heights on this program. You should also work on forging mental toughness by pushing through tough workouts. Just be smart about it. You know your body. Even though this program is a great guide, you must always stay in touch with your inner coach and change your training according to how you feel when you wake up each day.

Remember, you should work about two breakthrough sessions into each week from weeks two through five. That means you will do up to eight breakthroughs. It's a good idea to conduct your breakthrough sessions with groups of single-sport athletes. These athletes will motivate you to push your performance and enjoyment to the stratosphere.

A note to swimmers: While your aerobic fitness is likely sky-high, the integrity of your ligaments and tendons is not as hardened as that of a runner or cyclist. Ease into those other two sports until you get your land legs.

As a high-level athlete, you won't be able to limit your training to four hours per week, as less-accomplished triathletes can. You're likely exercising more than that already. Even the easiest adaptation training you'll start with in weeks one and two will total about 5 hours and 45 minutes. During the moderate-to-hard training of weeks three and four, you'll ramp up to about 9 hours and 45 minutes weekly. That may not sound like a lot to some of you, but this program is all about quality over quantity.

Don't get caught up in the overtraining syndrome that befalls so many age-group triathletes, however. Trust me, most age-groupers get to the starting line in an over-trained state. Be optimally rested as well as trained, and you will have a significant edge on that competition. To give you sufficient rest, your event-week training will take just 2 and a half hours.

I'm sure you also know how important rest days are. So take at least two days completely off each week. On those days, you can perform active recoveries such as walks, but no swimming, cycling, or running.

As a final rest strategy, do not perform strength sessions on back-to-back days.

WEEK 1: ADAPTATION

Monday: Rest

Tuesday: Swim for 45 minutes in Zone I; strength train for 20 minutes

Wednesday: Run for 30 minutes in Zone I

Thursday: Bike for 60 minutes in Zone I

Friday: Strength train for 40 minutes

Saturday: Bike for 45 minutes in Zone I

Sunday: Swim for 45 minutes in Zone I; run for 60 minutes in Zone I

WEEK 2: ADAPTATION

Monday: Rest

Tuesday: Swim for 40 minutes in Zone II (Benchmark); strength train for 20 minutes

Wednesday: Run for 30 minutes in Zone I

Thursday: Bike for 60 minutes in Zone II (Benchmark)

Friday: Strength train for 40 minutes

Saturday: Bike for 45 minutes in Zone I

Sunday: Swim for 45 minutes in Zone I; run for 60 minutes in Zone I

WEEK 3: MODERATE TO HARD

Monday: Rest

Tuesday: Swim for 60 minutes in Zone IV; run for 45 minutes in Zone III; strength train for 20 minutes

Wednesday: Bike for 2 hours in Zone II (use a portion of this workout as your Benchmark)

Thursday: Swim for 30 minutes in Zone I; run for 45 minutes in Zone II (Benchmark)

Friday: Bike for 45 minutes in Zone I; strength train for 40 minutes

Saturday: Bike for 45 minutes in Zone IV

Sunday: Swim for 40 minutes in Zone II; run for 90 minutes in Zone I

WEEK 4: MODERATE TO HARD

Monday: Rest

Tuesday: Swim for 60 minutes in Zone IV; run for 45 minutes in Zone III; strength train for 20 minutes

Wednesday: Bike for 2 hours in Zone II

Thursday: Swim for 40 minutes in Zone II (Benchmark); run for 45 minutes in Zone II

Friday: Bike for 45 minutes in Zone I; strength train for 40 minutes

Saturday: Bike for 45 minutes in Zone IV

Sunday: Swim for 40 minutes in Zone II; run for 90 minutes in Zone II (use a portion of this workout as your Benchmark)

WEEK 5: HARD

Monday: Rest

Tuesday: Swim for 30 minutes in Zone II; run for 30 minutes in Zone I; strength train for 40 minutes

Wednesday: Bike for 30 minutes in Zone III

Thursday: Swim for 20 minutes in Zone I; run for 45 minutes in Zone IV

Friday: Bike for 60 minutes in Zone I; strength train for 20 minutes

Saturday: Brick workout and test triathlon: Swim for 30 minutes in Zone II, bike for 75 minutes in Zone II, and run for 30 minutes in Zone II or Zone III

Sunday: Swim for 20 minutes in Zone I

WEEK 6: EVENT

Monday: Rest

Tuesday: Bike for 30 minutes in Zone II; run for 30 minutes in Zone II

Wednesday: Swim for 30 minutes in Zone II

Thursday: Run for 20 minutes in Zone I

Friday: Rest

Saturday: Swim for 20 minutes in Zone I; bike for 20 minutes in Zone I

Sunday: Seize the race day!

TRACK YOUR PROGRESS

Sometimes, no matter how hard you try to adhere to your carefully constructed triathlon program, you instead find yourself rearranging your sock drawer for the umpteenth time or getting sucked toward the freezer for an ice cream fix—double scoop.

How do you recapture enthusiasm for the exercise and diet goals that were so passion-driven when you first started? A simple, self-styled manual known as a Success Journal can prop you up on those off days and keep your passion afire over the long haul. "In fitness, it's the small, measurable steps that matter," says Susan Kleiner, PhD, RD, a sports nutritionist at High Performance Nutrition in Mercer Island, Washington, and coauthor of *Power Eating and Fitness Log.* "Making progress in our exercise and diet—and tracking that on paper—motivates and inspires us with confidence."

In addition to being a motivator, a Success Journal is also evidence of how much training progress you're really making. "Document what you actually end up doing week to week throughout the year," says six-time Ironman World Triathlon champion Mark Allen. "What we plan to do and the reality of what we actually end up doing can be worlds apart."

So record the basic statistics about your performance in each sport: Note the location, duration, intensity, and average heart rate or speed of each workout as a way to track your benchmarks and strive to better them over the weeks. Keep track of what you eat and how much water you drink. Mark down the weight, sets, and reps in your strength training—even comments about the way your clothes fit.

Periodically reviewing your Success Journal can remind you of what works for you and what doesn't. "Look at the results of your training and then change the program for the upcoming weeks . . . to reflect how your own body has responded to the training," says Allen. "It is through this constant process of refinement that you become your most valuable resource for success, both in training and in other areas of your life."

You should look forward to tracking and celebrating everything that's going well in your program. Get fired up! Just like the rest of your triathlon quest, this should be fun and passion-driven, never guilt-induced.

Your Success Journal is a forum for constructive fitness lessons and positive workout experiences only; it's not a place to beat yourself up. "Focusing on the positives, rather than the negatives, is more motivating and productive in the long run," says Dr. Kleiner. "That will make you feel successful, and you can build on those successes."

Keep a daily record of everything you're doing to bring yourself closer to your fitness goals, whether it's completing your long bike ride of the week, drinking eight glasses of water a day, taking your vitamins, or walking instead of driving to your local market (yes, it can be done!).

As you journal, tune in to how you feel and what's making your training experience so special for you. "Research shows that writing down things that deeply motivate you on a personal level keeps you on track," says sports psychologist Linda Bunker, PhD, of Charlottesville, Virginia.

Make copies of the worksheet on page 187 and fill them out as often as you can for the next six to eight weeks, using the "Success Journal Sample Entries" (page 186) as a guide. Or pick up a nutrition and workout logbook, such as Kleiner's *Power Eating and Fitness Log* or Tony Svennson's *Total Triathlon Almanac 4*.

Keep your journal in your gym bag and spend a few minutes after every workout writing down your successes. Or write at the end of the day, before bed. Pick a time when you'll be relaxed and excited about recording your accomplishments. "Writing in your journal should be a seamless part of your day," says Dr. Bunker.

Finally, customize your Success Journal so that it completely reflects your fitness life and you as a person. Build it into a thick, rich, inspiring scrapbook that includes a "before" photo of yourself (with an "after" photo placeholder), a copy of your registration form for your triathlon—anything that motivates you. Perhaps create a workout tape of your favorite songs or recipes for the healthy foods you truly love. Note how these things are specifically about you and how they make you feel.

TAKE A SEASONAL APPROACH

Have you ever noticed that the first day of the year seems to be an awfully ill-timed date to embark on your New Year's training resolutions? You're essentially proclaiming, "I'm going to get fit and melt away these fruitcake-induced love handles . . . in the dead of winter!" Few people emerge victorious after such a proclamation.

That's why a Triathlete-in-Training does things differently. By subtly modifying your weekly training plan as the seasons change, you can achieve better fitness and weight-loss results, reduce exercise-related injuries and pain, avoid frustrating plateaus, and bolster your exercise motivation throughout the year.

This modification is known as seasonal periodization, and it is how most world-class endurance athletes design their annual training programs. The human body follows very precise rhythms throughout the year, which have been shown to vary according to the seasons. "Periodization is an exercise concept in which your year is divided into periods, each having a specific approach based on weather conditions and how your body and mind are feeling," says Joe Friel, masters athlete, fitness expert, coach with more than 30 years of personal and team experience, and author of *The Cyclist's Training Bible*.

There is plenty of scientific evidence supporting the efficacy of this approach, but it also makes good sense, doesn't it? In winter, your desire to work out is at its annual low. In spring, you begin feeling more upbeat and motivated to exercise. In summer, your body is most receptive to the effects of exercise. And in fall, you begin to mentally and physically wind down again. Your exercise program should mirror those psychological and physiological ebbs and flows by changing throughout the year. Here's how.

WINTER

Food-filled holidays pop up every two to three weeks, and your metabolism is at a literal standstill. Plus, it's impractical and unnatural to be outside slogging through workouts in the cold and wet. This is when most professional athletes take a month or two almost completely away from exercise. You may want to consider doing the same.

Try this approach: During winter, reduce your exercise intensity and frequency by as much as 50 percent of peak summer levels. You'll emerge in spring feeling fresher and more mentally prepared for training.

SPRING

As the weather warms and the days grow longer, most people experience a noticeable rise in their willingness to exercise. Spring, therefore, is the time to ramp up your training program.

Keep your basic training structure the same, but increase the intensity of one or two workouts a week to comfortably challenging levels. For example, your Wednesday run may remain at the same duration, but include two or three intervals in which you run a little faster for two to three minutes at a time.

SUMMER

This is when you should really get that bootie moving, investing the most time and energy in your health and fitness. You may add two to four more intervals to your Wednesday run, going at a harder pace than in spring. Or you may increase the length of your Saturday bike ride. Such adjustments will pay enormous dividends in health, fitness, and weight loss without causing you undue fatigue and pain.

AUTUMN

As the days progressively cool and shorten, it's time to slow your body down. If you've followed the seasonal program, you will have a wonderful base of cardiovascular fitness upon which to sail into fall. You don't want to completely stop your exercise; just rein it in. Your exercise plan in autumn should fall somewhere between your winter and spring programs in terms of intensity and duration.

Follow this seasonal program and you'll enjoy your exercise more, achieve better long-term results, and each year, celebrate a firmer belly and fewer aches rather than bellyache about another year gone by.

RAMP UP TO LONGER EVENTS

One of the wonderful aspects of the triathlon is that it almost invariably inspires you to try to do better or give more each time you participate.

The longer the triathlon, the smarter and more patient you must be in your training. With the increase in physical demands on your body, setting your goals too high can lead to injury and burnout. So while you should always challenge yourself, you must balance that with knowing yourself and being smart. Reasonable jumps, such as from a sprint distance to an Olympic distance or from an Olympic distance to a half-Ironman, require six to eight weeks of consistent, injury-free training that is at least twice as frequent as your training for the lesser level. In other words, if you trained for 4 hours a week for a sprint-distance triathlon, you need to do at least 8 hours of weekly training for the Olympic distance and, yes, 16 hours for the half-Ironman. However, training frequency does not double again for the Ironman; that event requires between 20 and 28 hours a week.

Keep these guidelines in mind, and the training programs in this chapter can continue to serve you throughout your life as a triathlete—whatever your Fitness Level and whatever your event.

SUCCESS JOURNAL SAMPLE ENTRIES

Date Wed. 4/15/15

Workout Early evening Zone I 30-minute run around Lake Laginitas.

Average Heart Rate 125

Average Speed 16.2 mph

Positive Experiences Ran the loop 54 seconds faster at the same heart rate! Focused on deep breathing. Sun shining off the lake. Beautiful. Classical music. Very calming and motivating.

Why I'm a Champion I was exhausted from work, but I got out there anyway. Ran the entire loop and felt strong. Amazed I didn't stop.

Valuable Lessons No knee pain—I think I've found my ideal running shoes. Drank a full glass of water an hour before, which made me feel much better. Also the long warmup made a huge difference because of the cooler weather. One key to getting out the door is to lay out my running clothes the night before.

Date Sat. 4/18/15

Workout 45-minute bike ride around Mount Tam.

Average Heart Rate 144

Average Speed 18.9 mph

Positive Experiences New bike riding really well. Mountain was beautiful today. Teamed up with Toby, Darin, and Paul, who made me laugh the whole way.

Why I'm a Champion While climbing, I maintained excellent grace under pressure. When the guys started going a little harder, I remained calm and composed and kept my form together. I ended up outclimbing them.

Valuable Lessons Those new Speedplay cleats have taken the pressure off my knees. Half a Balance Bar and half a bottle of Cytomax not only improved my performance but also helped me recover faster. Heart rates are lower while pedaling in the saddle.

SUCCESS JOURNAL

Date _____

Workout _____

Average Heart Rate _____

Average Speed _____

Positive Experiences _____

_____

_____

Why I'm a Champion _____

_____

_____

Valuable Lessons _____

_____

_____

_____

Date _____

Workout _____

Average Heart Rate _____

Average Speed _____

Positive Experiences _____

_____

Why I'm a Champion _____

_____

_____

Valuable Lessons _____

_____

_____

_____

10
FUEL YOUR ACTIVE BODY

"If we could give every individual the right amount of nourishment and exercise—not too little and not too much—we would have found the safest way to health."

—HIPPOCRATES

Hippocrates' wisdom about diet and exercise is as valid today as it was 2,400 years ago. Of course, in modern vernacular, we'd just say, "You are what you eat." And if you plan on being a triathlete, you need to eat like one. Specifically, you need extra carbohydrates to provide the fuel for training and events, vitamins and minerals to help convert those carbohydrates to usable energy, and protein for adding new muscle. Plus you need some fat to keep cell membranes healthy and to produce important hormones. The best way to meet these nutritional needs is not with a gym bag full of energy bars and Gatorade. It's with a balanced diet, fine-tuned for your triathlon goals and calorie needs, and it's not as hard to plan or execute as you might think.

As a Triathlete-in-Training, you are doing some things differently now. You are burning more calories for fuel as you increase the amount of aerobic exercise you do each week and build muscle with your strength-training sessions. You may not be following the training schedule of a super-elite athlete—who may work out up to six hours a day and burn 5,000 calories—but there's a lot you can learn from the way the pros eat to help give you an edge throughout your training and on race day. Here's what you need to know to properly fuel your active body. At the end of this chapter, I put all of this together into a complete and easy-to-use meal plan.

CARBOHYDRATES: YOUR BODY'S PREFERRED FUEL

Carbohydrates—sugars and starches—are important because they're your body's main source of fuel. Carbs are easily converted to glucose, your muscles' preferred source of energy in most cases. In limited amounts, glucose can be stored in muscles and in the liver as glycogen, which is simply chains of glucose. Your intake of carbohydrates influences how long your body can go before it runs out of glucose—what marathon runners refer to as "hitting the wall."

Let's back up for a minute and talk about energy production. Your body's main fuel currency is a substance called adenosine triphosphate, or ATP for short. All fuels—carbs, fats, and proteins—need to be converted to ATP before they can be burned for energy.

During rest, the body gets slightly more than half of its ATP from fatty acids and most of the rest from carbohydrates, along with a small percentage of amino acids from protein breakdown. During physical activity, the body adjusts its mixture of fuels. Your muscles never use just one single fuel. How much of which fuels they use during exercise depends on the duration and intensity of the activity and the degree to which the body is conditioned to perform that activity.

During exertion, glucose that is stored in the liver and muscles as glycogen is released into the bloodstream. Your muscles use both of these glycogen stores to fuel their work. How much glycogen is stored depends on how many carbohydrates a person eats. The more glycogen the muscles store, the longer the stores last during activity. When glycogen is depleted, the muscles become fatigued. Glycogen depletion usually occurs about two hours after the onset of intense activity. Studies have confirmed that high-carbohydrate diets enhance endurance by enlarging glycogen stores. In one study, runners eating a diet high in fat and protein and low in carbohydrates had a maximum endurance time of 57 minutes; those eating a diet of about 50 percent of calories from carbohydrates lasted 114 minutes; and those eating a high-carbohydrate diet (83 percent of calories) were able to run for 167 minutes.

During moderate, rather than intense, activity—the kind you'll be doing for most of your triathlon training—your muscles will derive their energy from both glucose and fatty acids. By depending partly on fatty acids, moderate aerobic activity conserves glycogen. For the first 20 minutes, the muscles use mostly glycogen. But after that, they increasingly use more fat for fuel. Still, they also use glycogen, and if the activity lasts long enough and is intense enough, muscle and liver glycogen will be depleted—the old hitting the wall. (By the way, you can avoid hitting the wall by consuming carbohydrates such as sports drinks or energy bars during any activity that lasts more than one hour.)

To maximize their available glucose, some athletes will carbo-load. That is, they will eat a high-carbohydrate diet of approximately eight grams of carbohydrate per kilogram of body weight (or about 70 percent of calories in their diet) for three days before their event. While carbo-loading may indeed trick your muscles into storing extra glycogen before a competition, I don't feel that it's necessary for your training program. A normal amount of carbohydrates—50 percent or so of your total calories—is adequate for most Triathletes-in-Training. The meal plans in this chapter show you how to meet these carbohydrate needs. However, if you experiment and find you do better switching to a higher-carbohydrate, lower-fat diet for a day or two before an event or heavy-duty training bout, that's fine, too. All you need to do is cut back on foods higher in protein and fats (such as meats and dairy products) and substitute high-carb foods (such as pasta, rice, or fruit juices).

PROTEIN: WHAT BUILDS MUSCLE

The protein we eat is broken down into amino acids and reassembled into whatever proteins our bodies need to make muscles, bones, skin, hair, and all the connective tissues that literally keep us from falling apart. Certain amino acids found in protein are considered essential, meaning our bodies can't make them; we can only get them from foods we eat. Animal sources of protein—meat, eggs, and dairy products—tend to provide a better balance of essential amino acids than vegetable sources. (Eggs are as close to a perfect protein as you can get.) That doesn't mean you can't survive on vegetable proteins. You can. You just need to mix and match vegetable sources to get a good balance—the old rice-and-beans routine. (Soy or rice protein powders are also a good choice.)

Physically active people use protein to build muscle and other lean tissue structures and, to some extent, to fuel their activities. The strength-training component of your

Triathlete-in-Training program is specifically geared to build muscle, which your body does through a process called remodeling. This process requires protein. During active muscle-building phases of your training—when you're working to put on muscle rather than to just maintain the muscle you already have—you may add between ¼ ounce and 1 ounce (between 7 and 28 grams) of body protein to existing muscle mass each day. For this reason, you'll need slightly more protein than your couch-potato cousin needs. That doesn't mean you need to load up on protein supplements or eggs-and-steak breakfasts. All you need is an adequate amount of high-quality protein.

The nutrition plan laid out in this chapter follows the Academy of Nutrition and Dietetics's recommended intake of 1 to 1.5 grams of protein per kilogram of body weight per day. This will ensure that you're getting enough protein to fuel the endurance component of your training program and to support the muscle-building portion of your training.

It's easy to calculate how much protein you need. Simply divide your weight in pounds by 2.2 to get your weight in kilograms. Then multiply that by 1 and 1.5 to find your daily protein range. So if you weigh 160 pounds, for example, your daily protein range is 73 to 109 grams—the equivalent of about 10 to 15 ounces of meat.

If you're a vegetarian, you may need to supplement your diet with a protein powder drink as a snack or even as a meal. Protein powders allow you to add protein to your diet without adding a lot of fat or extra calories. Soy protein offers lots of health

HOW MUCH PROTEIN ARE YOU GETTING?

When you eat packaged foods, you can check the label to see how much protein is in them. Foods that contain at least five grams per serving are good sources of protein. To help you ballpark the rest of your diet, use this guide. The following foods note grams of protein.

1 cup milk (any type) = 8 g

1 ounce meat (any type) = 7 g

1 ounce fish (most types) = 7 g

1 large egg = 7 g

½ cup beans (most types) = 7 g

1 ounce cheese (any type except cream cheese) = 7 g

2 tablespoons peanut butter = 7 g

1 serving starch (1 slice bread) = 3 g

1 serving most vegetables (½ cup) = 2 g

benefits, including lowering your risk for heart disease and certain cancers. It can also help lower cholesterol. However, some people say rice protein powders are easier to digest than soy- or whey-based powders. Try all three and see which you like best. (See my recipe for a Power Smoothie, made with your choice of protein powder, on page 197.)

FATS: FOR THE LONG HAUL

Fat isn't all bad. In fact, we actually *need* some of it. That's because two types of fatty acids, linoleic and linolenic, are essential, meaning that our bodies can't make them. We can get them only through foods. The main sources of these essential fatty acids are vegetable oils, seeds, nuts, and fish. Our bodies require fats to make cell membranes and certain hormones and to absorb the fat-soluble vitamins A, E, D, and K.

Fat is a highly concentrated source of energy—it provides more energy per gram than any other food source. There are 9 calories in 1 gram of fat compared to only 4 in a gram of protein or carbohydrate. That's one reason fats have gotten a bad rep: Eat too much of them and you'll get fat.

But just because fat is high in calories doesn't mean it's a good source of quick energy, as anyone who's eaten a big fatty meal before a race can tell you. An active person who eats a fat-rich diet with little carbohydrate sacrifices athletic performance and will find that his body starts to break down protein stores to get the glucose it needs from amino acids. This is far from ideal and over time can actually lead to muscle loss.

That said, your body *can* use some fat for energy, but that fat comes from body stores, not from your most recent meal. In fact, body stores are of tremendous importance as a source of energy, especially as you become fit. It is training—repeated aerobic activity—that produces the adaptations that permit the body to draw heavily on fat for fuel. Just 20 minutes or more of aerobic activity, three or more times each week, stimulates even the untrained body to adapt by packing its cells with more fat-metabolizing enzymes and by improving the ability of the heart and lungs to deliver oxygen. That's what allows trained athletes to go longer before hitting the wall. Unlike glycogen stores, fat stores can fuel hours of activity without running out.

Luckily for most of us, we have enough body fat to fuel lots of triathlons. We just have to get to a point of fitness to be able to use it efficiently.

I recommend a diet that offers 25 percent of calories from fat, mostly from unsaturated, non-trans fatty sources—the kind that doesn't cause heart disease and may even help prevent it. That includes fish and vegetable sources, the best of which are fatty fish such as salmon and olive oil or canola oil. Nuts are also good sources, with walnuts and almonds topping the list. Avocados, olives, sunflower seeds, pumpkin seeds, sesame seeds, and soybeans also fit the bill.

VITAMINS AND MINERALS

Vitamins and minerals are important no matter what your fitness level. Research suggests that in the long run, taking a daily vitamin-mineral supplement can help prevent chronic disease. Taking a good multi can even help your athletic performance—if you take it regularly (not if you pop it just before the race!). A multivitamin protects you from becoming deficient in any one nutrient, which can lead to low energy levels. That's because vitamins and minerals are involved in many of the chemical reactions that release energy from fuels.

Some of the B vitamins, for example, act as shuttle buses to move carbohydrates as they go through the process of breaking down into energy. So if you're short on any one of the B vitamins, the process can slow down. The minerals magnesium and iron also play major roles in energy production. Iron, for example, transports oxygen throughout the body. People who are short on either mineral are tired and lack endurance.

You can get all the Bs you need in a good multi. As a guide, look for one that has about 30 milligrams of B6, 400 to 800 micrograms of folic acid, and 100 micrograms of B12. It should also contain at least 200 milligrams of magnesium.

Even though iron is important, experts recommend supplemental iron only to certain groups of people. The main one is premenopausal women. That's because these women lose iron every month during menstruation and have a hard time making it up. If you're a premenopausal woman, don't take more than 18 milligrams of supplemental iron a day without a doctor's diagnosis of your iron status. If a blood test shows that you have low iron levels, your doctor will prescribe supplemental iron, perhaps even in large amounts, in order to get you back on course. If you're iron deficient and get it corrected, you'll be pleasantly surprised at how much more energy you soon have!

Athletes can lose a bit of iron through sweat or through the breakdown of blood cells caused by impact from sports like running. Muscles also have a high demand for iron-containing molecules in their cells. Still, most men don't require supplemental iron and shouldn't take it. Too much iron can be harmful.

Vitamin E deserves special mention because it helps to reduce the damage to muscles that can cause delayed soreness after intense exercise—a problem almost every athlete over age 50 knows about. It's called oxidative damage. One study showed that taking 300 milligrams of vitamin E daily reduced exercise-induced oxidative damage in cyclists. I suggest you get this amount in your multi or take a separate supplement, preferably one that contains natural mixed tocopherols, including tocotrienol. (Those are the scientific names for forms of vitamin E.) Nuts, seeds, and wheat germ are also good food sources of vitamin E.

PREWORKOUT NUTRITION

You want to feel energized—not tired—going into a workout, so you can get the most benefit out of your hard work. I've found that the best way to do that is to have a snack one to two hours before working out. This allows you to start your workout with enough glucose in your bloodstream to get you going and keep you going without feeling weak or shaky. The snack should be 200 to 300 calories (but may go up to 400 calories depending on your daily calorie intake) and should provide mostly carbohydrates, along with some protein or fat. Some ideal snacks that fill the bill: energy bars, crackers and peanut butter, raisins and nuts, yogurt, or half a turkey sandwich.

You should also make a point to drink water before you begin, especially if you sweat a lot. You'd be surprised how much even a little dehydration can contribute to a sense of fatigue. It actually makes it harder for your blood to deliver oxygen to your muscles and can make your arms and legs feel heavy.

The general rule of thumb is to drink *before* you feel thirsty, because you can lose up to 2 percent of your body weight as sweat or urine before your thirst mechanism sets in. If you tend to sweat a lot during your workouts, you may need 10 to 15 glasses (8 ounces each) of fluid a day.

4 STEPS TO OPTIMUM HYDRATION

Here's a simple four-step fluid schedule to help you stay properly hydrated.

1. Two hours before you exercise, drink 3 cups of fluid.
2. Ten to 15 minutes before you exercise, drink 2 cups of fluid.
3. Every 15 minutes during exercise, drink 1 cup of fluid.
4. After exercise, drink 2 cups of fluid.

You can also weigh yourself before and after a workout or race to see how much fluid you've lost and how much you need to replenish. One pound of body weight equals roughly 2 cups (500 milliliters) of fluid.

Does all that fluid have to be water? Actually, no. Sports drinks such as Gatorade contain half the sugar found in sweetened teas, sodas, or fruit drinks, along with small amounts of sodium and potassium, two minerals lost during sweating. So they are a better choice than these other drinks. But if you routinely drink sports drinks instead of water, the calories can really start to add up. I'd stick to no more than 16 ounces of sports drinks a day, even on heavy training days, and get most of your fluids from drinking water.

RACE DAY NUTRITION

The big day brings with it a different set of concerns. If you have a nervous stomach, don't overeat or overdrink. Stick with routines that have worked for you in the past, whenever possible. If you're planning on using caffeine to boost your endurance and you don't normally drink coffee, beware. Coffee is a natural laxative. It may have you running places you didn't intend—like to the bathroom.

Some people don't eat any solids the day of an event—they stick with liquid foods. The advantage here is that there is less chance of cramping or diarrhea. A liquid meal substitute two or three hours before competition can supply some of the fluid and carbs needed, if you can't tolerate solids. Or you can have a Power Smoothie. Follow the hydration schedule on page 196 and stick with water or a sports drink. One beverage to avoid is orange juice. Because it's so acidic and highly concentrated in sugar, large amounts can cause stomach cramping.

POSTWORKOUT NUTRITION

Right after a workout or an event, drink at least two cups of water. And eat a high-carbohydrate snack to replace the glycogen stores you likely used up during your exercise. All you really need is a bagel or a cup of fruit juice within half an hour of finishing.

POWER SMOOTHIE

This is my own personal recipe for a preworkout shake that keeps you energized throughout your workout or race. Simply place these ingredients in a blender and blend to the desired consistency. Note that any generic protein powder will do; you don't need to spend your money on expensive designer protein powders.

2   cups ice
1   cup water or low-fat milk
2   tablespoons peanut butter
½   cup yogurt
¼   banana
2   heaping scoops protein powder (using the scoop that comes with the powder)

FIGURING OUT YOUR CALORIC NEEDS

How many calories a day do you need as a Triathlete-in-Training? Experts estimate that a man on this program will burn about 41 calories, and a woman about 37 calories, per kilogram of body weight per day. (To convert pounds to kilograms, divide by 2.2.) So a man who weighs 160 pounds will burn 2,981 calories a day. A 140-pound woman would burn 2,354 calories a day.

You can see how exercise helps maintain weight. Because you're burning so many calories from your training, you get to eat a relatively high number of calories and not gain weight. (If you are trying to lose weight, use your goal weight, not your actual weight, for this calculation.)

Now that you know roughly how many calories you need to get per day, you can find the meal plan ahead that's right for you. Each meal plan offers a few choices for every meal so that you can use the plan for a number of days. Beyond that, you can use this meal plan as a guide to help you come up with your own meal plans to meet your nutritional needs.

Note that if you're lactose intolerant or don't like to drink milk, you can substitute another beverage. Just make sure that you take a calcium supplement that provides 1,000 milligrams a day.

MEAL PLANS

2,000-CALORIE DIET
(50% CARBS, 25% PROTEIN, 25% FAT)

BREAKFAST

1 medium-size bagel
2 tablespoons reduced-fat cream cheese
2 strips turkey bacon, Canadian bacon, or soy bacon, or 1 ounce smoked salmon
1 small fruit or ½ cup juice
1 cup fat-free milk

TOTAL: 57 g carbohydrate, 18 g protein, 9 g fat, 435 calories

SNACK

¾ cup fat-free yogurt

⅓ cup low-fat granola

TOTAL: 36 g carbohydrate, 10 g protein, 2 g fat, 204 calories

LUNCH

2 slices whole wheat bread

2 ounces sliced low-fat turkey breast, lean pork, or chicken breast, or ⅔ cup tuna

1 ounce Swiss cheese

Lettuce and tomato

1 tablespoon reduced-fat mayonnaise

1 cup cubed cantaloupe

TOTAL: 45 g carbohydrate, 27 g protein, 16 g fat, 450 calories

SNACK

4 tablespoons dried fruit

10 almonds

TOTAL: 32 g carbohydrate, 3 g protein, 6 g fat, 190 calories

DINNER

6 ounces broiled salmon steak, ½ small broiled chicken breast, or 6 large broiled shrimp

½ cup baked beans

⅔ cup rice

1 cup broccoli

1 cup cooked carrots

½ cup low-fat ice cream

TOTAL: 80 g carbohydrate, 58 g protein, 24 g fat, 653 calories

TOTALS FOR DAY: 250 g carbohydrate, 116 g protein, 57 g fat, 1,932 calories

2,500-CALORIE DIET
(50% CARBS, 25% PROTEIN, 25% FAT)

BREAKFAST

1 medium-size bagel

2 tablespoons reduced-fat cream cheese

4 strips turkey bacon, Canadian bacon, or soy bacon, or 2 ounces smoked salmon

1 large fruit
½ cup juice
1 cup fat-free milk

TOTAL: 87 g carbohydrate, 20 g protein, 12 g fat, 560 calories

SNACK

1½ cups fat-free yogurt
⅔ cup low-fat granola

TOTAL: 72 carbohydrate, 21 g protein, 3 g fat, 408 calories

LUNCH

Large hoagie roll
3 ounces sliced low-fat turkey breast, lean pork, or chicken breast, or ¾ cup tuna
2 ounces Swiss cheese
Lettuce and tomato
1 tablespoon reduced-fat mayonnaise
1 cup cubed cantaloupe

TOTAL: 60 g carbohydrate, 41 g protein, 16 g fat, 600 calories

SNACK

2 tablespoons dried fruit
10 almonds
1 cup fat-free milk

TOTAL: 29 g carbohydrate, 8 g protein, 6 g fat, 220 calories

DINNER

8 ounces broiled salmon steak, ½ medium broiled chicken breast, or 9 large broiled shrimp
½ cup baked beans
⅔ cup rice
1 cup broccoli
1 cup cooked carrots
½ cup low-fat ice cream

TOTAL: 80 g carbohydrate, 62 g protein, 24 g fat, 688 calories
TOTALS FOR DAY: 328 g carbohydrate, 152 g protein, 61 g fat, 2,476 calories

3,000-CALORIE DIET
(50% CARBS, 25% PROTEIN, 25% FAT)

BREAKFAST

1 medium-size bagel

2 tablespoons reduced-fat cream cheese

2 strips turkey bacon, Canadian bacon, or soy bacon, or 1 ounce smoked salmon

1 large fruit

½ cup juice

1 cup fat-free milk

TOTAL: 87 g carbohydrate, 18 g protein, 9 g fat, 525 calories

SNACK

1½ cups fat-free yogurt

⅔ cup low-fat granola

TOTAL: 72 g carbohydrate, 21 g protein, 3 g fat, 408 calories

LUNCH

Large hoagie roll

3 ounces sliced low-fat turkey breast, lean pork, or chicken breast, or ¾ cup tuna

2 ounces Swiss cheese

Lettuce and tomato

1 tablespoon reduced-fat mayonnaise

1 cup cubed cantaloupe

TOTAL: 60 g carbohydrate, 41 g protein, 16 g fat, 600 calories

SNACK

4 tablespoons dried fruit

10 almonds

1 cup fat-free milk

TOTAL: 45 g carbohydrate, 11 g protein, 6 g fat, 280 calories

DINNER

11 ounces broiled salmon steak, ½ large broiled chicken breast, or 1 dozen large broiled shrimp

1 cup baked beans

⅔ cup rice

1 cup broccoli

1 cup cooked carrots

1 cup low-fat ice cream

TOTAL: 110 g carbohydrate, 103 g protein, 44 g fat, 1,058 calories
TOTALS FOR DAY: 374 g carbohydrate, 194 g protein, 78 g fat, 2,871 calories

FOUR DIETS WORTH TRYING

There is so much noise out there about newfangled ways to eat and new diets to try that it's hard to separate fact from fiction—and fad from trend. I believe there are four valuable diets to consider when seeking to improve your health, elevate your energy, and increase your performance.

THE PALEOLITHIC DIET (MORE COMMONLY KNOWN AS THE PALEO DIET)

We're simply modern cavemen and cavewomen—or so say proponents of this diet, also known as the caveman diet and the hunter-gatherer diet.

This is a way of eating that emulates what we ate during the Paleolithic era. The idea behind it is simple: We evolved on certain foods, and those are best for our health. The thinking is that foods that have appeared in our diets since the agricultural revolution 10,000 years ago—such as grains, dairy, and refined sugar—are not healthy, because our bodies are not equipped to digest them properly. Paleo proponents believe that these can lead to health-related issues such as diabetes, obesity, and heart disease.

Many triathletes swear by this diet, claiming they have more strength and energy—and better health and recovery times.

Here are the general guidelines for the Paleo diet:

- Lean meats such as fish, lean beef, and other animal protein compose a foundation of this diet. Anywhere from 15 to 35 percent of one's daily intake should come from these foods.

- Fresh fruits, berries, and nonstarchy vegetables ought to compose 45 to 65 percent of your overall daily caloric intake.

- Nuts and seeds are allowed, since they would have been a key component of the hunter-gatherer diet.

- No alcohol or coffee. This one is tough for many triathletes who crave that early-morning, preworkout coffee or evening glass of wine. But if you're going strict Paleo, you've got to go cold turkey on coffee and alcohol.

- No refined sugar. Ironically, many triathletes consume sports drinks and energy bars that are loaded with refined sugars. If you're going to follow the Paleo diet, then you need to check labels and do away with refined sugars. Personally, I have had incredible results—in the form of better health, more energy, and fewer illnesses—by eliminating refined sugars from my diet.

- No dairy.

- No grains.

- Very little salt.

Here are some sample meals, courtesy of http://eatdrinkpaleo.com.au

Spinach and Boiled Egg Chopped Salad With Avocado

1	bunch fresh spinach	¼	cup Spanish onion, finely chopped
	olive oil	½	cup halved cherry tomatoes
3	garlic cloves, finely diced	½	avocado, sliced
2	teaspoons lemon juice		sea salt and black pepper
2	hard-cooked eggs, chopped		

In a large skillet over medium-high heat, add the olive oil and sauté the spinach, garlic, and lemon juice. Place the wilted spinach in a large bowl.

Add the eggs, onion, tomatoes, avocado, and a pinch or two of salt and pepper. Add additional lemon juice and olive oil to taste. Makes one serving.

Grilled Salmon with Fennel, Orange, and Black Olive Salad

2	salmon steak fillets		½	cup chives, chopped
	sea salt and black pepper		¼	cup black olives, chopped
	coconut oil			mustard
½	fennel bulb, sliced			lemon
1	orange, sliced			olive oil

Preheat the grill or broiler.

Season the salmon with salt and pepper and brush with the coconut oil. Grill or broil the salmon for 2 to 3 minutes on each side.

In a large bowl, combine the fennel, orange slices, chopped chives, and olives. In a small bowl, mix together the mustard, lemon, and olive oil. Pour over the salad and mix to coat evenly. Serve with the fish.

MEDITERRANEAN

Heart healthy—that is the primary benefit of the Mediterranean diet. A fun and rewarding diet to explore, it can also lead to better overall health and greater enjoyment of food.

The Mediterranean diet is based on the traditional way of eating in countries around the Mediterranean Sea. We're talking fresh fish, fresh vegetables, olive oil, wine—what's not to love?

There are a few key components to the Mediterranean diet:

- Plant-based foods such as legumes, fruits, vegetables, and whole grains form the basis of the diet.
- Healthy fats that come from fish, olive oil, and nuts are emphasized.
- Meats should be limited to fish and poultry; you should eat red meat no more than once a week.
- Replace salt with other herbs and spices to reduce sodium intake.
- Drink a glass of red wine now and then.
- Enjoy meals in the company of others, and make an experience out of cooking and eating. Who can argue with that?

It makes sense that this is such a popular diet among triathletes. A diet high in quality proteins and fats and low in refined carbohydrates and sugars will power any triathlete training program. Moreover, food should be a source of pleasure, never a source of guilt. It should be enjoyed and celebrated with others. Some studies show that when you are in good company and in good spirits, your digestion improves. Here are some sample meals, courtesy of *Good Housekeeping*.

Chickpea Salad

7½   ounces canned chickpeas (half of a 15-ounce can), rinsed and drained

2   teaspoons olive oil

¼   cup chopped white onion (save the remaining onion for the Chicken Kebabs, see below)

¼   cup chopped green bell pepper (save the remaining pepper for the Chicken Kebabs, see below)

1   tablespoon sliced black olives

¼   teaspoon ground black pepper

1½   tablespoons apple cider vinegar

2   cups romaine lettuce leaves

In a bowl, combine the chickpeas, oil, onion, bell pepper, olives, black pepper, and vinegar. Mix thoroughly. Serve over the lettuce leaves.

Chicken Kebabs

4   ounces chicken breast

¼   cup fat-free Italian dressing
       white onion remaining from the Chickpea Salad recipe (see above)

1   green bell pepper remaining from the Chickpea Salad recipe (see above)

10   grape tomatoes

1   (6") whole wheat pita

2   tablespoons hummus

Preheat the grill or broiler.

Slice the chicken into small chunks for skewering. Place in a bowl with the Italian dressing and marinate for at least 30 minutes to overnight.

Slice the onion and bell pepper into chunks.

Alternate pieces of marinated chicken, onion, pepper, and tomatoes on skewers. Place on the grill or broiler and heat until meat is thoroughly cooked.

Toast the pita on the grill. Cut it in half and open to form a pocket. Spread the hummus in the pita. Serve with the chicken and vegetables.

Serve with 1 cup fat-free milk mixed with 1 tablespoon strawberry drink mix. For added refreshment, freeze the flavored milk into a Popsicle mold the night before and enjoy this as a healthy dessert! Make three Popsicles and save the remainder for dessert on other days.

GLUTEN FREE

A gluten-free diet is one that eliminates all gluten, which is a protein found primarily in wheat. For people with celiac disease (CD), the presence of gluten causes damage to the small intestines, resulting in various health problems. This condition affects roughly 1 percent of Americans, and some reports find that this number is rising.

Because of the increased attention on the gluten-free diet, many people who do not have CD are adhering to these diets. Some triathletes swear that it increases energy levels and reduces body weight.

The bad news is, this is a tough diet to follow, since wheat and related grains, such as rye and barley, are increasingly hard to avoid. We're talking about pasta, breads, bagels—common staples of active athletes. The good news is, this diet consists primarily of foods like fish, meat, fruits, vegetables, nuts, corn, and potatoes. These are foods that will power a healthy triathlete.

Here are some sample meals, courtesy of simplygluten-free.com.

Gluten-Free Mongolian Shiitake Noodles

8	ounces gluten-free linguini		4	cups thinly sliced green cabbage
2	tablespoons vegetable oil		3	medium carrots, grated
1	medium red onion, thinly sliced		¼	cup San-J Mongolian Sauce
8	ounces shiitake mushrooms, stems removed, caps sliced		½	teaspoon red-pepper flakes
			3	green onions, thinly sliced

Bring a large pot of salted water to a boil and cook the linguini according to the package directions. Drain and rinse with cold water.

Heat the oil in a large skillet or wok over medium-high heat. Add the onion and mushrooms and cook, stirring occasionally, for 10 minutes, or until soft and browned. Add the cabbage and carrots and cook, stirring, for 2 minutes.

Add the sauce, pasta, and pepper flakes. Cook, stirring, for 1 to 2 minutes, or until heated through. Garnish with the green onions.

Gluten-Free Crunchy Chicken Waldorf Salad

1 package (1 ounce) freeze-dried grapes
½ cup walnuts, toasted
½ cup celery, thinly sliced
1 medium apple, finely chopped
1 cup chopped cooked chicken

3 tablespoons mayonnaise
1 tablespoon fresh lemon juice
   Salt and black pepper
   Lettuce leaves

In a large mixing bowl, combine the grapes, walnuts, celery, apple, chicken, mayonnaise, and lemon juice. Season to taste with salt and pepper. Serve the salad on lettuce leaves.

VEGAN

This diet excludes any food containing animal protein—in any form. In other words, you don't just eliminate meat, fish, and poultry. You also eliminate anything made with animal products, such as butter, honey, and even gelatin. Some follow a vegan diet for health reasons, others for ethical reasons. Either way, this is a diet that has its advantages and disadvantages.

A vegan diet eliminates a lot of unhealthy foods such as saturated fat and cholesterol, which can have a positive effect on your health. The downside of the diet is that because you eliminate so many foods, you may risk not getting enough amino acids, vitamin B_{12}, or calcium. However, with proper planning and execution, you can combine proteins (such as rice and beans) and take vitamin supplements to get enough B_{12} and calcium.

Here are some sample meals, courtesy of allrecipes.com.

Red Lentil Soup

1 tablespoon peanut oil
1 small onion, chopped
1 tablespoon minced fresh ginger
1 clove garlic, chopped
1 pinch fenugreek seeds
1 cup dry red lentils
1 cup cubed butternut squash, peeled and seeded
⅓ cup finely chopped fresh cilantro

2 cups water
7 ounces coconut milk (half of a 14-ounce can)
2 tablespoons tomato paste
1 teaspoon curry powder
1 pinch cayenne pepper
1 pinch ground nutmeg
   Salt and black pepper

Heat the oil in a large pot over medium heat. Add the onion, ginger, garlic, and fenugreek and cook until the onion is tender.

Add the lentils, squash, and cilantro to the pot. Stir in the water, coconut milk, tomato paste, curry powder, cayenne pepper, and nutmeg. Season to taste with salt and pepper. Bring to a boil, reduce the heat to low, and simmer for 30 minutes or until the lentils and squash are tender.

Summer Vegetable Ratatouille

½	cup olive oil	1	yellow bell pepper, chopped
2	onions, sliced into thin rings	1	red bell pepper, chopped
3	cloves garlic, minced	1	bay leaf
2	zucchini, cubed	4	sprigs fresh thyme
1	medium eggplant, chopped		Salt and black pepper
2	medium yellow squash, chopped	4	roma (plum) tomatoes, chopped
2	green bell peppers, chopped	2	tablespoons chopped fresh parsley

Heat 1½ tablespoons of the oil in a large pot over medium-low heat. Add the onions and garlic and cook until soft.

In a large skillet, heat 1½ tablespoons of the oil and sauté the zucchini in batches until slightly browned on all sides. Remove the zucchini and place in the pot with the onions and garlic.

Sauté the eggplant, then sauté the yellow squash and bell peppers one batch at a time, adding 1½ tablespoons of the oil to the skillet each time you add a new set of vegetables. Once each batch has been sautéed, add them to the large pot.

Add the bay leaf and thyme. Season to taste with salt and pepper and cover the pot. Cook over medium heat for 15 to 20 minutes. Add the tomatoes and parsley and cook for another 10 to 15 minutes, stirring occasionally. Remove the bay leaf and adjust the seasoning before serving.

JUICE FASTING

There are strong opinions on both sides of the juice-fast argument. Some swear by it. Others believe it's pure marketing. I happen to be a big believer in a monthly three-day vegetable juice fast as a way to detoxify and cleanse the body. Because triathletes train more, they tend to eat more. I like the idea of giving my body a break from solid food once a month. I normally finish a juice fast feeling clearheaded and more aware of the foods I eat.

If you try a juice fast, keep these things in mind.

- Eliminate or greatly reduce the amount of exercise during your juice fast. You will not have the kind of energy you need for strenuous exercise, and it can be dangerous to work out with lower blood sugar levels.

- Only juice pesticide-free vegetables. Proponents of the juice fast believe it can help detoxify your body. But if you juice vegetables treated with pesticides, then you are not giving your body an opportunity to fully detoxify.

- The best ingredients to use are beets, celery, carrots, kale, and cucumber.

- Add fruits sparingly to improve taste. Pure vegetable juices can be tough to swallow. Apples are a great addition to vegetable juices.

PRODUCT RECOMMENDATIONS

In my quest for a competitive advantage over the last 20 years, I have tried and tested almost every conceivable product. While I do not have all the answers, I have found the following products to be among the best performing.

SPORTS & RECOVERY DRINK: Osmo (www.osmonutrition.com). This is a newcomer to the market. Osmo's hydration and recovery products are science driven, based on the peer-reviewed work of exercise physiologist Dr. Stacy Sims. Osmo has a light, refreshing taste, and the products are easy to digest.

SPORTS GEL: Honey Stinger Organics (www.honeystinger.com). Many energy gels contain refined sugars and unhealthy ingredients. This line of gels is certified organic, gluten free, all natural, and all awesome.

ENERGY BAR: With so many choices in energy bars, how does one make an intelligent choice? You cannot go wrong with Pro Bar (www.theprobar.com). They are non-GMO, organic, and all natural—as well as easy to digest. And they taste amazingly good.

11
STAY INJURY FREE

"The art of life is the art of avoiding pain; and he is the best pilot,
who steers clearest of the rocks and shoals with which it is beset."
—THOMAS JEFFERSON

If you're sick or in pain, how on earth can you live with passion and perform as a triathlete—or even as a human being? The problem with pain, injury, and illness is that we are so good at adapting to and working around them that imperceptibly, over time, we learn to live with them. Many of us, for example, continue to sit for hours at work and simply deal with our sore back for years on end rather than see a doctor or specialist and find out how to put an end to the pain.

Some people may fear that training for a triathlon will increase their risk of becoming sick or injured. After all, a triathlon is a physically demanding feat. This chapter outlines simple strategies to reduce the risk of sports-related pain and injury and to strengthen your immunity so you can ward off illness. Follow these strategies along with the training program in this book and your body will become stronger, more flexible, and less susceptible to injury. Although I emphasize injury prevention in this chapter, I also cover how to identify and treat some common sports injuries and pain, particularly those related to triathlon training.

PREVENTING PAIN AND INJURY

You finally had this triathlon training thing down. You were on a regular schedule, working out three or more times a week. Your weight was plummeting, and your performance and confidence were soaring—you couldn't remember the last time you felt so fantastic. Then a sharp pain in your hamstring during an overzealous interval on the track stopped you dead in your tracks.

Injuries are no fun. They cost us time and money, and perhaps worst of all, they prevent us from doing things we love—from living fully. The fact is, more than 10 million sports injuries are treated each year in the United States, according to *The Merck Manual*. Such injuries are a serious problem, but they don't simply befall us from bad luck. They are usually the result of one of four things.

1. Bad exercise habits
2. Lack of strength
3. Use of improper gear
4. Poor exercise technique

Follow these simple guidelines to avoid most sports injuries while at the same time strengthening your body and shielding yourself from future problems.

EXERCISE SMART

Preventing most sports-related pain and injury ultimately comes down to exercising smart. The program laid out in this book gives you the tools to do just that. For example, according to the American College of Sports Medicine, a warmup is necessary to prepare the body for exercise by increasing heart rate and bloodflow to working muscles. How to properly warm up is covered in Chapter 4.

Exercising smart also means paying attention to your internal cues, which I emphasize throughout this book. Most injuries can be averted by listening to your body, which will send warning signals well in advance of injury. You may feel a twinge in your calf or that "something just isn't right" in your hamstring. If that's the case, skip your run! Really. Although you must be honest with yourself—and comfortably challenge yourself—you never want to push past that line. It's better to ease off for a day with a minor strain than to be out of commission for weeks with a severe injury.

Taking a day off or stopping during a workout isn't wimping out. The world's best athletes do it all the time. So should you. According to the American Institute of Preventive Medicine, "If you continue to exercise when injured, further damage can leave you laid up for weeks or months and may even affect you for years afterward." Be smart, and your body will reward you for it.

STRENGTHEN YOUR BODY

One of the most effective ways to avoid sports-related injuries is to incorporate strength training into your weekly program. No matter what your Fitness Level, I recommend you do two strength-training workouts a week. It's an insurance policy against most injuries. By lifting weights or using resistance machines, you will build up the resiliency of your tendons, muscles, and ligaments, which are especially vulnerable to sports injuries. Refer to Chapter 8 for the essentials of strength training.

GET IN GEAR

Using the proper exercise gear—as outlined in Chapter 3—will go a long way in preventing injury. For example, the right cycling shorts can reduce the risk of chaffing, the running socks I recommend prevent blisters, and proper cold-weather gear can avert muscle cramps or, worse, hypothermia.

"The equipment you use should be in good working order and should fit your body," says Warren Scott, MD, founder and chief of the Division of Sports Medicine at Kaiser Permanente Medical Center in Santa Clara, California. "For example, if you are a cyclist, and your bike does not fit you, each time you turn the pedals, you are placing negative stress on your knees, hips, and back. That inevitably leads to pain and injury. Go to a bike shop and have them fit you properly on your bike."

Similarly, if you're a runner, make sure your shoes are right for your running style and are in good condition. Get a new pair of running shoes every 200 to 400 miles or after four to eight months of training, whichever comes first.

FOCUS ON PROPER TECHNIQUE

Using poor technique during exercise can lead to an array of injuries. When running, for example, too high of a vertical bounce can cause knee pain or injury, because you place too much impact stress on your body when you land with each step. Spend a few minutes to learn how to shuffle along more smoothly, and you will dramatically reduce your risk of knee pain. (Refer to page 104 for more information on proper running form.) For each triathlon sport, I take you through the proper technique to help you perform better *and* prevent injuries.

REST

When you take time away from physical exercise, you allow your muscles to recover and repair, which is an essential preventive measure against sports injuries. That's why as you mapped out your training program in Chapter 9, you were instructed to set aside your rest days along with your workouts.

TAKE HOT BATHS

Partaking of a deep soak has been a tradition since pre-Roman antiquity and for good reason. Little will do more to wash away the stresses of daily life and help you recover from your training.

I experienced my first super-hot soak in Japan, where I was competing in a triathlon. After the event, my hosts insisted I take a traditional "Japanese hot bath." They all accompanied me into the actual bathing chamber, beaming with pride that I had won the event and eager to see how I would respond to this therapy.

The water was so hot, I could barely move. But, of course, I smiled and nodded to all of them in the semicircle around me. It was almost painful.

But when I emerged from that tub, every muscle in my body was more relaxed than ever before. The next day, I was almost completely recovered from my triathlon.

By vasodilating your circulatory system, a hot bath allows fresh blood to enter your capillary beds and bring in healing oxygen and nutrients to your tissues while flushing them of waste products. This is an effective therapy, but it must be done with caution. Regulate the water temperature so it's never hotter than 105°F. If you are pregnant, elderly, or suffer from diabetes, gout, high blood pressure, or any other health condition, absolutely consult with your doctor before doing this.

GET BODYWORK

A complete training program includes preventive therapies such as deep-tissue massage, chiropractic, and acupuncture. These effective therapies not only prevent injuries but also improve long-term body function and keep you feeling your best. Many world-class athletes have bodywork up to six times a week to maintain flawless physical functioning. But for most people, bodywork is a luxury. Rates can be upward of $80 an hour, which may seem too stiff to have someone work out your stiffness.

Yet as research about the healing benefits of bodywork continues to surface, some experts believe this form of therapy is one you can't afford to do without. Science has shown that massage, for example, can help heal muscular injuries, reduce the risk of injury, and improve your performance in exercise and daily life.

"Years of improper stretching, driving, sitting, standing, walking, carrying groceries, talking on the telephone, and working at the computer all lead to pain, injury, and general discomfort," says alternative medicine expert Andrew Weil, MD, author of the best-selling *8 Weeks to Optimum Health* and *Spontaneous Healing.* "Indeed, many of us have forgotten how good our bodies can feel until we get expert bodywork."

My mother has a healthy perspective on bodywork: She regards it as part of her monthly budget—a utility bill to maintain her "most prized possession." And remember, massage or physical therapy may be covered by your health insurance. Although not all insurers provide this coverage, it may be worth doing some research to find a plan that does.

Here is an overview of the most popular and effective forms of bodywork and important considerations for each.

MASSAGE THERAPY. This is the most popular variety of bodywork and varies from an invigorating rubdown to deep-tissue massage geared to more serious athletes.

A massage does more than leave you feeling relaxed and refreshed; a good massage therapist will check over your body and ferret out problems before they become injuries. For example, she might find that your hamstring is tight and work to loosen it up. Your therapist should ask you questions about your body and focus on areas that are painful or not functioning optimally.

For a low-cost treatment option, look into massage schools in your area. The students need the experience and school credits, and I've found that they often do a better job than seasoned pros because they're trying harder! Even small neighborhood shops and beauty salons offer 10-minute massages for as little as $10.

ROLFING. Rolfing is massage—caffeinated. This form of deep massage was developed by Ida P. Rolf, a biochemist and therapist who claimed she found a correlation between muscular tension and pent-up emotions. Rolfing is generally intended to "restructure" the tissue that connects muscles to muscles, called fascia, and typically consists of 10 intensive sessions in which the practitioner applies firm—even slightly painful—pressure with the fingers and elbows to specific parts of the body. This form of bodywork is wildly popular among more serious triathletes.

Though you should check with your doctor before trying any intensive therapy, this form of bodywork is said to help people with chronic injuries or long-standing problems of bad posture and chronic back pain. It can also help diminish habitual muscle tension. For a referral in your area, contact the Rolf Institute at (800) 530-8875 or visit www.rolf.org.

ACUPUNCTURE. Emperor Shen Nung, the father of Chinese medicine, documented theories about circulation, pulse rate, and the heart more than 4,000 years before European medicine even began exploring these areas. His insights led to the development of modern acupuncture, the insertion of fine needles into very specific areas of the body's surface to influence physiological functions.

Shen theorized that the body has an energy force running throughout it, known as chi (pronounced "chee") and that the flow of chi in the body influences a person's health.

Acupuncture has brought relief to millions of people, including scores of triathletes and single-sporters. In addition, the National Institutes of Health has reported that there is clear evidence that acupuncture is an acceptable alternative to some conventional treatments for stroke rehabilitation, headache, menstrual cramps, fibromyalgia, lower-back pain, carpal tunnel syndrome, and asthma. The bottom line: It's worth experiencing at least once.

CHIROPRACTIC. This form of bodywork has long been stigmatized, but it has become more mainstream as access to higher-quality chiropractors has increased. According to the American Chiropractic Association, the practice and procedures of chiropractic specifically include the adjustment and manipulation of the articulations and adjacent tissues of the human body, particularly of the spinal column.

Good chiropractic treatments can be very good, but bad treatments can be exceedingly bad, even dangerous. That is why it's imperative to choose a highly respected, certified, and experienced chiropractor before you let that person anywhere near your neck. After getting chiropractic treatments around the world, I've learned one universal truth: Your chiropractor should do muscle-tissue work around your neck and back before adjusting those areas. Why? If your muscles are tight when your spine is adjusted, those tight muscles will simply pull your spine right back out of alignment.

Chiropractic work is best left to certified experts. Never attempt to do chiropractic on yourself or others.

Whatever bodywork you decide to get, follow these important tips.

- Relax fully during your bodywork. The more you can calm your mind and muscles, the more benefit you will get from the session. Focus on breathing deeply and clearing your mind.

- Because bodywork can be an intimate experience for some people, choose someone with whom you feel eminently comfortable.

- Get bodywork on rest days rather than on heavy training days.

- You know your body better than any therapist. If something doesn't feel right, tell him or her to stop. Communication is paramount, and you are the paying client.

Your body is the most wondrous piece of machinery you will ever own. Treat it as such. During your triathlon training, get bodywork tune-ups at least once every two weeks. You'll not only feel better but also perform better.

AVOIDING BACK PAIN

Back pain hits most of us at some point in our lives and deserves some extra coverage here. Preventing back strain and injury is the key to staying pain free. Although training for a triathlon will strengthen your core area, including your back and abdominal muscles, you must treat your back better at work as well.

The average person—including Triathletes-in-Training—sits for more than half the day, according to the University Health Network in Toronto, Canada. That's not good news for your back. The human body wasn't designed for long periods of sitting. It evolved as a machine for hunting and gathering and for running from danger. Our increasingly sedentary lives have placed new and unnatural stresses on our bodies. Even active triathletes suffer from pain arising from work-related sitting.

"The simple act of sitting places hundreds of pounds of pressure per square inch on your lower back," says Walter Lightner, DC, a chiropractor at Tahoe Yoga and Wellness Center in Truckee, California. "Your low back is an area very susceptible to injury, and over time, too much sitting can cause serious pain and irreparable damage."

Your circulatory system is designed to deliver oxygen to your body and to remove waste products from ongoing chemical reactions, such as the breakdown of food. Dr. Lightner says that when you sit at your desk for more than an hour, these waste products begin to build up in your lower back and legs. "The lack of physical movement reduces circulation," he explains, "and these waste products cannot be flushed out. This can lead to chronic pain and injury."

By exercising more and smarter with this program, you will loosen and strengthen your back—but that may not be enough. Here are four supplementary things you can do to reduce pain, increase comfort, and prevent injury caused by sitting at work for extended periods.

MAINTAIN BETTER POSTURE

The best preventive measure against sitting-related pain and stiffness is a simple shift in how you sit. Keep your ears, shoulders, and hips in a straight line, with your head held up and your stomach pulled in.

Your chair should have a straight back or, better yet, lower-back support. Chairs should swivel so that you can avoid twisting at the waist, and they should have comfortable armrests.

While sitting, your knees should be a little higher than your hips to reduce the pull on your lower back. A small pillow or rolled towel placed behind the lower back will relieve some pressure while you're sitting at your desk.

TAKE FIVE

You've probably heard that you should take periodic de-stress breaks throughout the day. Aim for at least five physical breaks away from your desk each day. I'm not talking about those seven-second shake-your-wrist breaks but sessions where you get up, do some deep breathing, clear your mind, and walk two or three flights of stairs.

Feel guilty about taking the extra time for your health? The corporate bottom line relies on a healthy and productive workforce—and you are a Triathlete-in-Training. You are adding to their bottom line. Take the time.

STRETCH YOUR CORE

During the workday, it's important to keep the muscles of your midsection—your lower back, abdominal, and buttocks muscles—loose and supple. Loosening these muscles every hour or so will go a long way toward reducing and preventing pain and keeping your muscles more flexible for those evening workouts.

But stretching the region around your lower back can be dangerous if you follow the old-fashioned touch-your-toes exercise routine, which can place stress on your lower back. Paul Conder, former chief designer at Microsphere, a company that designs ergonomic furniture in Vancouver, British Columbia, offers these stretches to loosen up your midsection safely and effectively.

Lying Back Stretch

1. Lying on your back, pull both knees to your chest and hold for 10 seconds.

2. Lower your feet to the floor and your arms to your sides. Slowly roll your knees over to one side until they touch the floor. Hold this position for 10 seconds while breathing deeply. Then repeat on the other side.

Back Bend

Stand with your feet a little wider than shoulder-width apart and knees slightly bent. Place both hands on the small of your back. Push your hips forward, feeling the stretch in your lower back and in the front of your hips.

Cobra

Lie facedown and push your upper body off the floor about two feet with your arms while keeping your pelvis and legs pressed into the floor. You'll need to find a private place to do this strange-looking stretch, but the rewards are well worth it.

INCREASE YOUR REVERSE CIRCULATION

Sitting all day also causes blood to pool in your legs due to the effects of gravity. It is essential for your good health to increase the reverse circulation of your legs.

One of the best ways to do this is to elevate your legs for a few minutes each day. Lie on the floor on your back with your buttocks against a wall and your legs straight up along the wall. Remain in this position for two to five minutes as you massage and shake out your leg muscles with your hands. This will, in effect, draw out all of the "old" blood. When you stand up, the fresh, oxygenated blood will rush back into your legs. This can provide tremendous relief and healing to your lower body, which has been put under stress from your training and hectic workday.

This strategy is a favorite among triathletes—you'll see me do it everywhere, including cafés, airports, and even business meetings. When people ask what I'm doing on the floor, I tell them I am training for a triathlon and need to stay loose. That keeps most people from raising their eyebrows.

TREATING COMMON INJURIES

Sometimes even the most careful athlete—who takes all the necessary precautions to prevent injuries—still gets hurt. When you suffer a sports-related injury, it's not wise to take matters into your own hands. For quick and proper healing, follow these guidelines.

GET AN EXPERT DIAGNOSIS RIGHT AWAY

The most valuable thing you can do is get an accurate diagnosis immediately so you don't inadvertently make the injury worse—say, by applying heat when you should apply ice. I cannot overstress the importance of seeing a specialist in the area of your injury rather than a general practitioner. If you suffer a foot injury, for example, see a podiatrist. If you experience shoulder pain from swimming, see a physical therapist who works with swimmers and understands how the shoulder is used in that sport.

Early in my career, I injured my lower back, and it has plagued me ever since, diminishing my quality of life more than I care to admit. In the first two years after the injury, I saw dozens of doctors and physical therapists around the world who prescribed stretching as the primary form of therapy. So, determined to beat it, I stretched my back into oblivion—at least two hours a day. My condition only worsened. It got so bad that one day, halfway into a six-hour ride, I couldn't turn the pedals anymore.

I finally found my way to Dr. Scott, who is not only a sports specialist but also an Ironman triathlete. Within 20 minutes, he told me that I had a chronic muscle tear. The treatment was *no* stretching. Stretching would just continue to aggravate the injury. I needed deep-tissue bodywork to realign the muscle fibers. Once I'd received it, I could stretch again. Had I met Dr. Scott three years before, I would have saved hundreds of hours, thousands of dollars, and untold amounts of heartache.

If you have an unresolved chronic injury, before you do anything else, seek out a proven sports injury expert to get a proper diagnosis.

SUDDEN VERSUS PERSISTENT

Injuries fall into two categories: acute and chronic. Acute injuries arise from mishaps, such as skinning your elbow in a bike crash, suddenly twisting your ankle while running, or, if you're like me, banging your head into the side of the pool because you weren't paying attention to the timing of a flip turn. You usually know exactly how an acute injury happened and have a much better chance at getting a proper diagnosis and starting treatment early. Acute injuries include concussions, broken bones, and sprains, as well as muscle, tendon, and ligament injuries. Each of these requires immediate medical attention and injury-specific treatment.

Here is my loose definition of a chronic injury: It's one that has been a huge pain in your rear end for more than four months. It may be an overuse injury such as tendinitis, shin splints, or plantar fasciitis (inflammation in the arch of the foot). Unresolved acute injuries may also become chronic.

Because chronic injuries have been with you for a relatively long period of time, they are the most frustrating. Your approach to resolving them must be deliberate and determined. The problem must be ferreted out, and it can take months to unwind the damage done. Often, with chronic injuries, compensatory issues are at work. For example, tight hamstrings that pull on your lower back may exacerbate chronic lower-back pain. In this case, you can treat your lower back ad infinitum, but until you loosen those hamstrings, your back will never fully heal. That is why you must approach these injuries holistically and under the guidance of a bona fide specialist who will make use of healing therapies that are appropriate for your injury.

TREAT YOUR INJURY FAST

Once you know the nature of your injury and the best treatment, jump right on it. The more you do to treat an exercise-induced injury in the first 72 hours, the quicker the injury will heal and the less likely it is to become a dreaded chronic condition.

RELY LESS ON DRUGS, MORE ON YOUR BODY

Although drugs may provide temporary relief from pain—which is an important adjunct to the initial healing process—over time, relying on drugs simply masks your problem and moves you no closer to resolving your injury.

After an appropriate amount of time for your injury, work with your doctor to use proactive methods—such as bodywork or physical therapy—to help heal the injury rather than dulling the pain with medication. Only treatments that promote healing will address the source of the pain and ultimately put a stop to it.

DON'T CRAMP YOUR STYLE

One mild type of acute injury that you can effectively prevent and treat on your own is the muscle cramp, which essentially is a painful involuntary muscle contraction that commonly occurs during or immediately after exercise. Muscle cramps can prey upon triathletes of any fitness level and can be agonizing and detrimental to performance.

Exercise-induced muscle cramps can be caused by various things: a low blood glucose level, fluid loss, electrolyte imbalance, inadequate conditioning, overexertion, or fatigue. Unfortunately, the exact physiological mechanisms underlying cramps are not definitively known.

Some popular theories center on abnormal control of the nerves responsible for protecting muscles from getting into a hyperactive state. According to experts, poor fitness, stretching habits, and dehydration may play a role. But research is pointing to another culprit.

"Studies using a technique that measures electrical activity of muscles both during and after exercise reveal that muscle fatigue is the most likely cause of cramping," says Liz Applegate, PhD, a nationally recognized expert on nutrition and performance and a faculty member of the nutrition department at the University of California, Davis. "Fatigue brings on a series of internal changes that cause the muscle to enter a state of enhanced excitability. Then the involved muscle suddenly shortens, resulting in a painful muscle cramp."

You can help relieve exercise-induced muscle cramps immediately by stretching the afflicted muscle. This helps relax the spasm. After that, rest, fluids, and assessment of vital signs are also important to rule out other causes of cramping, such as heatstroke. If you experience recurrent cramping during or after exercise, speak with your doctor.

Of course, as with any other workout-related pain or injury, prevention is the best medicine for exercise-induced cramps. Your first level of defense is to develop a solid aerobic base of fitness by consistently following the Triathlete-in-Training program laid out in this book—and by increasing your physical activity gradually, especially if you were sedentary before beginning the program. This helps to get your muscles conditioned so they're better prepared for the rigors of exercising at higher intensities and long durations.

Your second level of defense is to drink adequate fluids before, during, and after exercise. That means downing two 8-ounce glasses of water before your workout, drinking 32 ounces every hour during exercise, and having two more 8-ounce glasses after your workout.

According to Ironman champion Tim DeBoom, preparing your muscles with an easy and gradual warmup is another important defense against sports cramps. "By easing into a chosen activity, I've found that my muscles work better and I rarely, if ever, cramp," he says. For information on how to warm up properly before exercise, see Chapters 4 and 8.

PREVENTING ILLNESS

Strengthening your immune system is one of the most valuable things you can do to stick to your training program and improve your quality of life. That means turning your immune system into a finely honed military commando unit!

It's part art, part science, and it begins where you spend most of your time, at home.

KNOW THAT HOME IS WHERE YOUR HEALTH IS

In an ever more chaotic and stressful world, our homes as physical and mental sanctuaries become increasingly important. Home is where we go to rest, to peel off life's heavy layers, and to recharge our bodies and minds. Because we spend roughly two-thirds of our lives at home, the quality of our living space directly impacts the quality of our lives. Most of us think about ways to boost our physical health, but few of us consider the health of our homes.

"Many people simply are not aware of how unhealthy their living environments might be," says Debra Lynn Dadd, author of home health books including *Home Safe Home*. "Individually, things such as toxic cleaners and reduced air circulation may have only a small impact, but collectively, they can have devastating effects on one's long-term health."

Here are several simple steps to boost the health of your home.

INCREASE AIR QUALITY AND CIRCULATION. I drive my wife crazy because I am constantly opening all the windows in our home to bring in fresh air. I've transformed our home into a low-grade wind tunnel. Granted I am likely going overboard, but I believe the quality of air inside your home is a key factor in your overall health. Your body depends on a rich, clean supply of oxygen to function properly and to maintain optimal health. Unfortunately, in an effort to conserve energy, most homes are equipped with airtight windows, heavily insulated walls, and even gaskets that seal up doors and windows. Although these advances are effective in keeping in heat and keeping out cold, they also trap contaminated, stale air inside your home.

Open your windows to increase cross-ventilation. Also, consider installing a high-efficiency particulate air (HEPA) filter in your home, which removes particles in the air by forcing it through screens with microscopic pores. These devices work well and aren't too expensive. An item like this is especially important if you live in a big city, where fresh air is harder to come by.

Better yet, get an ionizer such as the Ionic Air Purifier from Sharper Image. Ever notice how the air outside feels especially clean and fresh after a storm? One reason is that the air is filled with negative ions. By sealing off our homes to the environment, the ion content inside can become unhealthful. A good deal of scientific research has shown that both the type and the quantity of ions in our air can have profound effects on our health. An ionizer can help to reestablish a healthy balance of ions in your home.

POLLUTION-PROOF YOUR HOME. We are all subjected to varying levels of air pollution each day. It's inescapable. But did you know that air pollution in your home can be up to five times worse than air pollution outside? This is due in large part to the fumes from products we use to clean our homes. Our bodies are not equipped to neutralize the chemicals found in many household items such as drain cleaner, for example, and that can negatively stress our immune systems, leading to higher incidences of illness and fatigue.

Shelley Cartwright, a home-health expert for the health and lifestyle Web site www.dreamlife.com, identifies three common household products that have a deleterious effect on the health of our homes.

1. **BLEACH AND OTHER CHEMICAL CLEANERS.** Many cleaners contain nasty ingredients (despite their upbeat names and cute mascots). Try to substitute natural products whenever possible, such as Orange Glo furniture cleaner or BioWorx glass cleaner. Sweep through your home and place all cleaning supplies in a box. Then exile that box to the garage or basement—away from your primary living spaces. A sealed storage bin in a closet will also work when living quarters are tight.

2. **COOKING HARDWARE.** Gas stoves and appliances release fumes into the air. If you use gas, make sure that rooms containing gas appliances are well ventilated. The by-product of burning gas is carbon monoxide. If you heat your home with gas, a carbon monoxide detector is a must—it could save your life. Also, from time to time arrange for maintenance checkups on your appliances to check connections for leaks.

3. **CANDLES.** Many candles release soot and other pollutants into the air. Those made with metal wicks are especially toxic, because they release lead into the air as well. Paraffin itself (a petroleum-based ingredient used to make candles) is known to be a pollutant. Try unscented, natural bee's wax candles instead.

GO GREEN. "Houseplants, especially spider plants and Boston ferns, can help reduce formaldehyde and other airborne pollutants in your home," says Dr. Weil. Remember, plants use carbon dioxide (CO_2) as fuel and release oxygen—which is the opposite of human metabolism (we breathe in oxygen and release CO_2). That's why plants make perfect additions to your home. Pick up some plants at your local greenhouse or grocery store, and spread them liberally throughout the house. You will breathe noticeably fresher air in a matter of days.

REMOVE YOUR SHOES AT THE DOOR. I learned this ritual while competing in Japan. Removing your shoes before entering the house may seem like a relatively small aesthetic detail, but its benefits go deeper. The Japanese place high importance on this symbolic act, which is viewed as a show of reverence for their living spaces—a physical way of separating the chaos and confusion of the world from the peace and sanctity of the home. An added benefit is that it keeps your home cleaner, too, because it prevents you from dragging dirt and pollutants such as lawn chemicals throughout your home.

KEEP STRESS IN CHECK

Research has shown that chronic anxiety can weaken your immune system, making you more susceptible to illness. Here are some simple ways to help you de-stress and boost your ability to ward off disease.

LOWER THE VOLUME. After a long, hard day and a tough exercise session, you just want to go home and relax. When you get there, the kids are running around, all the lights are blazing and shining in your eyes, the doors are open—allowing the sound of traffic to enter your home—and the stereo is blaring rap music. If you close the door, sit the kids down, soften the lights, and play relaxing music, you can transform your home into a calm, nurturing one in minutes. Tune in to the volume level of your home right now, not just the sounds but the sights as well. Sometimes we don't realize how stressful our home environment is until we lower the volume. By doing this at least twice a week, you will notice a huge difference.

LAUGH. Laughter positively affects your physical and mental health. According to heart disease researchers, 40 percent of heart patients are less likely than healthy people to laugh in various situations.

"When you laugh, there are opium-like chemicals released by your brain," says Michael Miller, MD, researcher and director of the Center for Preventive Cardiology for the University of Maryland Medical System in Baltimore. Dr. Miller gave 300 people questionnaires to test their humor responses in various everyday circumstances and concluded, "These [chemicals] give you a feeling of well-being or even euphoria. We believe this causes you to relax and your blood vessels to dilate. Laughter lowers blood pressure and your pulse rate. My advice is to laugh heartily for at least five minutes a day. Try to see the funny side and take life less seriously."

Did you know that the average child laughs 300 times a day, whereas the average adult laughs only 7? Give yourself plenty of opportunities to laugh: Read entertaining books, watch comedies on TV, and share funny stories from your training with your exercise buddies.

CREATE NEW DAILY RITUALS. Our lives are shaped by daily habits. There are rules we follow automatically, whether or not they're good or bad for us. For example, when faced with choices of where to eat, some of us just default to the nearest fast-food joint. Or, without thought, we spring out of bed and begin checking e-mails and worrying about our day, without even greeting our spouse.

One of the best ways to start your day off on the right foot, so to speak, is to walk outside in the morning and spend a few moments taking in the fresh air. While you do this, quietly commit to yourself that you will remain as calm and as balanced as possible throughout your day. You'll find yourself in better spirits and more in control of your life.

DRINK YOUR WAY TO HEALTH

Although your environment and your habits have an effect on your health, so does what you feed your body. Chapter 10 outlines the specific nutrition needs of an active Triathlete-in-Training. Here I want to mention two ways you can use food and fluids to keep you feeling your best.

HYPER-HYDRATE. Many of us are in a slightly dehydrated state most of the time. Once every two weeks, drink as much water as your body can handle. This will flush out many toxins in your system and rehydrate the cells in every corner of your body. The day after you hyper-hydrate, you should feel appreciably healthier and more energetic.

SUPER-JUICE. I find juicing to be a powerful adjunct to a high-energy life, and I believe it can reduce the onset and duration of most bacterial infections. At the very first hint of flulike symptoms, my wife whips up what has become legendary in our household for preventing illness. Use a juicer to make this drink. It serves two.

Alexandra's Amazing Tonic

2	medium beets		3	celery stalks
1	grapefruit		1	2" x 2" piece fresh ginger
2	oranges		1	medium onion
1	lemon		4	cloves garlic (yes, it's antisocial, but trust me on this one!)
3	carrots			

Almost immediately upon drinking Alex's concoction, you will feel your immune system shift into overdrive. (I drank roughly 44 of them while writing this book, and I consider that the primary reason I didn't get sick during the editing process!)

12
PUT YOUR MIND TO IT

"A hero is no braver than an ordinary person,
but he is brave five minutes longer."

—RALPH WALDO EMERSON

Triathlon training will strengthen not only your body but also your mind in ways you never dreamed possible. Here are the mental actions integral to becoming both a better triathlete and a mentally tough, more self-confident human being. Practice them in your training and in your daily life.

ACCEPT PERSONAL ACCOUNTABILITY

You control your body. You make choices each day that result in the body you do or don't want. Blaming others—your boss, your spouse, your kids, your television—just disempowers you. Remember that you alone have the power to change your life right this very moment, and you've already wielded that power by taking on this triathlon challenge.

DEEPEN YOUR SELF-BELIEF

Do you know that the bumblebee should not be able to fly? I'm serious. After a series of tests, analyses, and observations, NASA scientists concluded that given the bee's body design and weight, there is simply no way the insect should be able to get off the ground. Thankfully, the scientists didn't tell the bumblebee, which blissfully takes to the air with little regard for humankind's most esteemed aviation experts.

We should all take a lesson from the bumblebee and refuse to allow others to define our limits. Critics will try to tear down our confidence and fill us with self-doubt. Yet often, those critics could not be more off-base in their assessments. Life is too short to let others dictate what we can and cannot do.

How do you tune out the critics and deepen your self-belief? The most permanent and powerful way I've learned is to build my body. In training for triathlons, the one thing that progressively grew in me, regardless of performance, setbacks, or outside opinion, was my self-esteem. I chronicled all of my successes, small and large, and my self-esteem grew steadily to the point where I believed I could do anything. You, too, can parlay fitness success into a durable self-confidence that will serve you well in daily life as well as in athletics. If you follow the program in this book, your body will show the effects, and you'll radiate confidence naturally.

ACTION ITEM: *On a week when you have relatively more free time, give a little extra focus to your training program. Push yourself a little more during workouts. Record your successes and every workout that you do in your Success Journal. Pursuing a challenging and admirable goal such as triathlon— and seeing your progress along the way—bolsters your self-esteem and critic-proofs you.*

SUMMON CONFIDENCE ON COMMAND

During moments of doubt or anxiety, maintaining confidence is paramount. However, it's precisely during those moments that we feel the least confident. The trick is to just hang in there until the stress or anxiety passes.

A mental technique known as *anchoring* is a quick and proven way to do this. "Anchoring involves focusing your attention, quieting your mind, drawing inspiration from past events in your life, and then bringing those feelings of confidence and optimism to the present moment," says Kate Hays, PhD, a Toronto psychologist and author of *Working It Out: Using Exercise in Psychotherapy.* When your confidence starts to slip, think back to one of your most challenging workouts and remember how you successfully completed it. Know that because you could achieve your goal then, you can do it again now.

Acting is another technique that transforms fear into confidence. Late in races, when pain reaches a crescendo, top athletes look thoroughly composed. Their secret is simple: They fake it. They simply act as if they *feel* fine, and they start believing that they *are* fine. Studies have shown that just pretending to feel positive emotions—for instance, by forcing a smile—elicits profound physical changes in the body, including the reduction of the stress hormone cortisol. Your motions determine your emotions. This illustrates the power of a strong mind-body connection.

ACTION ITEM: *The next time you find yourself in a difficult situation, fake total confidence. Take a deep breath, assume a strong position with both feet planted firmly on the ground, and smile. When you control your mood, you've gone a long way toward controlling the situation.*

DEVELOP GRACE UNDER PRESSURE

I will never forget the image of Australian runner Cathy Freeman in the 400-meter at the 2000 Summer Olympics in Sydney, Australia. Rounding the final bend for the finish, in a dead heat with her competitors, Freeman took a deep breath, raised her shoulders, lengthened her stride, and, like a Thoroughbred horse, swept out in front of the other runners. In the most painful part of her race, with the best racers in the world bearing down on her, Freeman found a way to gather her strength, literally in midstride, and win the Olympic gold medal. It was one of the most awesome displays I've ever seen.

"During moments of stress or pain," says Freeman, "most people tend to lose composure and focus, but I've found ways to summon up my best during those times. And it gives me a distinct edge in my sport and in my daily life." Responding with your best when you're feeling your worst is known as grace under pressure. It works to your advantage in any stressful situation, be it a traffic jam, a tense meeting, a tough workout, or even a national tragedy.

Many people took note of the astounding grace under pressure that Mayor Rudolph Giuliani showed when terrorists struck New York City on September 11, 2001. Calm and in charge, Giuliani dealt with the crisis as he strode through panicked crowds and held press conferences. Had he not been as well equipped—or as willing—to deal with adversity, New York may have been a lot worse off.

One's ability to deal with adversity has been quantified in what is known as the Adversity Quotient, or AQ. Essentially, your AQ determines how much control and hopefulness you can maintain during difficult times. And it can be improved with practice, according to Paul G. Stoltz, PhD, who coined the term in his book *Adversity Quotient*.

The following steps will help you increase your AQ to boost your grace under pressure during exercise, at your triathlon event, and in your life.

1. BREATHE. Take three very deep breaths in through your nose and out through your mouth while relaxing all of your muscles. Research has shown that the simple act of taking a deep, diaphragmatic breath can reduce your blood pressure and heart rate and give you a stronger sense of self-control.

2. COMMIT. Quietly vow to yourself that you'll rise to the occasion by remaining calm, cool, and composed. This step is powerful—you reassure yourself that you are in control.

3. ASSESS. Take an objective look at the situation: Is it truly as bad as you are making it out to be? Maintaining a healthier, broader perspective reduces your anxiety and boosts your AQ, enabling you to respond to stress more effectively.

4. THINK. Most of us tend to react to stress, and in doing so we let it control us. Instead, you should take responsibility for your anxiety. The word *responsibility* essentially means that you have the *ability* to *respond* however you want in any given situation. Strive to respond productively when faced with stress or anxiety.

"Character cannot be developed in ease and quiet. Only through experience of trial and suffering can the soul be strengthened, ambition inspired, and success achieved."

—HELEN KELLER

5. ACT. Do something constructive to resolve the conflict that's causing your stress. In a traffic jam, take the time to pull over in a safe place and call to let others know you'll be late. In a triathlon, if you experience a rough spot in the run, stop and take a few deep breaths and literally shake off the stress. Then stand up straight with confidence and put a genuine smile on your face. You'll be amazed by how much better you'll feel when you return to the run after such a reset.

CHANNEL STRESS INTO POSITIVE ACTION

Just as feelings of frustration, fear, and anger can render us powerless, they also can motivate us to extraordinary action. The next time you work out, identify a couple of things that are really bothering you. Visualize your negative emotions as a powerful red fuel pouring into your heart and lungs. Let the fuel fill you with energy. Focus that energy into efficient forward motion and visualize the fuel burning off as your workout progresses. As you cool down, let all of the remaining negative fuel just evaporate into the air, and picture an empty tank.

BELIEVE THAT YOU CAN BOUNCE BACK

Believing that you can get right back onto your program after a setback is essential to long-term success. Personal case in point: When I took time off to write this book, I lost a lot of my high-end physical fitness. But I always knew I could regain it. That made it a great deal easier to start training again after my downtime.

Perhaps the most effective and immediate strategy for getting back on track is putting the past behind you. The ability to immediately leave the past in the past is the hallmark of every great champion. Even if you haven't exercised in a month, know that you can go out your front door and start a run right now. You can cycle a few miles tomorrow morning. You can dive back into the water.

You are in control, and you can come back anytime you want. Wake up each day anew and do your very best on that day.

The average person loses focus during stressful situations. Remember that you're not average. You're a Triathlete-in-Training.

13
SEIZE THE RACE DAY

"There is only one real failure in life that is possible, and that is not to be true to the best we know."

—FREDERICK FARRAR, AMERICAN WRITER AND EDUCATOR

Race day is your time to shine, a culmination of all of your hard work and determination. It is your day to have fun—and to be heroic. It is a moment of truth in the most positive sense of the term. Many truths will be revealed to you on this day. You'll know what I mean when you cross the finish line and when you reflect on your race after it's over.

Race day will be one of the more exciting and inspiring days of your life, and you'll want to feel nothing less than on top of the world. Here's how to give and get your best on event day, whether your goal is to win in your age group or merely to finish.

RACE TIMELINE

Obviously, on race day you want to feel as strong, fit, confident, and well rested as possible. This time-based checklist will help you fully prepare with the least amount of worry. It begins one day before the race and leads you from the starting line to the finish.

24 HOURS

ATTEND THE PRERACE TALK. This question-and-answer session is typically held the day before the race and is a great opportunity for you to ask a race official any questions

YOUR EVENT DAY CHECKLIST

Here's a list of everything you'll need to take with you on race day.

Directions to the event: I cannot tell you how many times I tried to find my way to a triathlon only to get there minutes after the start. *Take directions.*

Backpack (to hold all of your clothes and accessories)

Warmup/prerace outfit: Most triathlons are held in the morning, so take loose, warm clothing in which to mill about. A light sweat suit or warmup suit will do the job. Or you may want to wear tight-fitting stretch pants, which warm your muscles without adding bulk to your legs, so you can even wear them when warming up on your bike.

Towel: This serves as your home base, to delineate your transition area and to clean any rocks or debris from your feet between sports. A nice, big fluffy towel is a relaxing thing to have in the hectic pace of the race. A simple bath towel works best. You may want to use a brightly colored one so that you can find it among the sea of towels.

Permanent black marker (to mark yourself for the race)

Swimsuit

Wet suit (if permitted)

Goggles: Also bring your antifog to prepare your goggles before the race.

Swim cap: You are required to wear the swim cap provided in your race packet for the swim leg of the event.

Race outfit (whatever you plan to wear for the swim, bike, and run portions of the race): As I mentioned in Chapter 3, some participants wear their swimsuits for the entire race, whereas others prefer to pull on bike shorts and a shirt over their suits for the bike and run portions.

Race number (preattached to your race outfit): Pin your race number onto the front of the shirt or jersey you plan to wear for

you may have about the event. Most questions asked at these meetings relate to the bike course, because that is the fastest and potentially most dangerous part of the race. You should find out the route of the bike course, whether there are any hazards such as metal grates or railroad tracks to watch out for, and whether the course is closed (meaning regular traffic will be rerouted away from the course) or open (meaning traffic will flow through the course as normal, so you'll need to be extra cautious).

PREP YOUR BIKE. Be sure the tires are clean of all rocks, glass, and other debris. Fill up your water bottles and insert them into the bottle cages. Tie your race number onto the top tube of your bike. (Your number will be in the race packet that you either received in the mail in advance of the race or picked up at the event site the day before the race. Either way, the packet should contain two race numbers—one for your bike and one for your shirt.)

the bike and run legs of the race. You can also use a race belt for your number. When using a belt, display your race number on your back during the bike leg, and then pull it around to your front for the run.

Bicycle

Bike helmet

Bike shoes

Bike gloves (optional but helpful for longer events such an Ironman event)

Tool kit and spare tire: If you get a flat tire during your warmup or the race itself, don't let that end your day. Be prepared to repair or replace the tire. Place the tool kit—complete with spare tube and tire levers—under the seat of your bike. You also need a pump with you; most are designed to attach to the bike's frame.

Running shoes

Running and biking socks

Sunglasses

Hat (optional)

Sunscreen (optional)

Food (energy bars/energy gels to give you a boost if your reserves run low during the race)

Water bottles

Postrace outfit: You may be modest and prefer not to strut around in your swimsuit or bike shorts once the race is over. If that's the case, bring a warmup suit to pull over your race duds, or simply use the same one you wore before the race began.

10 TO 12 HOURS

WIND DOWN. The night before the race, you're likely to be keyed up. To get a good night's sleep, begin winding down around 8 p.m. by lying down and watching TV or reading. Try to be asleep by 10 p.m. so you feel well rested in the morning.

3 HOURS

ARISE, TRIATHLETE! You want to give yourself enough time to fully wake up so you feel completely energized by the start of the event. Plus, having an extra hour or so to prepare for the race will make the day much more enjoyable. Even if you follow this checklist to a T, you'll find that things take longer than you anticipate—like setting up your transition area and standing in line at the porta-potties before the race begins.

WALK. Stroll outside, take a few deep breaths, and mentally center yourself for the spectacular day ahead. Reflect on all of your great training, relish the moment, and get excited.

HYDRATE. Drink one 8-ounce glass of water to rehydrate yourself after sleep.

2.5 HOURS

EAT A PRERACE MEAL. Have a light breakfast—a bagel, a smoothie, an energy bar or two, or whatever feels most comfortable to you. This allows you to digest the food before the race. Drink three cups of water to properly hydrate and a cup of coffee or two if you wish, to get primed for your event.

STRETCH. Start to loosen up using the stretches described in Chapter 8.

1.5 HOURS

HEAD TO THE RACE SITE AND CHOOSE YOUR TRANSITION SPOT. Securing the best transition area can be an event in itself and often resembles a 19th-century land grab. That's why it's preferable to arrive a little early.

SET UP YOUR TRANSITION AREA. Find a spot that feels comfortable and allows you to easily move from swim to bike and bike to run. You'll likely be in close quarters with your fellow participants, but no worries: Just lay down your towel to claim your space. Rack your bike in the provided rack, pump your tires, and spread out your equipment. You may want to look around to see how some of the more experienced triathletes set their transition spot. Place an extra bottle of water on your towel to remind you to carry it with you on the first half mile of your run.

PREPARE YOUR GOGGLES. Rub your antifog onto the inside and outside of the lenses of your goggles. Leave it on for a couple of minutes and then rub it off.

GET MARKED. Rather than wait in line for the body markers, have a friend or fellow racer mark you with your permanent black marker. Then return the favor and mark him, too. Just be sure to use the same size numbers and placements used by the official body markers. At almost every triathlon I've been in, they write your race number on your left shoulder and left calf. But check someone who's been officially marked just to be sure.

1 HOUR

WARMUP. Begin your physical warmup for the race. Take an easy 10- to 30-minute ride—called spinning—with a few light accelerations. Begin at the starting line so you can check out the course and map your way out of the transition area. Afterward, go for a 10- to 15-minute jog.

Once you're fully warmed up, return to your transition area and make sure all of your gear is in the proper place. Stretch those muscles that feel particularly tense to you. This is also a good opportunity to top off your energy stores with a carbohydrate drink or energy gel—and to take that all-important last-minute bathroom break.

20 MINUTES

WARM UP FOR YOUR SWIM. Saunter down to the water to warm up your swimming muscles. Try to find an area where fewer people are swimming, to avoid prerace collisions. You don't need to swim too long or hard; just warm up your upper body. Do a few accelerations, or pickups, of 20 to 30 seconds each and finish with three to five minutes of easy swimming. The quick sprints will help to get your body prepared. Forgo these and, trust me, you'll feel it during your swim.

5 MINUTES

PREPARE TO START. Make your way back to the start and do some last-minute stretching and limbering up: Swing your arms like windmills to loosen your shoulders, do some neck rolls to release any tension in your neck, and stretch or massage any other areas that feel particularly tight or sore. To stretch your lower back, lie on your back and lift your legs off the ground, bringing your thighs in toward your upper body. Then pull your knees to your chest for 2 to 3 seconds. Stretch your quadriceps while standing by lifting your lower leg behind you and pulling the heel of your foot into your buttocks. Make sure to keep your knees in line with each other as you hold the stretch for 2 to 3 seconds. Then shake out your leg and repeat on your opposite leg.

Once you're limber, take your place at the start. Triathlons generally begin in age-group waves, so locate your wave and file in. If the race organizers don't announce where each wave should gather, ask a race instructor where to go or look for the group of racers wearing the same color swim cap as yours.

DO A FINAL MENTAL PREPARATION. No matter how fit or prepared you are, you will get prerace butterflies. They're completely natural; everyone gets them. As in any stressful situation, however, mental preparation is less about the *presence* of butterflies than about getting them to *fly in formation.*

Channel your nervousness, doubts, and fears into efficient, calm, forward action. Take a few moments before the start to clear your mind and relax. *You're ready.* Anchor to the feelings of confidence instilled by all of your training. Now is the time to move all of your doubts and fears aside and open yourself up to the day you want to have.

If you find that you're very nervous, pull back and regain some perspective by looking around you. Many people regard the triathlon atmosphere as the best part of the sport. Scan the crowd of spectators and fellow participants. You will see smiles, laughter, and excitement. Draw energy from them. All triathletes know that everyone entered in the event has sacrificed a lot to be there, so they're incredibly supportive of one another. Tap into that energy and use it to overcome your nervousness and to enjoy the day more fully. Find those people who look a little nervous, and give them a hearty pat on the back. Triathlon is an individual pursuit, but you're out there with these other people who are each individually striving for their own greatness. Support them. They'll return the favor during the event.

30 SECONDS

BREATHE. Take three very deep breaths, clear your mind, and say to yourself, "Stay present in each moment, give your best every step of the way, and *have fun*!"

You're ready to roll.

A TRIO OF TRIATHLON TACTICS

If there are three things to focus on during your event, they should be refueling, breathing properly, and having fun. Those three things will get you to the line the fastest and in the best spirits.

REFUEL. If your triathlon lasts less than one hour, all you'll need to consume is water. You may want to carry one or two packets of energy gel on the bike just in case you feel you need the extra hit of sugar.

If your event lasts longer than one hour, you'll definitely need supplementary fuel in the form of energy gels, energy bars, or carbohydrate drinks. The general rule of thumb is to consume between 200 and 500 calories per hour after the first 45 minutes of your triathlon event.

BREATHE. During the excitement of a triathlon, you may forget to breathe deeply. Yet in terms of physical performance and comfort, maintaining a deep, rhythmical breathing pattern during your event is the second most important thing you can do, after staying well-hydrated. You must maintain good oxygen exchange throughout your entire race.

STAY IN THE MOMENT—AND HAVE FUN. No matter how meticulously you plan, not everything will go perfectly on race day. There will be times when you'll think there's absolutely no way you can finish. Every seasoned triathlete has experienced that feeling dozens of times. That's why a valuable skill to develop—in triathlons as in life—is to be open to every experience on race day: Do your best but embrace your mistakes, and have the ability and ego strength to push yourself and laugh at yourself at the same time. By staying present during your race, you can attend to any issue that may arise, whether it be dehydration, shallow breathing, or a tight hamstring.

Focus on doing your best every step of the way. Sometimes your best may be rocketing along through six-minute miles; sometimes it may be walking. At all times, just commit to going for another minute or another few steps, and then reassess. You'll find that if you break down the race to the immediate moment and take just a few more steps, you'll be more inclined to keep going. I've made these "minute-long promises" to myself throughout an entire Ironman run. They work like magic. By giving your best in every moment, you string together a series of your bests that invariably produces your very best performance.

Finally, remaining in the moment allows you to fully appreciate your experience rather than keeping your mind on the finish line. Enjoying every part of your triathlon and encouraging others along the way will make the process a great deal more rewarding to you. And when you can break through your fears and finish your triathlon, you gain the confidence to break through your fears and achieve great things in your life as well.

TRIATHLON RULES AND ETIQUETTE

Choose your starting position wisely. If the triathlon you've entered has a mass start (meaning all racers start at the same time) rather than starting in age-group waves, place yourself in the crowd according to your goals and ability. If you're a beginner who's there just to finish, start in the back so you don't get trampled. Likewise, if you're a strong swimmer and a contender, begin in the front of the pack so you don't end up trampling those in front of you.

DO NOT DRAFT ON THE BIKE. Unless you are competing in a "draft legal" event (which isn't likely), you cannot follow behind another cyclist to gain a drafting advantage. You can draft only in the swim and the run. Stay at least 10 bike lengths behind the rider in front of you.

KEEP YOUR HELMET BUCKLED WHENEVER YOU'RE TOUCHING YOUR BIKE. This means before you unrack it after the swim leg and until you rerack it after the bike leg. Take this rule very seriously—you can be disqualified for violating it.

DO NOT CROSS THE CENTER LINE. This speaks for itself. People have been killed crossing the center line during the bike leg of the triathlon. I don't care how competitive you are or how fast you want to go, never, ever do it.

BE AWARE OF OTHERS. This is particularly important on the bike. Nobody wants road rash. Stay aware at all times.

TREAT THE VOLUNTEERS WITH COURTESY AND RESPECT. Thank them when they give you water during the race, and follow their instructions without griping if they ask you to do something—like head to the swim start early.

AVOID THE URGE TO GO NUDE. You'd be amazed at what some people will do in transition areas! I've seen some seriously naked people over the years, and though they invariably give me a good laugh, the officials don't find them so funny.

RACE WALK-THROUGH

THE START

The start of a triathlon, unfortunately, can be the most physically and mentally stressful part of the race. If you are a strong, confident swimmer, you may want to position yourself near the front of the field so that you can swim with the better swimmers. However, if you are a slower swimmer or if you're nervous about open-water swimming, start the race out on the periphery. This will allow you to avoid that frenzied mass start and get into your own rhythm.

THE SWIM

When the gun goes off, settle into a nice, easy pace. One of the more common errors people make in triathlons is going out too fast during the swim. Your objective is to exit the water feeling strong and confident, not panic-stricken.

After the first minute, blend into the pack, which will have settled into a less frenetic pace. This will allow you to take advantage of the drafting effect. Drafting, or following behind someone else, is a savvy way to conserve energy. By breaking through the water, the person in front of you makes it easier for you to pass through that space. This can save you up to 30 percent in energy expenditure, because water is 1,000 times denser than air. So if you feel comfortable drafting someone else in the swim, do so.

If you bump into other swimmers, don't panic; you may want to stop swimming and take a couple of breaststrokes, get your bearings, and continue swimming. Keep in mind that nobody is out there to hurt you. Everyone is just trying to find his or her own little area in which to swim. You're all in this together.

Swim at a nice, steady pace and maintain good form. Remember to swim from your hips; they constitute your engine. Focus on your glide. You want to feel sleek, efficient, and under control.

The best thing you can do during the swim is to maintain physical and mental equanimity: deep, calm breathing and a loose, relaxed body. You may even want to talk to yourself: "Stay loose. Breathe." Trying to stay relaxed may seem counterintuitive—particularly if you are out to notch a good time—but if you watch world-class athletes during top performances, you will see that even in the midst of great effort, they appear composed.

As you approach the shore, stand up and exit the water when you can feel the ground with your hand during your swim stroke.

THE FIRST TRANSITION

As you emerge from the swim, you'll feel a little wobbly. That's perfectly natural. I've seen top pros get out of the water looking like babies taking their first steps. Most of your blood will still be in your arms, shoulders, and back, so your legs won't work too well in those first few steps.

For this reason, it isn't a good idea to sprint out of the water into the transition area. It's better to stand up slowly, walk for 10 to 15 seconds, and then begin jogging to your spot. That will allow your body to more efficiently transition from a horizontal position to a vertical position, making the rest of your race more comfortable.

As you approach your transition spot, remove your wet suit (if you're wearing one), goggles, and swim cap and set them on your towel. (Please don't hurl your items discus-like. You won't save any time, and you'll likely lose them in the Transition-Area Vortex, a force more powerful at making objects disappear than the Bermuda Triangle.)

If you have a race outfit other than your swimsuit, pull it on. Buckle your helmet and don your shades.

If you're cycling in running shoes, put them on and go. If you're using clipless pedals, strap on your cycling shoes—assuming they aren't already attached to the bike. (Some people attach their cycling shoes to the pedals before the race and strap them on while on the bike to save time. This skill takes practice.)

Pay extra attention to your breathing during transition so that you can reoxygenate your body and calm your mind before the bike portion begins.

THE BIKE

As you roll your bike out of the transition area, be aware of the other participants who are also trying to exit. Mount your bike and begin riding.

With the crowd cheering you on, you may be tempted to sprint out of the transition area. You can wave and high-five the crowd, but try not to sprint. It's to your advantage to ride the first few kilometers of the bike portion at a conservative pace. Here's why: Your body requires some time to move its attention and blood supply from your shoulders and arms to your legs. By building your effort slowly through the bike portion, you will not only go faster but also feel appreciably better.

On the bike, drink some water or an energy-replacement drink after about 10 minutes of pedaling. Try to maintain good form on the bike and keep your breathing deep, diaphragmatic, and into your belly. Ride at a nice, strong, steady pace based on how you feel. Encourage the other bikers as they go by—or as you pass them!

WHAT IF I "FLAT"?

Getting a flat tire during your event can test your resolve and your grace under pressure. I was tested in a race in Tahiti when, in second place overall and bearing down on the leader, with three kilometers to go on the bike, my front tire went flat. I was so close to the transition area that I decided to keep riding rather than take the time to fix it. I can't repeat the steady stream of obscenities that flowed forth from my mouth, in multiple languages, but I can tell you that my reaction was totally counterproductive. My heart rate rose, my blood pressure skyrocketed, and I lost control of a great race.

The best thing you can do when you realize you have a flat tire is to calmly dismount your bike, take a very deep breath, and relax. Your race isn't over—you never know what's going on up ahead of you. Stay calm, move quickly, and fix your flat tire.

Tahiti notwithstanding, I've come back from flats to win races. You can do the same.

With roughly one kilometer to go on the bike, move your attention to the run. Shift into an easier gear and ramp your effort down a level, or spin out your legs. Sit up and stretch your back and your calves. You can even clip out of your pedals and shake out your legs. Don't worry about losing time. Those 30 seconds of stretching will give you a minute in the run and make you feel much better.

THE SECOND TRANSITION

As you enter the bike-to-run transition, dismount your bicycle and walk or jog it to your transition spot. Rack your bike and take off your helmet. Slide off your cycling shoes and slip on your running shoes. Acknowledge your support crew with as much energy as you can muster. Put on your running hat (if you plan to wear one), pick up your water bottle, and jog out of the transition area.

The overwhelming consensus in triathlon is that "T2," or the second transition, is the less pleasant of the two. Your legs may feel as if they were filled with lead. That's the bad news.

The good news is that this feeling is entirely natural. Everyone is in the same boat as you are.

THE RUN

This is the final leg of your journey. The run portion of your triathlon will likely be the most challenging because of the accumulated fatigue from the swim and bike portions of the event. Be mentally prepared for that.

It's perfectly acceptable to walk for the first half-mile of the run. Beginning with a walk will serve as a gentle wake-up call to your running muscles and will give you a brief mental break after your swim and bike ride.

You will feel better as the run progresses. Stay calm, cool, and composed as you stride along with strong, confident, graceful fluidity. Also, be sure to drink plenty of water during your run.

Late in the run is where the most attrition occurs. Yes, you want to finish, but please don't risk your health in your determination to do so. If you feel any sharp shooting pains or recurring dizziness or light-headedness, by all means stop immediately.

However, if you simply feel fatigue and aches and pains as a result of exertion, push right through that. In fact, I have discovered this one incontrovertible truth about tri-

THE POWER IN MONITORING POWER

Arguably the biggest and most damaging mistake triathletes make during events is over-pushing the bike leg. If you push your body too hard, you will experience a decline in performance (and enjoyment) over this leg of the race—and you will have a slower and more difficult run.

The best way to manage the bike leg is to measure your power output. This ensures that you put out just enough power to perform your best without hurting your performance by overdoing it.

There are several devices that measure power: SRM (www.srm.de), PowerTap (www.powertap.com), and Stages Cycling (www.stagescycling.com). They are not cheap, ranging from $700 to $1,400. However, if you are interested in maximizing your performance—and enjoyment—of the sport, and if you hope to race longer triathlons, you may want to explore power meters.

It's important that you work with a trained professional to test your power output on the bike. This person will bring you into a lab and identify your optimal power range based on heart rate and other factors. Once you know this range, you simply watch your power meter during the bike leg of the triathlon. If you stay in your range, you will ride with power and strength and get off the bike feeling fresh for the run.

athlon, and all organized athletic events for that matter: The more you challenge yourself, the deeper you dig, the more richly rewarded you are at the finish—and for the rest of your life.

Over the final 500 meters of your event, push past what you thought was impossible. Smash to pieces all of your doubts, fears, limits, and excuses—break free from those constraints as you soar across the finish line. Remember the scene in the movie *Forrest Gump* where Forrest seems to run off his leg braces? Pretend you're Forrest.

THE FINISH

The final 100 meters of your triathlon event will indeed be very special. Relish your accomplishment. Triathlon gives you the opportunity to experience feelings of courage and heroism. Let your feelings of achievement and excitement well up and explode forth. You may even want to high-five the crowd. Yes, I'm serious—they'll love it, and it will make you feel like the rock star that you are. Remember, to the spectators, you are among the fitness elite. The fact that you're crossing the finish line at a triathlon is mind-boggling to most people watching the event.

14
NOW WHAT? THE MORNING AFTER AND THE REST OF YOUR LIFE

"The pursuit of truth and beauty is a sphere of activity in which we are permitted to remain children all of our lives."

—ALBERT EINSTEIN, PHYSICIST

You've done it! You've scaled the summit, so to speak, and you not only have emerged alive, you likely feel more invigorated than ever. Congratulations! What you did was nothing short of extraordinary. Believe it or not, you are now in the top 1 percent of the fitness pyramid—in the world.

You invested a good deal of your time and energy into this quest. You are probably thinking, "Now what?" Do you train for another triathlon? A single-sport event? Should you do nothing at all?

After your event, you may feel what are called postrace blues. This is a well-identified psychological and physiological phenomenon that even Olympic champions suffer from. Postrace blues are the feelings of emptiness, confusion, and even depression that can occur after an individual undertakes a long mental or physical buildup to an event. It can hit as soon as the day after the event. The greater the investment in the endeavor, the higher the predisposition toward, and depth of, postrace blues.

Some may simply be burned out from the experience and quit exercising altogether. Others will remain inspired by the journey and continue to do triathlons and organized races as a means to stay healthy, fit, energetic, and youthful. Indeed, I hope you fall into the latter category. If you train for and do just one athletic event per year for the rest of your life, you'll live longer and better. That, I assure you.

However, it isn't necessary to continue doing athletic events to maintain your health and fitness. The mission of this book was to encourage you to complete just one triathlon—and that the process of doing so would provide you with an array of life-altering benefits.

You indeed finished your event, and without a doubt your life has changed in the process. But all you really need to do to maintain good health for the rest of your life is simply apply the concepts of smart exercise from this book to a two- to four-hour-a-week exercise program. That's it. Remember: The six to eight weeks you already invested in your body have created a foundation of fitness upon which you can maintain optimal health and fitness for decades to come.

If you want to maintain a higher level of fitness and have decided to do more triathlons, then good for you! That's a decision you'll never regret. Simply go back to Chapter 4 and graduate to the next level program. This time use your experience to train a little harder and a little smarter. If you're ready to move beyond Fitness Level IV, get yourself a copy of *The Triathlete's Training Bible* by Joe Friel. This book is the definitive guide to competitive-level triathlon performance. Who knows: You could wind up a sponsored professional. You may become such a success in your age group that companies begin giving you athletic gear at sharply discounted rates—just to have you use their stuff! Hey, why not?

Regardless of what you decide, ultimately the answer to "Now what?" can be found in the soul of your quest. Throughout this book, you were encouraged to focus on the process—on the enduring qualities of self-actualization, achievement, courage, compassion, confidence, stress management, self-esteem, and a seize-the-day sense of adventure. Those are your "Now whats." Whether or not you feel it or believe it, you are a different person now. Your habits, your waistline, your diet, your dreams have likely changed for the better.

You are a Triathlete. If you can be that, you can be anything. The world is your oyster. Sure, it's a cliché. But it's absolutely true.

FINAL THOUGHTS AND INSPIRATION

I have always believed that training for organized athletic events helps all kinds of people lead healthier, more passionate, more deeply fulfilled lives. Doing an athletic event is a quest that inspires, motivates, and compels us all to give, and be, our best.

I am also a believer in the power of the human spirit. I have watched seemingly ordinary people do unmistakably extraordinary things. To refresh my memory every year, I travel to the big island of Hawaii to watch the Ironman Triathlon World Championships. If you get the chance, watch the NBC coverage wire to wire one year. You'll be deeply moved by the heroic, indomitable spirit of these people. You may even be moved to tears. I am. Every year.

Although you should use the advice in this and other books to learn more about your body, there is one expert who knows best: you. Always trust your instincts and let your body have the final word when it comes to how you move, how you eat, and how you live your life.

That is what the triathlon is all about: giving you a supreme sense of self-reliance, showing you in a tangible way that you are capable of anything you set your mind to. It will help you take control and live exactly the way you want, on your terms, so that you can live your best life.

In training for and completing your triathlon, you likely received a lot of support along the way. Now that the event is over, it's your chance to give back and pass along what you have learned. To the extent that you can inspire and instruct those around you to lead better lives—by sharing your secrets and your passions—do so. Offer to give advice to newcomers in organizations such as Team in Training to benefit leukemia or breast cancer. Get kids involved in triathlon by starting a club in your hometown. Compel your friends to do just one triathlon; hand them this book. You can even do something as simple as high-fiving a stranger as you run by on a morning jog. This can be a very powerful affirmation of what they're doing.

These things solidify your long-term commitment to your health while inspiring others to reach new heights, boosting the collective health of our world. There is no greater gift than that. And, as Americans, we have never needed each other's help more in the areas of overweight and exercise.

I hope this book has given you the tools you need to keep the passion afire in your workouts—not only for these two months but also for life. I hope your individual quest to train for and complete a triathlon has helped you achieve a higher level of well-being, self-confidence, self-esteem, and personal fulfillment.

As you take the next step, remember this maxim: Motivation follows action. This whole process began with a single step. Don't be afraid to take that first step toward reaching your dreams, whatever they may be. That step will lead to another and another, giving way to momentum with a life of its own, one that leads you inexorably to that hallowed finish line where fulfillment, exhilaration, and pure unadulterated joy await you.

Seize the day, seize the moment. Take that step.

I wish you all the best.

TRIATHLON TALK

AN ENLIGHTENING AND ENTERTAINING GLOSSARY OF TERMS

One obstacle many of us face in reaching our health and fitness goals is making sense of the commonly used jargon—understanding exactly what the heck people are saying. Even as an experienced athlete, I don't understand much of what in God's name is being said.

Here is an example: "During your next cross-training session, do a descending set of reverse pyramid intervals. That'll increase your basal metabolic rate. Afterward replenish your depleted glycogen stores with a high-glycemic food unit."

Translation: "Run strong and enjoy your bagel."

By better understanding the language that is used in health and fitness circles, you will get more out of what you read, you will make more informed choices about what you buy, and you'll have a lot more fun! Here is a list of commonly used health and fitness terms.

Antioxidants (n): Vitamins A, C, and E and the minerals zinc and selenium. Antioxidants protect your cells by reacting with the oxygen (*anti* means "against"; *oxy* means "oxygen"). Normally, we think of oxygen as a positive thing—after all, it's what we breathe. But oxygen has a dark side. Here's why: When you exercise, oxygen enters your bloodstream at an accelerated rate. This can oxidize your cells, similar to how the paint on your car might oxidize by being exposed to the elements. There is now enough research to support supplementation with an antioxidant formula each day to help counteract the negative effects of oxygen.

Basal metabolic rate (BMR) (n): This is a measurement of how many calories you expend at rest. For example, a 120-pound woman might burn 1,500 calories per day. Some people are blessed with higher BMRs and tend not to put on body fat as easily. (Yes, we dislike these people!) The good news is that your BMR can be increased through exercise. By working out in the morning, you increase your metabolism, which helps to burn more calories through the remainder of your day.

Bonk (v): To hit the wall or, in extreme cases, to blow sky high. This term was coined by marathon runners who would run out of energy, or hit the wall, between the 18-mile and 20-mile marks in marathons. It was later discovered that these athletes had simply run out of muscle glycogen. When you bonk during exercise, you literally feel like you've run out of gas. To prevent this from happening, consume a small snack an hour before exercise and 200 to 300 calories per hour during exercise in the form of a sports drink or energy gel. On race day you'll need to consume even more—200 to 500 calories per hour—because you'll be operating at a higher intensity.

DQ'ed (v): To be disqualified. A few things can get you disqualified from a triathlon, such as drafting on your bike. Play it cool and keep your distance from the cyclist in front of you. Unbuckling your cycling helmet while handling your bike can also get you DQ'ed.

Endorphin (n): This word is abbreviated from *endogenous morphine*, which means "a morphine produced naturally in the body." Your body produces endorphins to counteract stress or pain. You've likely heard the term *runner's high*. This is a state associated with the endorphin rush brought on by the act of running. Exercise is a form of positive stress and brings about the production of endorphins. It's also one reason why you're a lot more agreeable to be around after a good workout!

Fish (v): To catch up with the swim specialists in triathlon events. Most of us lose lots of time relative to others in the swim, but that's okay. We end up fishing the faster swimmers on the bike and run, anyway. In other words, reeling them in. A very good feeling.

Flip it (v): To turn around on the bike. If you are cycling, and you and a friend have pedaled too far ahead of another friend, turn to your buddy and say, "Hey, Sally, we'd better flip it and go find Brad." Cooler than cool.

Go large (v): To give your all. To pull out all the stops and give your very best in a workout or event, as in "Yeah, I was awesome—I went so large in that run!"

Pickups (n): A series of short sprints. For example, you could do a few pickups as part of your warmup for the swim leg of your event. These are essentially quick accelerations where you pick up the pace and then take it slow for a bit before the next pickup.

Rocket fuel (n): Food that makes you feel great and go strong. Examples of rocket fuel are peanut butter, coffee, and ice cream (this combination is only to be eaten the night before a big training day or event). During training, rocket fuel would be something like Cytomax energy drink or an energy gel.

Sets/reps (n): Strength-training terms. Reps, short for repetitions, is the number of times you lift a weight or perform an activity. Sets is how many groups of those repetitions you do, normally with a period of 20 seconds or more of rest in between each set. So, two sets of 10 reps of crunches would mean two separate groups of 10 crunches each.

Spin out (v): This means to do some easy pedaling with little or no resistance. It's helpful to spin out as part of your warmup and cooldown.

Spot reduction (n): One of the more common myths in the health and fitness marketplace. The notion here is that by working on a certain area of your body, you can lose fat in that area. For example, situps help you lose the fat on your stomach. Unfortunately, spot reducing has never been supported by credible research: You simply cannot lose fat around your abs by doing situps. That's why most of those abdominal machines do not work for people who are overweight. The best way to reveal your abdominal muscles is to burn the fat around them, and for that you must do regular aerobic exercise.

T1 and T2 (n): Stands for transition 1 and transition 2. In the sport of triathlon, T1 is when you're moving from the swim leg to the bike leg of the race, and T2 is when you go from the bike to the run. Learning to make smooth transitions is key to your success in a triathlon.

Take a digger (v): To fall. A term commonly used in mountain biking, as in "Dude, you were riding so well until you took that digger and landed on your frontal cortex!" Needless to say, diggers are to be avoided. To do that, work on your riding technique—balance and coordination—and always be aware of your surroundings.

Thermogenic (n): Thermogenesis is loosely defined as the production of heat in an animal body by physiological processes. Many popular nutritional supplements boast a fat-burning effect by increasing your resting metabolism or thermogenesis. The problem is that these supplements usually contain harmful, and sometimes dangerous, stimulants such as ephedrine. The reality is that thermogenic supplements do not increase your metabolism anywhere near as much as a simple walk around the block would. Stick to exercise and avoid the pills. You'll save money and protect your health.

Wheelsucker (n): This is a person who rides right behind you on the bike to take advantage of your draft. In cycling, this is not only legal, but also smart. But if someone is doing this during a triathlon event, that's illegal. If you're just out there to have fun, however, then let them do it—they probably desperately need the relief—and take it as a compliment to your impressive strength! But if it's annoying you, simply say, "Hey there, wheelsucker, get off my wheel." That'll take care of the situation.

RECOMMENDED READING

The following are what I consider to be the definitive guides on the sport of triathlon and health and fitness in general.

- **SWIMMING:** Sheila Taormina, *Swim Speed Strokes for Swimmers and Triathletes* (Velo, 2014)
- **CYCLING:** Joe Friel, *The Cyclist's Training Bible* (Velo, 2009); Emily Furia and the editors of *Bicycling* magazine, *The Big Book of Bicycling* (Rodale, 2010)
- **RUNNING:** Steve Magness, *The Science of Running* (Origin Press, 2014); Nicholas Romanov and Kurt Brungardt, *The Running Revolution* (Penguin Books, 2014)
- **TRIATHLON (THE NEXT LEVEL):** Joe Friel, *The Triathlete's Training Bible* (Velo Press, 2009)
- **SPORTS NUTRITION:** Matt Fitzgerald, *Racing Weight* (Velo Press, 2012)
- **GENERAL NUTRITION:** Roberta Larson Duyff, *American Dietetic Association Complete Food and Nutrition Guide* (Houghton Mifflin Harcourt, 2012)

- **MIND-BODY:** Jim Afremow, *The Champion's Mind* (Rodale, 2014)
- **EXERCISE MOTIVATION:** Joe De Sena, *Spartan Up!* (Houghton Mifflin Harcourt, 2014)
- **PILATES:** Rael Isacowitz and Karen Clippinger, *Pilates Anatomy* (Human Kinetics, 2011)
- **YOGA:** Sivananda Yoga Vedanta Centre, *Yoga: Your Home Practice Companion* (DK Adult, 2009)
- **STRETCHING:** Kristian Berg, *Prescriptive Stretching* (Human Kinetics, 2011)
- **WELLNESS/HEALTH:** Andrew Weil, *8 Weeks to Optimum Health* (Ballantine Books, 2007)

CUSTOMIZED BENEFITS AND SAVINGS FOR YOUR NEXT TRIATHLON

Active.com—one of the industry's most popular resources to register online for triathlons nationwide—offers unique benefits for triathletes.

Active Advantage (http://advantage.active.com), a premier athlete membership program, offers daily discounts and benefits to get you to your next triathlon. Accessed online, the program delivers discounts on airfare (including bicycle equipment waivers for some airlines), lodging, rental cars, sports gear and apparel, and race entries.

ACKNOWLEDGMENTS

Thank you to my wonderful agent Jane Dystel—and to Mark Weinstein and the Rodale team for your unwavering commitment to impeccable work.

INDEX

Boldface page references indicate photographs. Underscored references indicate boxed text.

A

Ab Crunch, 118, 148, **148**
Abdominal muscles
exercises for, 118, 147–49,
147–49, 148
six-pack, 148
Ab machines, 148
Accountability, accepting personal,
231
Active-isolated stretching (AIS),
114–15
Acupuncture, 216–17
Adenosine triphosphate (ATP), 190
Adrenaline, 61
Adversity Quotient, 234
Aerobic cycle, 56
Aerobic exercise
combining with strength
training, 20
fat metabolism, 193
running as, 99–100
warmup for, 53
for weight loss, 125
Aerobic fitness
building with running, 19
exercising in target heart rate
zone, 56
Aero position, 88, **88**
Age
as excuse, 28–29
muscle loss with aging, 116
Air quality and circulation,
increasing, 225–26
AIS, 114–15
Alcohol, 203, 204
All-or-nothing approach, 33

Amino acids, 191, 193
Anatomical adaptation, 119
Anchoring, 232, 242
Antifog solution, 38–39, 70, 240
Anxiety
immune system weakened by,
227
over workouts, 107
taking responsibility for your,
234
Arm Swings, 121, **121**
Arm warmers, 46–47
ATP, 190
Autumn, training program for, 185
Avocado
Spinach and Boiled Egg Chopped
Salad with Avocado, 203

B

Back
lower-back exercises, 150–51,
150–51
stretches
Back Bend, 220, **220**
Cobra, 118, 147, **147**, 220,
220
Lying Back Stretch, 115, **115**,
118, 120, 150, 220, **220**
Upper-Back Stretch, 118, 130,
130
upper-back exercises, 130–34,
130–34
Back Bend, 220, **220**
Back pain, avoiding
breaks, taking throughout the
day, 219

posture, 218–19
stretching, 115, 219–20, **220**
Back Squat, 128, **128**
Ball Drape, 118, 147, **147**
Banana
Power Smoothie, 197
Bath, hot, 214–15
Beach, running on, 103
Belt, sports, 48
Benchmarks, 164–65
Benefits of triathlon training,
1–13
inspirational, 9–13
becoming your best, 9
hero to your kids, 12
motivation to others, 12
sense of purpose, 9
setting positives in motion,
12–13
life changing, triathlon as,
10–11
mental, 5–8, 7
mood improvement, 6
motivation to exercise, 6–7
productivity increase, 5–6
strengthening weaknesses,
7–8
stress management, 6
physical, 2–5
energy increase, 4
health improvement, 5
injury prevention, 4–5
longer life, 5
weight loss, 2–3
workout efficiency, 4
younger look and feel, 3–4
social, 8
Bent-Knee Pushup, 142, **142**

Biceps exercises, 152, **152**
Biceps Stretch, 152
Bicycle
    cost, 40
    fit, 83–87, **85**, 213
    indoor bike trainer, 41
    mountain bike, 40–41
    prerace prep, 238
    selecting, 39–40
    tandem, 21
Bike shoes, 42–43
Bleach, 226
Blues, postrace, 251–52
Body fat
    burning
        for abdominal appearance,
            148
        with aerobic exercise, 125
    energy stored in, 193
Body image, 2
Body markers, 240
Bodywork, 215–17
    acupuncture, 216–17
    chiropractic, 217
    cost, 215, 216
    massage therapy, 215–16
    rolfing, 216
    tips for, 217
Booties, 47
Bouncing back, 235
Bra, sports, 48
Breakfast
    meal plans
        2000-calorie diet, 198
        2500-calorie diet, 199–200
        3000-calorie diet, 201
    race day, 240
Breaks, taking throughout the day,
    219
Breakthrough sessions, 166–68
Breathing
    power, 61–62
    prerace, 242
    for sense of self-control,
        234
    during strength training,
        116–17
    in swimming stroke, 74
    triathlon tactics, 243
Bricks, 104, 164
Bridge, 151, **151**
Buchanan Moment, 39
Bulking up, 123
B vitamins, 194

C

Cable Squat, 127, **127**
Caffeine, 197
Calf exercises, 144–46, **144–46**
Caloric needs, calculating, 198
Calories
    burned in
        fun activities, 24
        running, 99
    consumed during race, 243
    in fats, protein, and
        carbohydrates, 193
Cap, 48
Carbohydrate drink, 241, 243
Carbohydrates, 190–91
    calories per gram, 193
    in postworkout meal, 56
Carbo-loading, 191
Celiac disease, 206
Checklist, event day, 238–39
Chest exercises, 140–43, **140–43**
Chest Fly, 141, **141**, 143, **143**
Chest Press, 118, 140, **140**, 143
Chest Stretch, 118, 140, **140**
Chicken
    Chicken Kebabs, 205
    Gluten-Free Crunchy Chicken
        Waldorf Salad, 207
Chickpeas
    Chickpea Salad, 205
Children
    being a hero to, 12
    laughter by, 228
    play, 24
    training with, 20, 20–21
Chiropractic, 217
Chronic fatigue syndrome, 61
Circatrigintan rhythms, 106
Circulation
    reverse, increasing, 221
    sitting effects on, 218–21
Cleaners, chemical, 226
Climate, as excuse, 30
Clothing. *See* Gear; *specific items*
Cobra, 118, 147, **147**, 220, **220**
Coffee, 197, 203
Cold-weather gear, 46–48, 102
Commuting, bicycle, 94
Confidence
    anchoring to thoughts of, 242
    building with
        benchmark workouts, 165
        breakthrough sessions, 166

    faking, 233
    summoning on command, 232–33
Contract, Fitness-For-Life, 65
Cooldown, 56, 109, 123
Core
    exercises for, 154–56, **155–56**
    stretching, 219–20, **220**
Cortisol, 233
Cost
    of bodywork, 215, 216
    as excuse, 29–30
    of exercise gear, 35–48
Course, reviewing, 163
Cramps
    muscle, 223–24
    stomach, 197
Cravings, sugar, 107
Creatine kinase, 114
Critics, 232
Cross-training, 3
Crunches, Simple, 156, **156**
Cycling, 83–98
    aero position, 88, **88**
    bike fit, 83–87, 213
        biomechanical synchronicity,
            84–85
        frame size, 84
        handlebar position, 86
        saddle position, 84–85, **85**
        seasonal changes, 87
        shoe/cleat alignment, 86–87
    body shaping, 3
    core strength and, 154
    flat tire, 91, 247
    gear, 43–44, 90, 94, 213 (*see
        also specific items*)
    group riding, 91–92
    hand signals, 89, **89**
    interval training, 57, 97–98
    mountain biking, 92–94
    power output, measuring, 248
    race walk-through, 246–47
    reverse loop, 86
    safety, 88–90, 91, 93–94
    technique, 87
    Training Zone I, 95–96
        endurance, 96
        soft-pedal, 95
    Training Zone II, 96–97
        hills, 96–97
        tempo, 97
    Training Zone III, 97–98
        indoor trainer, 98
        short intervals, 97–98

Training Zone IV, 98
triathlon rules and etiquette, 244
to work, 94
workout, 86, 95–98
Cycling gloves, 44
Cycling shorts, 43

D

Dairy products, 202–3
Dehydration, 196, 223, 228
Detoxifying, with juice fasting, 208–9
Diagnosis, proper injury, 221–22
Diarrhea, 197
Diets, 202–8
    gluten free, 206–7
    high carbohydrate, low fat, 191
    Mediterranean, 204–5
    Paleo, 202–4
    vegan, 207–8
Dinner meal plans
    2000-calorie diet, 199
    2500-calorie diet, 200
    3000-calorie diet, 202
Distance
    of competitions, 22
    training by time and intensity
        instead of, 55
Doctor, working with your, 167
Dogs, 100, 107
Drafting, 244, 245
Dumbbell Curl, 152, 152
Dumbbells
    benefits of, 117
    suggested weights, 119
Dumbbell Squat, 124, 124

E

Eggs
    as protein source, 191
    Spinach and Boiled Egg
        Chopped Salad with
        Avocado, 203
Elevating your legs, 221
Embarrassment, 26–27
Endurance
    cycling, 96
    running, 105, 109
    swimming, 80

Energy
    increase with triathlon training, 4
    lack as excuse, 25–26
Energy bars, 191, 209
Energy gel, 209, 241, 243
Enjoying the journey, 31
Equipment. See Gear
Essential amino acids, 191
Etiquette, triathlon, 244
Event, choosing, 161–62
Event day checklist, 238–39
Excuses, 15–33
    background lacking in sports, 30, 32
    boring nature of exercise, 24–25
    climate, 30
    cost, 29–30
    distance and time of competition, 22
    embarrassment, 26–27
    energy lack, 25–26
    Excuse List, compiling, 16–17
    first step, 32
    guidance lack, 32–33
    injury, pain, or illness, 27–28
    motivation lack, 22–24
    physical shape, 30, 32
    rebuttals to, 17
    support is missing, 29
    time limitations, 17–21
    weight, stature, or age, 28–29
Exercise(s)
    abdominal, 147–49, 147–49, 148
        Ab Crunch, 118, 148, 148
        Ball Drape, 147, 147
        Cobra, 147, 147
        Roman Chair Run, 149, 149
        Weighted Crunch, 149, 149
    biceps, 152, 152
        Biceps Stretch, 152
        Dumbbell Curl, 152, 152
    as boring, 24–25
    calf, 144–46, 144–46
        Floor Calf Raise, 145, 145
        Lying Calf Stretch, 144, 144
        Seated Calf Raise, 146, 146
        Stair Calf Raise, 145, 145
        Standing Calf Stretch, 144, 144
    chest, 140–43, 140–43
        Bent-Knee Pushup, 142, 142
        Chest Fly, 141, 141, 143, 143

Chest Press, 118, 140, 140, 143
Chest Stretch, 140, 140
Pushup, 142, 142
core, 154–56, 155–56
    Pelvic Tilts, 155, 155
    Plank, 155, 155
    Side Plank, 155, 155
    Simple Crunches, 156, 156
family, getting fit with, 20, 20–21
getting back into swing, 33
hamstring, 135–39, 135–39
    Hip Lift, 136, 136
    Lying Hamstring Stretch, 135, 135
    Single-Leg Hamstring Curl, 138, 138
    Stability Ball Leg Curl, 136, 136
    Standing Hamstring Curl, 139, 139
    Standing Hamstring Stretch, 135, 135
    Standing Leg Curl, 137, 137
intensity, 55, 58–59, 77, 108–9, 166
location of, 25
lower-back, 150–51, 150–51
    Bridge, 151, 151
    Lying Back Stretch, 115, 115, 118, 120, 150, 220, 220
    Superman, 150, 150
morning workout, 19
motivation to exercise, 6–7
Pilates, 156–60, 157–60, 158
    The Hundred, 157, 157
    One-Leg Circle, 159, 159
    Single-Leg Stretch, 160, 160
quadriceps, 124–29, 124–29
    Back Squat, 128, 128
    Cable Squat, 127, 127
    Dumbbell Squat, 124, 124
    Leg Press, 129, 129
    Lunge, 118, 125, 125
    Step Up, 126, 126
stopping when injured, 212–13
Superman, 118
triceps, 153, 153
    Overhead Triceps Press, 153, 153
    Triceps Stretch, 153, 153

Exercise(s) *(cont.)*
   upper-back, 130–34, **130–34**
      Lat Pulldown, 133, **133**
      One-Arm Row, <u>118</u>, 130, **130**
      Pullover, 132, **132**
      Seated Cable Row, 134, **134**
      Seated Overhead Press, 131, **131**
      Upper-Back Stretch, 130, **130**
   volume, increasing, <u>33</u>

F

Fab Five routine, <u>118</u>
Faking confidence, 233
Family, getting fit with, <u>20</u>, 20–21
Fasting, juice, 208–9
Fatigue
   chronic fatigue syndrome, 61
   muscle, 223–24
   Training Zones and, 56
Fats, 193–94
   calories from, 193–94
   in Mediterranean diet, 204
   sources of, 194
Fatty acids, 190, 193
Fennel
   Grilled Salmon with Fennel, Orange, and Black Olive Salad, 204
First step, taking, 32
Fish
   Grilled Salmon with Fennel, Orange, and Black Olive Salad, 204
Fitness elite, 8, 249
Fitness-For-Life Contract, <u>65</u>
Fitness Level, 49–51
   benchmark workouts, 165
   breakthrough sessions, 166–67
   brick workouts, 164
   calculating, 50
   description of levels, 51
   training programs, 168–81
      Fitness Level I, 169–72
      Fitness Level II, 172–75
      Fitness Level III, 175–78
      Fitness Level IV, 178–81
Flat tire, <u>91</u>, <u>247</u>
Flexibility
   improving with Pilates, 156, <u>158</u>
   strength training and, 116

Floor Calf Raise, 145, **145**
Fluids
   hydration schedule, 196
   for illness prevention, 228
Focus, shifting, <u>33</u>
Food. *See also* Nutrition; *specific foods*
   liquid, 197
   postworkout meal, 56
   race day, 197, 240
   race week, 163
   recipes, 203–8
Friends
   exercise buddies, 63–64
   group cycling, 91–92
Fruit
   Alexandra's Amazing Tonic, 229
   juice fasting, 209
   in Mediterranean diet, 204
   in Paleo diet, 203
Frustration, 107
Full 40 routine, 119–23
Fun, exercise as, 24–25

G

Gear, 35–48
   antifog solution, 38–39, <u>70</u>, 240
   belt, 48
   bicycle, 39–40
   bike shoes, 42–43
   cap, 48
   cold-weather, 46–48, 102
      arm warmers, 46–47
      booties, 47
      gloves, full-length, 47
      leg warmers, 46
      rain outfit, 47–48
      warm hat, 48
      wet suit, 48, 75
   cost, 35–48
   cycling gloves, 44
   cycling shorts, 43
   event day checklist, <u>238–39</u>
   goggles, 38
   heart rate monitor, 46
   helmet, 41–42, 90, <u>244</u>
   impulse buying, <u>39</u>
   indoor bike trainer, 41, 98
   injury prevention and, 213
   mountain bike, 40–41
   music, <u>47</u>, 48

   racing suit, 37
   running/cycling socks, 45–46
   running shoes, 45, 101–2, 213
   sports bra, 48
   sports top, 43–44
   sunglasses, 44
   swim cap, 37–38
   swimsuit, 37
   30-day wish list, <u>39</u>
   toolkit, 45, 90
   warmup suit, 36
Gloves
   cycling, 44
   full-length, 47
Glucose, 190, 193, 195
Gluten free diet, 206–7
Glycogen, 56, <u>125</u>, 190–91, 193
Glycogen depletion, 190–91
Goggles, 38, <u>70</u>, 240
GPS devices, 46
Grace under pressure, 233–34
Growth hormone, 119
Guidance, lack of, 32–33
Guilt, <u>33</u>

H

Half-Ironman, 22, 179, 185
Hamstring exercises, 135–39, **135–39**
Hand signals, cycling, 89, **89**
Hat, warm, 48
Health
   improvement, with triathlon training, 5
   as priority in life, 18
Heart rate
   calculating maximum, 57
   target zones, 56–60
   unusually elevated, 107
Heart rate monitor, 46, 55, <u>104</u>
Heatstroke, 224
Helmet, 41–42, 90, <u>244</u>
HEPA filter, 225
Hero to your kids, 12
High-efficiency particulate air (HEPA) filter, 225
Hills
   cycling, 96–97
   running, 105
Hip Lift, 136, **136**
Hitting the wall, 191

Home environment, boosting
        health of, 225–27
    air quality and circulation,
        225–26
    houseplants, 226–27
    pollution avoidance, 226–27
    volume lowering, 227
Household production, unhealthy,
    226
Houseplants, 226–27
The Hundred, 157, **157**
Hydration
    benefits
        health improvement, 228
        muscle cramp prevention, 224
    race day, 240
    schedule, 196

I

Illness
    as excuse, 27–28
    preventing, 224–29
        food and fluids, 228–29
        health of home environment,
            boosting, 225–27
        stress management, 227–28
Immune system, strengthening,
    224, 227
Indoor bike trainer, 41, 98
Injury
    acute and chronic, <u>222</u>
    causes of, 212
    as excuse, 27–28
    exercising when injured, 212–13
    preventing illness, 224–29
    running, 100
    treating common, 221–24
        diagnosis, getting proper,
            221–22
        medication use, 223
        muscle cramps, 223–24
        quick treatment, 223
Injury prevention, 211–29
    active-isolated stretching, 114–15
    benefits of triathlon training, 4–5
    bodywork, 215–17
        acupuncture, 216–17
        chiropractic, 217
        massage therapy, 215–16
        rolfing, 216
        tips for, 217

core strengthening, 154
dumbbell use in strength
    training, 117
exercising smart, 212
hot baths, 214–15
proper exercise gear, 213
rest, 214
running location choice, 102–3
running warmup, 108–9
strength training, 213
swimming technique, 69
technique, focus on proper, 214
Inner coach, 108
Inspirational benefits of triathlon
    training, 9–13
Insurance, health, 215
Intensity, workout/exercise, 55,
    58–59, 77, 108–9, 166
Interval training, <u>57</u>
    cycling, <u>57</u>, 97–98
    running, 110–11
    swimming, <u>57</u>, 77–78, 80–81
Ionizer, 225–26
Iron, 194–95
Ironman, 22, 185

J

Journal, 181–83, 186–87, 232
Juice
    juice fasting, 208–9
    juicing for health improvement,
        228–29

L

Lat Pulldown, 133, **133**
Laughter, 227–28
Leg Press, 129, **129**
Legs, elevating, 221
Leg warmers, 46
Lentils
    Red Lentil Soup, 207–8
Life changing, triathlon as, <u>10–11</u>
Lifting to failure, 119
Liquid foods, 197
Listening phase, of workout, 54–55
Location of exercise, varying, 25
Longevity, 5
Lower-back exercises, 150–51,
        150–51

Lunch meal plans
    2000-calorie diet, 199
    2500-calorie diet, 200
    3000-calorie diet, 201
Lunge, <u>118</u>, 125, **125**
Lying Back Stretch, 115, **115**, <u>118</u>,
        120, 150, 220, **220**
Lying Calf Stretch, 144, **144**
Lying Hamstring Stretch, 135, **135**

M

Magnesium, 194
Markings, race day, 240
Massage therapy, 215–16
Meal plans, 198–202
    2000-calorie diet, 198–99
    2500-calorie diet, 199–200
    3000-calorie diet, 201–2
Meat
    in Mediterranean diet, 204
    in Paleo diet, 203
Mediterranean diet, 204–5
Menstruation, 194
Mental actions, 231–35
    bouncing back, 235
    channeling stress into positive
        action, 235
    grace under pressure, 233–34
    personal accountability, 231
    prerace, 242
    self-belief, 231–32
Mental benefits of triathlon
        training, 5–8, <u>7</u>
Minerals, 194–95
Mirror, rearview cycling, 89
Mood improvement, with triathlon
        training, 6
Motivation
    attitude approach for workouts,
        23–24
    benchmark workouts, 164–65
    dogs as, <u>100</u>
    excuses for lack, 22–24
    to exercise, 6–7
    external, 23
    following action, 254
    getting back into fitness swing, <u>33</u>
    of injury, pain, or illness, 27
    intrinsic, 22–23
    of others, 12
Mountain bike, 40–41

Mountain biking, 92–94
Muscle(s)
    bulking up, 123
    fuel for, 190–91
    iron demand by, 195
    loss
        with age, 116
        with fat-rich, low
            carbohydrate diet, 193
    oxygenating, 53
    protein to build, 191–92
    warming up, 52–53
Muscle cramps, treating, 223–24
Muscle fatigue, 223–24
Muscle soreness
    reduced with vitamin E, 195
    running and, 106
    static stretching and, 114
Muscle tension, 216
Muscular imbalance, 105, 117
Mushrooms
    Gluten-Free Mongolian Shiitake
        Noodles, 206
Music, 47, 48

N

Neck Rolls, 122, **122**
Negative split, 60
Nutrition, 189–209
    caloric needs, calculating, 198
    carbohydrates, 190–91
    diets, 202–8
        gluten free, 206–7
        Mediterranean, 204–5
        Paleo, 202–4
        vegan, 207–8
    fats, 193–94
    juice fasting, 208–9
    meal plans, 198–202
        2000-calorie diet, 198–99
        2500-calorie diet, 199–200
        3000-calorie diet, 201–2
    postworkout, 197
    preworkout, 195–96
    product recommendations,
        209
    protein, 191–93, 192
    race day, 197, 240
    recipes, 203–8
    vitamins and minerals, 194–95

O

Obstacles. *See* Excuses
Olives
    Grilled Salmon with Fennel,
        Orange, and Black Olive
        Salad, 204
Olympic-distance triathlon, 22,
    178, 185
One-Arm Row, 118, 130, **130**
One-Leg Circle, 159, **159**
Orange juice, 197
Oranges
    Grilled Salmon with Fennel,
        Orange, and Black Olive
        Salad, 204
Osteoporosis, 99
Overhead Stretch, 120, **120**
Overhead Triceps Press, 153, **153**
Overtraining, 55, 165, 179
Oxidative damage, 195
Oxygen delivery to your body, 53,
    61, 243

P

Pace
    running, 105, 108–9
    swimming, 76
Pain. *See also* Injury prevention
    back, 115, 218–21
    as excuse, 27–28
Paleo diet, 202–4
Peanut butter
    Power Smoothie, 197
Pelvic Tilts, 155, **155**
Periodization, 183–84
Personal trainers, 36
Perspective, 31
Pesticides, 209
Physical benefits of triathlon
    training, 2–5
Physician, working with, 167
Pilates, 156–60, **157–60**, 158
Plank, 155, **155**
Plantar fasciitis, 103
Plants, 226–27
Plateau, 60, 166
Play, 24–25
Pollution, 226–27
Pools, standard sizes of, 77

Popularity of triathlon, 28
Posture, 154, 218–19
Potential, glimpsing your true, 9
Power breathing, 61–62
Power meters, 46, 248
Preoxygenating with warmup, 53
Pressure, grace under, 233–34
Priorities, setting, 17–18
Productivity increase, with triathlon
    training, 5–6
Progress, tracking, 181–83
Protein, 191–93, 192
    for building muscle, 191–92
    calories per gram, 193
    daily amount needed, 192
    in Paleo diet, 203
    sources of, 191–93, 192
    in vegan diet, 207
Protein powders, 191, 192–93, 197
Pullover, 132, **132**
Purpose, sense of, 9
Pushup, 142, **142**

Q

Quadriceps
    exercises for, 124–29, **124–29**
    Standing Quad Stretch, 118, 121,
        121, 123

R

Race day, 163, 237–49
    checklist, 238–39
    nutrition, 197
    prerace talk, 237–38
    timeline, 237–42
        5 minutes, 241–42
        1 hour, 240
        1.5 hours, 240
        10-12 hours, 239
        30 seconds, 242
        3 hours, 239–40
        24 hours, 237–38
        20 minutes, 241
        2.5 hours, 240
Races/racing
    choosing an event, 161–62
    postrace blues, 251–52
    race walk-through, 244–49

bike, 246–47
finish, 249
first transition, 245–46
run, 248–49
second transition, 247
start, 244
swim, 245
ramping up for longer events,
185
rules and etiquette for triathlons,
244
simulating race conditions, 104
tactics, 242–43
to train, 60
training timeline, 161–63
Racing suit, 37
RAD, 43, 87
Rain outfit, 47–48
Rate of perceived exertion, 58–59
Reasons to do triathlon, 1–13
Recipes, 203–8
Alexandra's Amazing Tonic, 229
Chicken Kebabs, 205
Chickpea Salad, 205
Gluten-Free Crunchy Chicken
Waldorf Salad, 207
Gluten-Free Mongolian Shiitake
Noodles, 206
Grilled Salmon with Fennel,
Orange, and Black Olive
Salad, 204
Power Smoothie, 197
Red Lentil Soup, 207–8
Spinach and Boiled Egg
Chopped Salad with
Avocado, 203
Summer Vegetable Ratatouille,
208
Remodeling, 192
Repetitions, number of, 119, 123
Reset, 76
Resistance band, 119
Responsibility, 234
Rest
breakthrough sessions and,
167–68
for injury prevention, 214
before race, 239
race week, 163
recovering from an event, 60
rest days in training programs,
168–81

Reverse circulation, increasing,
221
Reverse loop, 86
Rice protein powders, 191, 193
Rituals, creating daily, 228
Rolfing, 216
Roman Chair Run, 149, **149**
Rotational adjustment device
(RAD), 43, 87
RPE, 58–59
Rules, triathlon, 244
Runner's high, 6, 99
Running, 99–111
benefits of, 99–100
body shaping, 3
core strength and, 154
dog as training buddy, 100,
107
freeing up time for, 19
gear, 45–46, 101–2, 213 (*see also
specific items*)
in groups, 104
interval training, 57
knowing when to say when,
105–8
location, 102–3
beach, 103
road/sidewalk, 103
track, 103
trails, 102–3
treadmill, 103
race walk-through, 248–49
safety, 107
strengthening your weaknesses,
105
stride-outs, 111
technique, 104, 214
tips from pros, 104
Training Zone I, 109
endurance, 109
walk, 109
Training Zone II, 110
long intervals, 110
tempo, 110
Training Zone III, 110–11
short intervals, 110–11
treadmill, 111
Training Zone IV, 111
water running, 27
workouts, 108–11
Running/cycling socks, 45–46
Running shoes, 45, 101–2

S

Safety
cycling, 88–90, 91, 93–94
open water swimming, 75
running, 107
Salad
Chickpea Salad, 205
Gluten-Free Crunchy Chicken
Waldorf Salad, 207
Grilled Salmon with Fennel,
Orange, and Black Olive
Salad, 204
Spinach and Boiled Egg Chopped
Salad with Avocado, 203
Salmon
Grilled Salmon with Fennel,
Orange, and Black Olive
Salad, 204
Scale, 3
Seasonal periodization, 183–85
autumn, 185
spring, 184
summer, 184–85
winter, 184
Seated Cable Row, 134, **134**
Seated Calf Raise, 146, **146**
Seated Overhead Press, 131, **131**
Self-belief, 231–32
Self-confidence, 11, 20, 231, 232–33
Self-esteem, 20, 232
Sense of purpose, 9
Shin splints, 103
Shoes
bike, 42–43
removing at your door, 227
running, 45, 101–2, 213
Shorts, cycling, 43
Shoulder Stretch, 116, **116**
Side Plank, 155, **155**
Simple Crunches, 156, **156**
Single-Leg Hamstring Curl, 138,
138
Single-Leg Stretch, 160, **160**
Sitting, effects of, 218, 221
Smoothie, 197
Snacks
meal plans
2000-calorie diet, 199
2500-calorie diet, 200
3000-calorie diet, 201
preworkout, 52, 196

Social benefits of triathlon training, 8
Social facilitation, <u>36</u>
Social networks, 64
Socks, running/cycling socks, 45–46
Soup
    Red Lentil Soup, 207–8
Soy protein, 191–92
Spinach
    Spinach and Boiled Egg Chopped Salad with Avocado, 203
Sports bra, 48
Sports drinks, 191, 196, 203, 209
Sports gel, 209
Sports top, 43–44
Spring, training program for, 184
Sprint-distance triathlon, 22, 77
Stability ball, 119
Stability Ball Leg Curl, 136, **136**
Stair Calf Raise, 145, **145**
Standing Calf Stretch, 144, **144**
Standing Hamstring Curl, 139, **139**
Standing Hamstring Stretch, 135, **135**
Standing Leg Curl, 137, **137**
Standing Quad Stretch, <u>118</u>, 121, **121**, 123
Statistics, triathlon participation, <u>28</u>
Staying in the moment, 243
Steps, running up, 103
Step Up, 126, **126**
Strava, 64
Strength training
    advice, 116–19
    after benchmark workout, 165
    benefits, 116
        building muscle with, 191–92
        injury prevention, 213
    combining with aerobic exercise, 20
    lifting to failure, 119
    for running, 105
    weight selection, 117–19
Stress
    channeling into positive action, 235
    grace under pressure, developing, 233–34
    loss of focus with, 233, 235
    physical on body
        cycling, 43, 83, 86, 88, 95, 213
        from daily life, 113
        injury from, 4–5
        interval training, <u>57</u>
        running, 101, 103, 213–214
        swimming, 69, 77
    positive of exercise, 106, 166, 168, 256
Stress management
    cycling, <u>94</u>
    handling stress effectively, 6
    laughter, 227–28
    lowering volume in home environment, 227
    physical activity, 22–23, 26, 67
    power breathing, 61–62
    rituals, creating daily, 228
    running, 99
    taking breaks, 219
Stretches
    Arm Swings, 121, **121**
    Back Bend, 220, **220**
    Ball Drape, <u>118</u>, 147, **147**
    Biceps Stretch, 152
    Chest Stretch, <u>118</u>, 140, **140**
    Cobra, <u>118</u>, 147, **147**, 220, **220**
    Lying Back Stretch, 115, **115**, <u>118</u>, 120, 150, 220, **220**
    Lying Calf Stretch, 144, **144**
    Lying Hamstring Stretch, 135, **135**
    Neck Rolls, 122, **122**
    Overhead Stretch, 120, **120**
    Shoulder Stretch, 116, **116**
    Single-Leg Stretch, 160, **160**
    Standing Calf Stretch, 144, **144**
    Standing Hamstring Stretch, 135, **135**
    Standing Quad Stretch, <u>118</u>, 121, **121**, 123
    Triceps Stretch, 153, **153**
    Upper-Back Stretch, <u>118</u>, 130, **130**
    Upper-Body Rotation, 122, **122**
Stretching, 113–16
    active-isolated (AIS), 114–15
    for back pain avoidance, 115, 219–20, **220**
    in bike-to-run transition, 247
    core, 219–20, **220**
    in Fab Five routine, <u>118</u>
    in Full 40 routine, 120–23
    goal of, 114
    for muscle cramp relief, 224
    Pilates, <u>158</u>
    prerace, 240, 241
    in seven-phase workout, 53
    static, 114
    yoga, <u>158</u>
Stride, running, 105, 111
Stride-outs, 111
Success Journal, 181–83, 186–87, 232
Sugar
    cravings, 107
    refined, 203, 204
Summer, training program for, 184–85
Sunglasses, 44
Superman, <u>118</u>, 150, **150**
Support system, 29, 63
Sweat, water loss from, 196
Swim cap, 37–38
Swimming, 67–82
    body position, **69**, 69–70
    body shaping, 3–4
    core strength and, 154
    drills, 78–79
        Buddy Up, 79
        Catch Up, 78
        Press the Body, 78
        Punch It, 79
    gear (see Gear; specific items)
    health benefits, 67
    interval training, <u>57</u>, 77–78, 80–81
    learning stages, 67–68
    masters programs, <u>76</u>
    open water, 74–76
        mass start, preparing for, 75–76
        pacing yourself, 76
        safety, 75
        swimming straight, 75
    race walk-through, 244–45
    stroke components, 71–74, **71–74**
        breathe, 74
        catch, 71, **71**
        entry/extension, 71, **71**
        pull, **72**, 72–73
        push, 73, **73**
        recovery, 74, **74**

technique, honing, 68–69
Training Zone I, 79–80
    endurance, 80
    R&R, 79
    technique work, 80
Training Zone II, 80–81
    long intervals, 80–81
    strength, 81
Training Zone III, 81
Training Zone IV, 82
warming up for race day, 241
workout, 77–82
Swimsuit, 37

T

Tactics, 242–43
Tandem bike, 21
Technique
    cycling, 87
    focus on proper, 62, 214
    running, 104, 214
    swimming, 68–69, 71–74
Tendinitis, 100
Time Journal, 18
Time limitations, 17–21
    freeing up some time, 18–21
    setting priorities, 17–18
    time-wasters, eliminating, 19
Timeline
    race day, 237–42
    training, 161–63
Tocopherols, 195
Toolkit, 45, 90
Top, sports, 43–44
Track, running on local, 103
Tracking progress, 181–83
Trails
    cycling on, 92–94
    running on, 102
Trainers, personal, 36
Training program
    benchmark workouts, 164–65
    breakthrough sessions,
        166–68
    brick workouts, 164
    duration of workouts, 168
    exercise buddies, 63–64
    Fitness Level I, 169–72
    Fitness Level II, 172–75
    Fitness Level III, 175–78

Fitness Level IV, 178–81
fitness levels, 49–51
getting the most from, 52–64
longer events, 185
overview, 49–65
power breathing, 61–62
putting technique first, 62
racing to train, 60
seasonal approach, 183–85
    autumn, 185
    periodization, 183–84
    spring, 184
    summer, 184–85
    winter, 184
seven-phase workout, 52–56
social network use, 64
starting, 164–81
Success Journal, 181–82,
    186–87
timeline, 161–63
tracking progress, 181–83
Training timeline, 161–63
one month, 162
one week, 163
race day, 163
two days, 163
two months, 161–62
Training Zones
cycling, 95–98
overview, 56–60
running, 108–11
swimming, 79–81
Transition area, 240, 246, 247
Treadmill, 103, 111
Triathlon Tale
    Egan, Sharon, 20
    Haley, Darryl, 16
    Keller, Martin, 26
    Maureen, 10–11
    Winans, Vanessa, 249
Triceps exercises, 153, **153**
Triceps Stretch, 153, **153**
TV, turning off, 18–19

U

Upper-back exercises, 130–34,
    130–34
Upper-Back Stretch, 118, 130,
    130
Upper-Body Rotation, 122, **122**

V

Vegan diet, 207–8
Vegetables
    Alexandra's Amazing Tonic,
        229
    juice fasting, 209
    in Mediterranean diet, 204
    in Paleo diet, 203
    Summer Vegetable Ratatouille,
        208
Vegetarian diet, protein
        supplements for, 192
Visualization, 162
Vitamins, 193, 194–95
Volume, lowering in home
        environment, 227

W

Walking, 109, 228, 240, 248
Warmup, 52–53, 118, 120, 212,
    224
    preoxygenating your body with,
        53
    race day, 241
    running workout, 108–9
    stop-and-go, 53
Warmup suit, 36
Water
    hydration benefits
        health improvement, 228
        muscle cramp prevention,
            224
    hydration schedule, 196
    postworkout, 197
    preworkout, 52, 196
Water running, 27
Weaknesses, strengthening, 7–8, 27,
    105
Weight
    as excuse, 28–29
    feeling good at any, 2
Weighted Crunch, 149, **149**
Weight loss
    aerobic exercise, 125
    benefits of triathlon training,
        2–3
Wet suit, 48, 75
Winter, training program for, 184
Work, cycling to, 94

Workout(s)
    attitude approach to, 23–24
    benchmark, 164–65
    breakthrough sessions, 166–68
    brick, 104, 164
    cycling, 86, 95–98
    duration of, 168
    exercise buddies, 63–64
    Fab Five routine, 118
    Full 40: Ultimate 40-Minute
        Stretch and Strength
        Routine, 119–23
        phase I: warmup, 120
        phase II: initial stretch, 120–
            22
        phase III: main set, 123
        phase IV: cooldown, 123
    getting more out of, 4
    intensity, 55, 58–59, 77, 108–9,
        166
    interval training, 57

location, varying, 25
morning, 19
musically enhanced, 47
nutrition
    postworkout, 197
    preworkout, 195–96
    race day, 197
as play, 24–25
running, 108–11
scheduling, 18, 168–69
seven-phases, 52–56
    cooldown, 56
    listening phase, 54–55
    postworkout meal, 56
    preworkout preparation, 52
    stretch, 53
    warmup, 52–53
    workout, 55
simplifying, 19
with strength and aerobic
    components, 20

swimming, 77–82
training programs by Fitness
    Level, 168–81
    Fitness Level I, 169–72
    Fitness Level II, 172–75
    Fitness Level III, 175–78
    Fitness Level IV, 178–81
Training Zones, 56–60
    cycling, 95–98
    swimming, 79–81
varying, 117

Y

Yoga, 158
Yogurt
    Power Smoothie, 197
Younger look and feel, with
    triathlon training, 3–4

ABOUT THE AUTHOR

Eric Harr considers himself "the happiest CEO alive." Eric is the founder and CEO of STAND, a new mobile platform that helps you connect with the people you care about—for the causes you love. It empowers you to put your compassion into action.

Prior to STAND, Eric founded Resonate, a social media and advertising agency; he was the former Founding Editorial Director of *VIV Magazine,* the world's first mass market digital magazine, founded with Fiji Water's David Gilmour; an on-air correspondent with CBS news; a syndicated columnist with the *Los Angeles Times*; and the author of five books including *The Real Truth about Social Media.*

Eric was also a professional triathlete ranked number 6 in the world. Recently at the age of 40, he finished 40th overall at the Ironman Triathlon World Championships in a time of 9:01:34. He's going back in 2016 to use the STAND platform and looks to raise a million dollars for a worthy charity—in the *under 9 hours* it takes him to finish the event.

To learn more, visit him at http://stand.tc.